ENTERTAINING WITH
HOUSE
& GARDEN

ENTERTAINING WITH
HOUSE
& GARDEN

**600 recipes for successful
menus and parties
compiled by Leonie Highton**

TREASURE PRESS

CONTENTS

First published in Great Britain by Cathay Books
for W H Smith & Son Limited

This edition published in 1983 by Treasure Press
59 Grosvenor Street
London W1

© 1979 Condé Nast Publications Limited

ISBN 0 907812 35 X

Printed in Hong Kong

INTRODUCTION

Of all the thousands of books published every year, cook-books have most reason to declare their interests. Is the book for the beginner or for somebody already well-versed in the culinary arts? Is it for the passionate lover of the cookery of the Balkans or for the stay-at-home discoverer of the traditional dishes of Old England? Well, then, a word about this particular cook-book.

First of all, it is wide-ranging, having six hundred recipes to challenge the most demanding of taste-buds. On the other hand, it doesn't claim to have every classic of the world's cuisines. Neither, indeed, is it a basic cook-book, although it does contain lots of good, simple recipes ideal for the beginner.

Essentially, this is a personal selection of favourite recipes drawn from the hundreds and hundreds which have appeared in the *Wine & Food* section of *House & Garden*. The recipes derive not only from some of the most notable chefs and restaurant-owners of our time but from unexpected enthusiasts who are better known in other walks of life. Michel Roux, chef-patron of Le Gavroche, one of the half-dozen most renowned restaurants in London, gives a recipe for Crabe Vahine, while Una Stubbs, far more publicized for her TV appearances than for her skills as a cook, provides a recipe for Veal and Dill Stew. Thus the cross-section is wide indeed.

PLANNING AHEAD

Any cook-book worth its salt must also be a book for entertaining—as well as an entertaining book, the compiler hopes. After all, every recipe, whether for what Noel Coward called 'something eggy on a tray' or a spectacular confection *à la française*, should be good enough to be served other than as a solitary repast or merely as a family meal in the kitchen.

Misanthropes and misogynists apart, most of us like to entertain. We plan our kitchens with an eye to ease not just of preparation but of serving, too. We design and decorate our dining-areas with a thought for the visual pleasure they will give us and our guests. We debate what is the best size and shape of the table for a party. Is a refectory table better for general conversation or a circular table? And if a circular table, what diameter will seat eight or ten in comfort? And what kind of chairs? Ah, the hours that can be spent on these matters!

Then there is the problem of movement of food from cooker to table. Is a hatchway between kitchen and dining-room essential? Or is it better to forget the dining-room altogether and use the space for a really large, comfortable, family kitchen which is decorative enough to eat in, even on party nights?

All these questions relate to what might be termed the tangibilities of entertaining and, to a large extent, they are governed by the physical limitations of your accommodation, budget and, of course, by the type of parties you are planning. If you frequently find yourself involved in formal business-type dinners, a separate dining-room, or at least a well-defined dining-area, is a must. But if your parties are casual, for family and close friends only, then an attractive, well-planned kitchen/dining-area is all you need. The only thing to remember in all this is that there are simply no rules. *Chacun . . .*

There are, however, a few basic guide-lines relating to the less tangible side of entertaining —how to create that elusive but essential quality for a party: atmosphere.

From an interior decoration point of view, lighting is probably the most important single factor governing this, and, fortunately, it is also the simplest to correct. Skilful lighting can hide a multitude of design imperfections as well as give a sense of well-being to guests. Many dining-rooms have a high, pendant lamp which covers the diners below with a harsh, unsympathetic glare. If you are prepared to go to the trouble and expense of

These dishes can be prepared entirely in advance.
**These dishes need only minimum attention before serving.*

PLANNING AHEAD

<table>
<tr><td>

BUFFET (WINTER)

Kipper pâté★
Sercial Madeira

———

Lang Syne Stew★
White Burgundy, like Meursault

———

Cheese
Dry rosé, such as Lirac or Tavel

———

Angel's hair gâteau★
Côteaux du Layon from Loire

</td><td>

GARDEN PARTY OR SUMMER BUFFET

Iced prawn soup★
Dry sparkling white, such as West German Pradikats-Sekt

———

Marinade of beef★
Salads
Claret (Médoc or Pomerol) or northern Rhône red (Côte Rôtie or Hermitage)

———

Cheese
Continue with main-course selection or take an older vintage of the same wine

———

Cherry tarts★
A heavy, sweet wine (as Kirsch is included in the recipe) such as the Portuguese Moscatel de Setubal

</td></tr>
</table>

revamping the lighting altogether, so much the better. If not, the quickest, cheapest and most effective solution is to install dimmer switches. For traditional and modern interiors alike, lighting operated by dimmers offers an attractive, flexible arrangement, which can be altered to suit the mood and type of party.

The table-setting itself is also important in creating a pleasant and cossetting atmosphere, for it reflects the care taken by host or hostess to ensure the enjoyment of his or her guests. The table should look pretty, without being fussy, and should definitely not be decorated with tall flowers or candlesticks which only serve to interrupt vision—and conversation—across the table.

The choice of food and drinks again depends on the type of party. In this chapter there are several suggested menus for different occasions which should act as a spring-board for your own inventiveness. The most important points to remember when planning a menu are: (1) it should have a well-balanced set of flavours, colours and textures, (2) it should be appropriate to the season and (3) it should not contain any dish which overtaxes your ability and/or confidence as a cook.

Although there is much pleasure to be gained in cooking for friends, it is a mistake to spend so much time on preparation that you are exhausted before the party has even begun.

Plan your menu well in advance, taking into account the amount of hidden time involved in preparation—and never choose three courses which all need last-minute attention. At least one course should be prepared entirely in advance. Again, when you are planning a menu, picture how many plates and dishes will have to be in the oven at any one time. This is something that even experienced cooks often overlook. Next, make sure that oven temperatures for the dishes you want to cook for your party are compatible. If you have a double oven, of course, so much the better. The problems of conflicting oven temperatures and last-minute stove-face panic can be avoided by devising a menu of three cold dishes, but this lacks vitality except on the very hottest of days.

A freezer is undoubtedly an advantage if you entertain on a large scale, and many of the dishes in this book can be frozen without worry, either in entirety or in part. There is no reason, for example, not to get ahead with making the pastry for a flan.

The majority of the following recipes were chosen because they are particularly suitable

Nineteen-twenties table in palisandra and poplar woods, with matching mirror, provides a handsome setting for a celebration buffet. Design by Olive Sullivan.

SUNDAY LUNCHEON (SUMMER)

Chilled cucumber and mint soup*
*Middle Loire white, such as
Vouvray or Montbuis*

———

Roast leg of lamb Spanish-style**
Caramel potatoes; Lettuce salad
Riojan red from northern Spain

———

Cheese
*An older vintage Riojan red than that served
with the main course*

———

Pears in coffee*
*Light sweet white Bordeaux,
such as St Croix du Mont*

EXTRA SIMPLE

Instant tomato bisque*
*Dry Italian white, preferably Riesling,
from Alto Adige*

———

Veal and Dill stew**
Jacket potatoes; herbed carrots
Cabernet red, such as from California

———

Cheese
Continue with main-course wine

———

Grapefruit cheesecake or Refrigerator log cake**
*Rich fruity West German, Auslëse quality from
Palatinate or an Austrian dessert style,
Beerenauslesen*

---

for lunch and dinner parties which, in all probability, is the type of entertaining most frequently undertaken by most readers. There are, however, a few recipes for barbecues and for picnics, and even for baking—for all those lovely old-fashioned tea parties.

The ten suggested menus which are given in this chapter are based on three courses and cheese (served *before* the dessert, as this affects the order of the wines), using recipes which, with the exception of the more straightforward vegetable accompaniments, can all be found in the ensuing pages. Those dishes marked with an * can be prepared entirely in advance. Those marked ** need only a little attention just before serving. Included in the chapter on Starters are recipes for canapés for drinks parties (which would also be good for light, pre-theatre parties), and elsewhere there are lots of recipes particularly suitable for buffet meals.

Here, then, is a sufficiency of recipes for entertaining on almost any scale you care to plan. And to aid you in your endeavours, Philip Shaw provides the following notes on choosing wine plus specific suggestions for wines to accompany the dishes in our menus:

A lace tablecloth and richly-upholstered chairs turn an at-home dinner for two into a special occasion. Design by Olive Sullivan.

It is important to plan party wines as far ahead as possible. This allows you to obtain the wine you want without taking second best and ensures that it is served to maximum advantage. The better off-licence chains give formal training to their staff, which can be a useful source of advice for the buyer, but this is sadly lacking in most supermarkets and other similar drinks outlets. The independent, often small, wine merchants are usually reliable sources, for they have the expertise and are eager to cultivate regular custom. Although many of the latter are on a mail-order basis, do not let this deter you, for their wine lists can be a mine of information and pleasure. For the finer vintages and the less usual wines, auctioneers provide a further useful source.

If wine orders can be combined with those of friends, possibly neighbours or work colleagues, there are two advantages. First, there will be little or no freight cost on any mail order wines. Second, there could be useful discounts on straight dozen bottle units.

When choosing your wines, remember to take bottle-size into account as, nowadays, there are considerable variations. The larger the bottle-size, the slower the rate at which the wine matures. A magnum—equivalent to two bottles—will show less development than the same wine in a conventional-size bottle,

WATCHING THE COST

Sardine eggs★
Portuguese dry white, like Vinho Verde

———

Kidneys à la Dubois★★
Noodles; Green salad
Dão red from Portugal or Côtes du Rhône

———

Cheese
Continue the same red as for the main course

———

Lemon sauce pudding
Inexpensive dessert Spanish white from Catalonia

WATCHING THE COST

Danish egg cake
Yugoslavian Riesling

———

Tuna rice ring★★
Continue Yugoslavian Riesling or select a low-priced Mosel from a fairly recent vintage

———

Cheese
Continue main-course wine

———

Plum jalousie★
Umbrian abboccato, like Orvieto

and half-bottles mature quickest of all. This is an important factor for Claret, Burgundy and Rhône. Litre, 1½ and 2 litre bottles usually show a small saving over the conventional 72 to 75cl bottle, but when sealed using a closure other than natural cork, they cannot be stored to any maturity advantage. All wines with natural corks should be stored in a horizontal position (including sparkling wines) in order that the wine stays in contact with the cork, thereby keeping the cork expanded and preventing oxidation of the wine. A constant temperature of around 13°C (55°F) is best for storage, whilst widely fluctuating seasonal variation should be avoided. A minimum-maximum thermometer is helpful. The storage space should be free from draughts and vibrations and, if possible, be naturally dark. If you are likely to move frequently or do not have such conditions, it would be prudent to store your wine with a merchant or with one of the warehouses which undertakes this service, but ensure adequate insurance cover at replacement cost.

When selecting wines, try for variety and interest to complement the food. It is more exciting for host and guest to experience several wines, rather than larger quantities of one wine. A simple rule to follow is: dry before sweet; white before red (except for desserts); and youth before age. Use half-bottles for starters or for matching with dessert courses if a full bottle size is too much. If any wine is left over, do not waste. Stopper immediately and, if possible, decant into a smaller-sized bottle (to reduce the amount of oxygen in the bottle, the ullage as it is termed). Use for casseroles and sauces at a later date or pour a little oil over which acts as a useful seal. Use a special stopper for sparkling wines which allows sparkling wines to be served without loss of effervescence over two or three meals.

Serve whites or rosés at about 12°C (54°F) but colder if they are sweeter, say 7°C (45°F). Fortified wines, with the exception of the drier styles, which are enhanced by light chilling, may be served at room temperature. If you forget to warm a red, do not try drastic action. Pour and explain. Friends will understand and the action of cupping the glass in the hand will quickly bring out the full flavour, both on the nose and palate. Normally, reds will best be enjoyed at about 16°C (60°F) although there is a trend occasionally to show a light style—perhaps a Nouveau like Beaujolais—just slightly chilled. This can be attractive but can accentuate acidity.

Some of the most memorable settings for meals are the simplest. Here, French cheeses and a basket of fresh fruit are served on a table of French country provenance.

BARBECUE PARTY

Gazpacho★
Fino sherry

———

Stuffed veal birds
Salads
Light red, such as Alsation Pinot Noir or
Burgundian red Mercurey

———

Cheese
Continue with main-course selection

———

Summer fruit bowl★
Demi-sec sparkling wine

PICNIC FOR DOWNLAND OR SEASIDE

Hors d'oeuvre roll★

———

Oiseaux en gelée★
Avocado salad★

———

Cheese

———

Coeur à la crème★
Fresh redcurrants

———

A light dry rosé, such as Tavel or Lirac from
southern Rhône, for all courses except dessert

Unless a wine is really old or in sparkling form, it will benefit from decanting. Even on a picnic, where one is unlikely to have a decanter, try to pour the wine into a clean vessel (which can be another wine bottle) and perhaps return it to the original. This will serve two objects: to aerate the wine and bring it to life and to remove the clear wine from any sediment that has formed. Classic reds, like vintage Port, Claret, some Rhônes and Burgundies, can be stood upright for a day before decanting which helps any loose deposit to slide down the bottle. Remove the top part of the capsule to below the lip which allows the wine to be poured without crossing the lead in the event that it is a lead closure. Use a long threaded corkscrew in order that it does not partially penetrate the cork and the latter fracture. Clean around the neck of the bottle after the cork has been drawn pre-decanting. Avoid using a wine basket, for the action of forcing a bottle into it increases the likelihood of disturbing any sediment.

In Britain Port tends to be enjoyed at the end of a meal, or after it, whereas in France it is more popular as an apéritif. Wood-aged Ports do not need decanting and are extraordinarily good value, the cheapest being Ruby, but more mellow and attractive are the Tawny and Late Bottled varieties. White Port is generally regarded as an apéritif. For really special dinner-parties, bottle-aged Port is the thing: a single vintage declared by a shipper two years after the harvest, or Crusted which is usually four years after the vintage. Vintage is best served after some fifteen years in bottle and Crusted after about six. Serve at room temperature.

Madeira should not be forgotten for parties, especially the drier styles for apéritifs and to accompany soups and pâtés, such as Sercial or Verdelho; the dessert styles of Bual and Malmsey are excellent finales to the meal.

Finally, the shape of the glasses is important. Tulip-shaped glasses are ideal for wine, for they allow the appearance to be appreciated to the full and the glass to be swirled to allow both the aroma (the grape smell) and bouquet (the development that has taken place), which jointly form *nose* in wine terminology, to be assessed. Fill to just over half full. These comments apply equally to sparkling wine as to table wine. A smaller quantity of wine should be poured in the case of fortified, such as Sherry, Madeira or Port.

Table after table of cheeses, cold meats and quiches, all ready for a stand-up party. Luxuriant plants and a pair of antique candelabra create a decorative setting. Design by Olive Sullivan.

SOUPS

French onion soup

1½ lb onions
1½ oz butter
1 tablespoon olive oil
½ small teaspoon sugar
1½ oz flour
3¼ pints good beef stock, hot
¼ pint dry white wine or cider
Salt and pepper
8 rounds of bread
2 oz Gruyère cheese cut into thin slices
1 tablespoon grated raw onion

Slice the onions very thinly. Heat the butter with the olive oil in a heavy pan, put in the onions and stir them around until they glisten. Cover for 15 minutes. Take off the lid, sprinkle in the salt, pepper and sugar, and stir well. Cook, uncovered, for 40 minutes, stirring often, until the onions are a rich golden-brown. Blend in the flour and cook, stirring for three to four minutes. Add the hot stock and the wine. Simmer with the lid half on for 45 minutes to an hour. Add more salt and pepper if necessary. Put the dried bread at the bottom of a warm tureen and pour the boiling soup over. Stir in cheese slices and grated onion.

SERVES 6. J.E. 1

Herbed onion soup

This soup is made in the lower half of a steamer while a chicken is being cooked in the top half.

4 medium-sized onions
¾ pint water
1 crumbled chicken cube
½ bay leaf
Bouquet garni
Any available poultry or white meat trimmings

Peel and slice the onions. Place all the ingredients in the lower container of a three-tiered steamer, and use as steaming liquid for the chicken above. It will pick up flavour from the chicken, reduce, and be well flavoured when you are ready to use it. Before serving, remove the bay leaf and bouquet.

SERVES 3. M.B. (2)

Sorrel soup

½ lb orange lentils
3 pints water
Handful sorrel leaves
Salt

Cook the orange lentils in water for about 20 minutes, until soft enough to put through a sieve or mouli.

Chop sorrel leaves fairly finely. (The quickest way is with a double-handled chopping knife.) Add the sorrel to the lentil soup and cook for a further 10 minutes. Taste and if necessary add salt—but add it carefully, as sorrel itself is very sharp in flavour.

If you like, just before serving add 3 tablespoons of cream.

SERVES 4-6. F.M.

Traditional French Onion Soup, laced with bread and gruyère cheese, is a warming start to a winter meal. (Recipe above.)

Zuppa di Verdura Toscana

Winter Tuscan soup

1 lb dried haricot beans (white)
½ celery
2 carrots
2 onions
½ cabbage
1 bulb fennel
2 courgettes
¼ lb cooked peas
6 slices of home-made-type white bread
Bayleaf
¼ lb bacon
3 pints chicken broth
1 tablespoon oil
1 oz butter
Salt and pepper

Cook beans, drain them, and put aside. Dice the bacon and the vegetables. Place oil, butter and bacon in a deep saucepan and fry for two minutes. Add the vegetables and cook for ½ hour, adding a ladle of chicken broth, as necessary. In soup tureen, place one layer of the cooked vegetables, then cover with two slices of bread. Repeat operation using the rest of the vegetables and beans, adding the remaining hot chicken broth. Serve with grated Parmesan cheese.

SERVES 6. J.B. (1)

Altdeutsche Erbsensuppe

Traditional German pea soup

6 oz green split peas
1 large onion, chopped
3 rashers of smoked back bacon, cubed
1 medium carrot, finely diced
1 large leek, finely chopped
1¾ pints beef stock
4 German frankfurters

Place the bacon cubes in a heavy casserole and fry until slightly browned. Add the onion, followed by the stock—home-made if possible. Then add the peas, carrot and leek, bring the soup to the boil and simmer until the peas are cooked.

Warm the frankfurters separately, but remember not to bring these sausages to the boil as they tend to split. Cut them into large chunks and add them to the soup, together with chopped fresh parsley. Add salt and pepper to taste.

SERVES 4. W.S.

Chestnut soup

3 oz smoked, streaky bacon, diced
1 small onion, sliced
1 carrot, peeled and sliced
1 stick celery, sliced
1 cooking apple, peeled, cored and sliced
1½ lb chestnuts, peeled
1½ pints chicken stock
Bouquet garni
Salt and freshly-ground black pepper
¼ pint single cream
1 tablespoon parsley, chopped

Gently fry the bacon until the fat runs, then stir in the vegetables and apple and fry until lightly browned. Add the chestnuts, stock, bouquet garni and seasonings, bring to the boil, cover and simmer gently for 45 minutes to 1 hour until the chestnuts are tender. Remove a few of the chestnuts for garnish. Purée the soup, return to the pan and check the seasoning. Stir in the cream and reheat but do not boil. Roughly dice the reserved chestnuts and sprinkle over the soup with the parsley.

SERVES 4-6. H.W.

Lettuce soup

1 oz butter
½ lb lettuce
1 small onion
¾ pint milk
1 tablespoon cornflour
Salt and pepper
Nutmeg
Sugar
¼ pint stock

Blanch lettuce for a few minutes in boiling salted water. Rinse well, drain and chop coarsely. Cook the chopped onion in the melted butter for five minutes. Add lettuce and stock, season well and cover. Simmer for fifteen minutes. Put through a blender or sieve and reheat with the milk. When boiling, stir in cornflour blended with a little milk, and bring back to the boil, stirring all the time. Simmer for five minutes and check seasoning, add about a tablespoon of sugar and a dash of nutmeg (or mace). Serve with finely chopped parsley or mint. Just before serving, an egg beaten into a couple of tablespoons of cream can be added.

SERVES 4. C.W.

Bouillabaisse
Provençal fish soup

5–6 lb fish
½ pint good olive oil
2 large onions, sliced
4 cloves garlic
1 lb tomatoes peeled
Salt and pepper
Parsley and fennel, chopped
Pinch saffron
Bay leaf
Thyme, orange peel and a clove
ROUILLÉ SAUCE:
1 green pepper
Oil
4 cloves garlic
¼ lb stale breadcrumbs
¼ pint fish stock

The important points to follow in making this soup are as follows: (1) A variety of fish must be used, some with firm flesh, some with soft, perhaps crustaceans and molluscs too. (2) The liquor must be boiled very fast to ensure amalgamation of olive oil and water. (3) Onions, garlic, tomatoes, parsley and saffron are always used. (4) The fish is served separately from the liquor, which, when consumed, is poured over pieces of garlic-rubbed toast and accompanied by *rouillé* sauce made as follows: remove seeds from pepper, chop and fry in oil until soft. Mash with crushed garlic cloves. Soak the stale bread in water, squeeze out and add. Put in a pan and stir in oil in which pepper was cooked plus the fish stock. You need about five or six pounds of fish in all, including, for example, red mullet, roach, gurnard, sole, whiting, haddock, cod, crawfish, lobster, prawns and clams. Gut, scale and wash the fish and keep whole where possible, including the heads. Heat half the olive oil in a large heavy saucepan, and brown the sliced onions, chopped garlic; then add the peeled tomatoes. Put in the firm-fleshed fish and cover with boiling water. Add salt and pepper, fennel, chopped parsley, a good pinch of saffron, perhaps a bay leaf, thyme, orange peel and a clove. Bring to, and keep at, a vigorous boil, adding the remaining olive oil, for 15 to 20 minutes. Towards the end of this time, add the softer fish and the clams, giving just enough time to cook. The secret is the fast boiling. After cooking, lift the fish out, whole if possible, and arrange on a dish (some of the softer fish will have disintegrated, thus giving body to the broth). The liquor is sprinkled with chopped parsley, and the whole served immediately.
SERVES 8–10. J.M.

Bouillabaisse, the famous fish soup of Provençe, is virtually a meal in itself. (Recipe above.)

Cullen skink
Scottish fish soup

1 pint water
¾ pint milk
1 lb whole peeled potatoes
4 small onions, whole
1 cup oatmeal or Quaker oats
1 oz butter
Salt and pepper
Sprig of parsley
1 lb white fish, preferably cod or fresh haddock
FOR POACHING THE FISH:
¾ pint water
¼ pint milk
½ oz butter
Salt and pepper

Prepare the vegetables. Put all ingredients (except fish and ingredients for poaching) into a large saucepan and bring to the boil, simmer until the potato and onions are cooked. This forms the basis of the soup.

To cook the fish, place in a buttered ovenproof dish and add the liquid for poaching, season and dot with butter. Cover with foil and put in oven at 350°F (gas 4) for 20 minutes or until it flakes easily. When the soup is cooked, add the flaked fish and serve garnished with chopped parsley. Alternatively, put the soup through a sieve or blender before adding the fish. This makes a smoother consistency.
SERVES 4. S.G.

Fiskesuppe
Fish soup

1½ pints fish stock
5 oz carrots
4 oz turnip (or parsnip and celeriac mixed)
Flour
7 fl oz milk

Prepare a good fish stock from head, skin and bones of white fish. Boil carrots, turnip (or parsnip and celeriac) in a little lightly-salted water. Cut them up and keep hot in a little of the water in which they were cooked. Add the rest of the water to the fish stock and bring to the boil. Thicken with flour mixed with

milk. Stir well and boil for 10 minutes. Add the root vegetable. A little sour cream and chopped chives may be added just before serving.
SERVES 6. C.W.

Crab soup

1 oz chopped onion
1 oz chopped green pepper
1 oz chopped celeriac
1½ tablespoons butter
2 × 14-oz tins chicken consommé
7-oz tinned tomatoes, drained and chopped
3 oz conchiglietti (tiny shells)
1 tablespoon chopped parsley
Good pinch salt
Dash pepper
7½-oz tin crab

Melt the butter in a large pan, add the onion, green pepper and celeriac. Cook until tender but do not brown it. Add the consommé, tomatoes, pasta, parsley, salt and pepper. Bring to boiling point, cover and simmer for half-an-hour. Drain and flake the crab; add it to soup and cook for not more than five minutes.
SERVES 4. W.G.

Watercress soup

2 bunches watercress
1 oz butter
1 onion
1 pint chicken stock
Parsley, thyme and bayleaf
Salt and pepper
1 tablespoon cornflour
½ pint milk
1 egg yolk
¼ pint double cream

Wash the watercress and break into pieces, removing any coarse stalks. Dry well and reserve a few sprigs for garnish. Heat the butter in a saucepan, add the chopped onion, and fry gently for 3 minutes until tender. Add the watercress and fry for another 2 minutes. Stir in the stock, herbs, and salt and pepper to taste. Bring to the boil, lower the heat, cover and simmer for 20 minutes. Remove the herbs and sieve or liquidize the soup. Return to a rinsed pan. Blend the cornflour with a little of the milk, and add it to the soup with the rest of the milk. Place over heat and bring to the boil, stirring until thickened, which will take about 3 minutes. Take off the heat. Mix the egg yolk with half the cream in a small bowl, and then beat the mixture into the soup. Return to very low heat and cook gently, stirring continuously. Do not boil as this will curdle the egg and cream.

Serve with a swirl of the remaining cream on each serving and a small sprig of watercress.
SERVES 4. M.N.

SOUPS

Zupa grzykowa
Dried mushroom soup

½ lb dried mushrooms
4 carrots
4 onions
2 sticks celery
1 teaspoon vinegar
½ lb macaroni
Salt and pepper
2 fl oz cream

Cover the mushrooms with water and soak overnight. Thoroughly wash and chop the vegetables and put in pan with the mushrooms, vinegar and seasoning. Add 2 pints water, bring to the boil and simmer for 40 minutes. Ten minutes before the cooking time is up, add the macaroni. Stir in the cream immediately before serving.
SERVES 4-6.   M.D.

White bean soup
Fasolia soupa

1 lb dried white beans
½ lb canned tomatoes
2 onions, finely diced
½ cup celery tops, diced
2 sprigs parsley, finely diced
3 small carrots, finely diced
½ cup fine olive oil
1½ teaspoons salt
A dash of coarsely-ground pepper
4 oz smoked bacon, finely chopped

Wash the beans and leave overnight in cold, salted water. Next day, drain off the water and tip the beans into a saucepan with 2 pints cold water. Bring to the boil, reduce heat and simmer gently for 1 hour. Add the remaining ingredients and simmer for a further 1½ hours. Garnish with parsley and a little paprika and serve.
SERVES 4.   D.V.

Cream of carrot soup

To give a slightly more unusual flavour, this recipe includes dill seed and white wine.
1 oz butter
4 oz onion, roughly chopped
1 clove garlic, crushed
1 lb carrots, roughly chopped
2 pints chicken stock
1 oz rice
½ teaspoon dill seed
3 fl oz white wine
3 fl oz double cream
Salt and pepper
Knob of butter
Chopped parsley

In a large saucepan melt the butter, then add the onion and garlic and cook gently for about 5 minutes until soft and translucent. Add the carrots, stock, rice and dill seed, cover and simmer for 30 minutes. Stir in the white wine and liquidize the whole mixture. Rinse the pan, add the liquidized mixture, then season to taste with salt and pepper, and adjust with the cream. Add the knob of butter and beat gently but do not boil before serving. Sprinkle with chopped parsley.
SERVES 6.   L.B./M.P.

Cold pea and mint soup

¾ lb cooked young peas
¼ pint yogurt
5 tablespoons soured cream
1 pint milk
1½ oz cooked lean ham or gammon
3 small mint leaves, finely chopped
Salt and pepper

Liquidize all the ingredients without seasoning. Then add salt and pepper to taste. Refrigerate well before serving.
SERVES 4.   M.M.

Iced cucumber soup

2 medium cucumbers
1 medium onion
3 pints chicken stock
2 oz butter
2 tablespoons flour
Salt and pepper
3 egg yolks
6-8 tablespoons double cream
2-3 drops edible green colouring
GARNISH
1 tablespoon mint or chives
3 tablespoons double cream, very lightly whipped

Peel cucumbers and cut into ½-inch slices. Simmer in pan with onion and stock for 15 minutes until soft. Put in liquidizer. Melt butter, add flour and cook until straw-coloured. Add the cucumber liquid. Stir until boiling. Season and simmer for 2-3 minutes.

Work the egg yolks and cream together. Take the soup off the heat and very slowly add 3-4 tablespoonfulls of hot soup to this mixture. Return to saucepan and reheat gently, without boiling, until soup thickens. Colour the soup very delicately and pour into the container ready for chilling. Cover the soup to prevent a skin forming and place in fridge.

When serving, pour soup into individual bowls, add a blob of lightly-whipped cream and sprinkle with the mint or chives. Serve with cheese straws.
SERVES 6.   M.L.

Summer bacon soup

1 knuckle smoked bacon
1 pig's trotter
Bayleaf, parsley and thyme
10 black peppercorns
1 onion stuck with 4 cloves
2 pints water
12 oz mixed summer vegetables
¼ pint sherry

Use a mixture of young carrots, peas and beans for the vegetables. Put the knuckle, trotter and herbs, peppercorns and onion into the water. Bring to the boil and simmer gently for 1½ hours. Strain and add the vegetables cut into dice. Cook until tender. Add the sherry and tiny pieces of bacon cut from the bone. Season and chill thoroughly.
SERVES 4-6.   M.N.

Green summer soup

1 pint pure apple juice
½ pint soured cream
½ medium green pepper
Cucumber (approx 3-inch chunk)
4 spring onions
4-6 oz cooked chicken
4 teaspoons cider vinegar
Salt
GARNISH
Lemon slices
Watercress leaves

Chill the apple juice and soured cream, then put into a basin and whisk together until smooth. Chop the vegetables and chicken into small pieces and add with the vinegar and salt to taste. Cover and chill for an hour to allow flavours to mingle. Serve in individual bowls, garnish with lemon and watercress.
SERVES 6-8.   P.M. (1)

Iced soup is a refreshing start to a luncheon on a hot summer's day. This one is Cucumber soup. (Recipe on this page.)

Green pepper soup

This soup is full of flavour and unusual enough to encourage your guests to ask what is in it. One thing to remember: you must sieve it (not difficult). It is not enough to purée it in the blender as this does not get rid of all the small pieces of pepper skin which would spoil the texture. Serve it hot or cold—I prefer it cold. If you are making it in advance, freeze it before adding the milk and cream. The milk should go in when you reheat the soup, the cream just before serving.

2 tablespoons oil
2 oz butter
8 oz green peppers, seeds and cores removed, then diced
2 onions, chopped
1½ oz flour
¾ pint home-made chicken stock or stock made with 2 chicken cubes
Salt and pepper
¾ pint milk
2 to 3 tablespoons single cream

Heat the oil in a saucepan, then add the butter. When it has melted, add the green peppers and onions and cook gently for 5 minutes. Blend in the flour and cook for 1 minute. Gradually stir in the stock and bring to the boil. Season and simmer, covered, for 30 minutes or until the vegetables are soft. Sieve the soup.

Return the sieved soup to the pan with the milk and heat through, adjust seasoning and just before serving stir in the cream. If serving the soup cold, turn into a tureen and leave to become quite chilled before swirling the cream across the top.

SERVES 4. M.B. (1)

Iced prawn soup

STOCK
1½ pints water
1 chicken stock cube
½ lb white fish, cut into large cubes
Pepper, freshly ground
Juice and thinly pared rind of 1 lemon
Pinch each of fennel, thyme, rosemary
SOUP
1 oz plain flour
1 oz butter
Stock—as above
3 tablespoons white breadcrumbs
1 lb shelled prawns
¼ pint white wine
Juice of ½ lemon
A little ground nutmeg
2 egg yolks
¼ pint single cream
Cucumber, finely chopped

Put all the stock ingredients into a saucepan and simmer for 15-20 minutes or until the fish is cooked. Meanwhile, cook the flour and butter together to form a smooth paste in another saucepan. Strain the stock onto the flour mixture and cook, stirring constantly until the mixture becomes thickened and smooth. Stir in the breadcrumbs (these give a pleasant light body to the soup).

Pound together, or liquidize, the pieces of white fish and about three-quarters of the prawns, adding a little of the wine if necessary to make the operation easier. Stir into the soup and add the wine, lemon juice and nutmeg to taste. Mix together the egg yolks and cream, stir in a few spoonfuls of the hot soup, then add this to the saucepan, stirring well over a gentle heat to complete the thickening for a minute or two.

Leave to cool, then refrigerate until well chilled. Before serving, add the rest of the prawns and garnish with diced cucumber.

SERVES 8. L.B. L.T. (2)

Avocado soup

½ pint well-flavoured chicken stock
2 avocado pears
2 tablespoons lemon juice
¼ pint single cream
¼ pint natural yogurt
3–4 tablespoons white wine
Salt and pepper

Make a well-flavoured chicken stock and cool. (This can be done in advance and frozen.) Peel the avocados, remove their stones and cut the flesh into large chunks. Put all the ingredients into a liquidizer, cover, and switch on to medium setting until a homogeneous creamy mixture is formed. Adjust the flavour with salt and wine. Put the soup into air-tight containers and store in the refrigerator until just before serving.

SERVES 4. L.B./H.B.

Avocado and carrot soup

1 avocado
1 small onion
1 10-oz can whole carrots
1 oz butter
2 pints of chicken stock
Concentrated orange juice
Chopped parsley
Salt and pepper

Finely chop the onion. Heat the butter, add the onion and fry gently until clear. Split the avocado in two lengthways, remove the stone and scoop out the flesh. Put avocado and onion in half the stock, bring to the boil and simmer for about 15 minutes. Drain the carrots and place in the liquidizer with avocado mixture and blend until smooth (or rub through a nylon sieve). Put into a saucepan, add the salt and pepper and remaining stock and bring to the boil. Remove from the heat and stir in the orange juice to taste (probably 1–1½ tablespoonfuls). Chill; decorate with parsley.

SERVES 6. M.M.

Avocado-prawn soup

3 ripe avocados
½ pint chicken stock
½ pint single cream
4 oz prawns
1 tablespoon finely chopped onions
Chives for garnish

Liquidize avocado flesh and a cupful of stock for the minimum time necessary to pulp the fruit. Place in a bowl, add other ingredients, stir to a smooth consistency. Chill for a day, garnish with chives and serve. (If made the day before, place avocado stones in mixture to prevent discoloration.)

SERVES 4. V.D./V.W.

Tomato and orange soup

1½ lb fresh tomatoes, blanched and seeded, or 1 14-oz can peeled tomatoes
1 onion
1 carrot
Juice of 4 oranges
Lemon rind
6 peppercorns
Bay leaf
1½ pints stock
¼ pint single cream

Roughly chop the onion and carrot and simmer in the stock with all the rest of the ingredients, except single cream and juice of oranges, for half an hour. Liquidize or strain through a sieve. Make a *roux* (by melting 1 oz butter and stirring in 1 oz flour), then add the liquid and juice from the oranges, and bring to the boil. Allow to cool, stir in the cream, and chill well. Garnish with chopped chives.

SERVES 4. M.M.

Tomato and cucumber soup

2 oz butter
1 medium carrot, peeled and diced
1 small onion, finely chopped
1½ lb fresh tomatoes
1½ pints stock
Salt and pepper
1 level tablespoon caster sugar
1 level tablespoon flour
½ cucumber
Single cream for serving

Melt half the butter in a large saucepan and add prepared carrot and onion. Cover and cook gently for five minutes. Add halved tomatoes, re-cover and fry gently for fifteen minutes to soften and extract tomato juice and to produce

The centrepiece of this Italian spread is a traditional, winter soup from Tuscany : Zuppa di Verdura Toscana. (Recipe on page 17.)

maximum vegetable flavour.

Stir in the stock, season with salt and pepper and sugar. Boil, then simmer gently for one hour. Draw off heat and rub the soup through a sieve. Press through as much of the soft vegetables as possible, discarding the remainder. Return the strained soup to the pan. Cream the flour with the remaining butter to make a *beurre manie*, add this gradually to the hot soup, stirring over low heat until soup is blended, thickened and boiling. Peel and slice the cucumber in half lengthwise. Discard seeds and dice the flesh. Add to a pan of boiling salted water, reboil and simmer for two minutes; this softens the cucumber and gives it a nice green colour. Drain and add to the tomato soup, check seasonings

and chill. Just before serving, swirl in a little cream, but *do not* stir in.
SERVES 6.   J.T.

Instant tomato bisque

1 large tin tomato soup
1 pint soured cream
Juice of one lemon
½ cucumber, finely sliced
¼ lb peeled prawns
Chopped chives

Pour soup into a bowl. Mix in soured cream and the juice of one lemon, to taste. Chill well. To serve, pour mixture into individual bowls. Add finely-sliced cucumber, prawns and sprinkle with chives.
SERVES 6.   M.M.

Piquant tomato soup

½ pint tinned tomato juice
½ pint good chicken stock
1 teaspoon powdered celery salt
½ crushed garlic clove
Half a bunch of watercress
6 large spinach leaves (without stems)
Finely-chopped mint

Mix tinned tomato juice with chicken stock. Add celery salt and crushed garlic clove.

Liquidize carefully-washed watercress with 2 fl oz of tomato-stock mixture and spinach leaves until a smooth purée. Then stir into the remaining tomato-stock mixture. Chill well. Before serving, sprinkle with finely-chopped mint.
SERVES 4.   M.M.

23

White gazpacho

4 cloves garlic
3 tablespoons of stale breadcrumbs
¾ pint milk
¾ pint chicken stock
3 fresh firm tomatoes
¼ pint wine vinegar
¾ pint water (approx.)
¼ cucumber
1 green pepper
1 red pepper
2 slices of bread
Salt and pepper

Chop the garlic and put the breadcrumbs with the garlic in a bowl and crush to a paste with a tablespoon of stock. Blend in the rest of the stock. Add ¼ cucumber, ½ green pepper, ½ red pepper and 2 tomatoes and liquidize. Allow the mixture to stand and marinate for two to three hours in a cool place. Add the cold boiled milk and the water. Add salt and pepper and the vinegar. Chill well.

Serve with bowls of the remaining diced tomatoes, green pepper, red pepper and cucumber. A bowl of croûtons can also be served. To make these, remove the crusts from the bread and cut into cubes. Beat an egg into a ¼ pint of cold milk. Dip bread cubes into this mixture and deep-fry in hot oil until golden brown. Drain thoroughly and serve when cold.
SERVES 6.　　　　　　　　　　M.M.

Gazpacho andaluz
Chilled tomato soup

1 clove garlic
Salt and pepper
3 tablespoons olive oil
2 tablespoons wine vinegar
1 oz fresh white breadcrumbs
1 lb tomatoes
Half a cucumber
1 large canned red pepper
1 small onion
½ lb ice cubes

Crush the garlic and place in a bowl with the salt, pepper, oil, vinegar and breadcrumbs and mix well so that the breadcrumbs absorb the oil and vinegar.

Peel the tomatoes, cut into quarters and remove the pips, peel the cucumber and cut into rough slices, remove any seeds from the pepper, peel and quarter the onion. Place all in a blender and reduce to a purée.

Stir the purée into the bowl and mix well. Add the ice cubes and leave in a cool place until ready to serve.

Serve with side dishes of diced cucumber, green pepper, fried bread and tomatoes.
SERVES 4–6.　　　　　　　M.B. (1)

Gazpacho is one of the most delectable of summer soups. Above are three versions to try, including one which is white.

Gazpacho

6 ripe tomatoes
1 large green pepper, seeds and core removed
1 large red pepper, seeds and core removed
2 cloves garlic
1 small cucumber, peeled
3 slices bread, diced
1 small onion
2 tablespoons wine vinegar
3½ fl oz olive oil
¾ pint tomato juice
Salt and cayenne pepper

Liquidize ¼ green pepper, ¼ red pepper, ½ cucumber, 1 clove garlic and four tomatoes. Strain into a bowl and stir in the tomato juice, vinegar, olive oil, salt and cayenne pepper. Blend in well and chill. For garnish: dice remaining tomatoes, cucumber, green pepper and red pepper and place each in small serving-bowls. Fry the diced bread in some butter and garlic until golden brown. Cool and serve in separate bowls.
SERVES 4.　　　　　　　　　　M.M.

Iced cucumber and avocado soup

½ pint milk
1 onion, chopped very finely
1 cucumber
1 oz butter
1 oz flour
2 ripe avocado pears
1 pint good chicken stock
Salt and white pepper
Blobs of soured cream for the top

Fry the chopped onion in the butter, very gently until it is soft but not brown. Stir in the flour, then add the milk and, stirring, bring to the boil.

Peel the cucumber, and cut it into very thin rings. Keep a few of these to float on the top for decoration. Whizz the rest up in a blender with the avocado flesh, and enough of the hot stock to keep it liquid. Put everything into the saucepan, and heat slowly to scalding point. Chill. Season to taste. Serve in individual cups, with a cucumber ring and a blob of soured cream in each one.
SERVES 4.　　　　　　　　　　P.L.

Jellied consommé rosé

3 pints rich brown stock
2 egg whites, whisked until frothy
2 egg shells, crushed
½ lb raw minced shin of beef (free of fat)
¼ pint red wine
½ oz gelatine

Make sure all the fat is removed from the stock when it is cold and the fat has risen to the surface in a firm layer. (The stock can be made in advance and frozen.) Put this stock into a clean saucepan with the egg whites, crushed shells, and the beef. Whisk lightly over a gentle heat until the mixture begins to simmer. Carefully remove the pan to the side of the heat to leave only one side gently bubbling for 5 minutes. At intervals of 5 minutes, and without further agitation, turn the pan gradually until each section has had its turn of gentle bubbling.

Remove from the heat and carefully (to disturb the crust of egg white as little as possible) pour the consommé through a double thickness of damp muslin set in a sieve over another saucepan. Discard the contents of the muslin. Add the wine to the consommé, and sprinkle the gelatine over the surface. Heat only to melt the gelatine, then pour into a suitable container and cool. Cover and chill well. If liked, the jellied consommé may be lightly broken up with a spoon before serving to increase the glittering effect.
SERVES 6.　　　　　　　L.B./J.E. (2)

Beef consommé

The basic stock for this consommé is made when a joint of topside is being cooked.

1 large beef bone
3 lb rolled topside
Dripping or cooking fat for browning
8 oz carrots
4 oz turnips
2 leeks
1 stick celery
1 oz parsnips
4 medium onions
6-8 whole cloves
Bouquet garni (bay leaf, large sprig of parsley, spray of thyme, a few peppercorns)
1 tomato
2 tablespoons salt
8-10 pints water

Ask the butcher to chop the bones to fit into the pot to be used (it must be very large), then brown them well in the dripping. Remove and set aside, then brown the joint of meat well on all sides and set it aside with the bones. Wash, peel and chop coarsely the carrots, turnips, leeks, celery, parsnips and *one* of the onions and brown these in the pan, adding extra fat if necessary.

Tie the herbs together loosely in a small piece of clean muslin. Peel the remaining onions and stud with the whole cloves. Cut the tomato in half across, sprinkle with a little sugar and brown well under the grill.

The basic preparation is now complete and the stock-making can proceed. Return the bones and meat to the pan with the browned vegetables, and add the 3 onions, the bouquet garni, tomato, salt and water. Bring to the boil, removing any scum which may rise to the surface by skimming with a metal spoon. Cover the pot and simmer for 45 minutes, then remove the meat for serving rare, cut in thin slices. (If liked, extra whole onions can be added to the pot for the last few minutes of the meat cooking and these can be served with the meat and a little of the juices for gravy.)

Continue to cook the bones and vegetables for a further 2 hours adding extra water if necessary, to ensure the bones are always covered.

TO CLARIFY THE STOCK

Remove the bones, strain off the liquid into a clean bowl and discard the vegetables. Cool the strained liquid, cover and chill well in the refrigerator for several hours to allow the fat to set in a firm skin on the surface. Carefully lift off this layer of fat which can be used for other cooking.

Put the skimmed stock into a clean saucepan and heat gently. Gradually

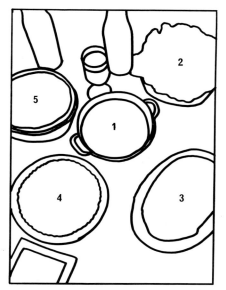

Beef consommé takes time to make but is well worth the effort for a light lunch or supper. **1** *Beef Consommé (see this page)* **2** *Lettuce salad sharpened with sliced radishes and spring onions* **3** *Glazed Carrots (page 112)* **4** *Peach Flan (page 145)* **5** *Cheese Pudding (page 44).*

whisk into the heating stock lightly whisked egg whites—1 white for every 1½ pints of stock. Continue to whisk the stock and the egg whites as the mixture heats. As soon as boiling point is reached, stop whisking and let the foam rise right to the top of the pan.

Turn down the heat or, if necessary, draw the pan off the heat to prevent boiling over. This operation may be repeated once or twice more to ensure the whole of the liquid has been reached by the egg white which traps solid particles as it coagulates.

Rinse out a clean white cloth in hot water and use it to line a sieve. Place the sieve over a clean bowl and pour the clarified stock through the cloth—slowly at first, keeping back the egg-white crust, then gently sliding the crust into the cloth and pouring through it. If the stock is not completely clear the first time, repeat the straining through the cloth and the egg-white crust.

The clarified stock is now ready for use in consommé.

The stock may be frozen and reserved for special occasions when there isn't time to carry through this lengthy process. If it is to be used within two or three days, it may be kept in the refrigerator. For a sparkling clear hot consommé, gently heat the stock and adjust the flavour to taste with madeira or sherry. Approximately 1 tablespoon is sufficient for 1½ pints. The consommé may be served plain or garnished. A few examples of some of the classic consommés are: Consommé à la Brunoise (tiny dice of cooked carrots, turnips, celery); Consommé Julienne (very thinly-sliced strips of vegetables cooked to a light brown in butter); Consommé à la Royale (fine dice of a savoury baked custard).

Allow between ¼ and ½ pint per person, depending on the substance of the rest of the menu. L.B.

Jellied bortsch

Although this soup is particularly good served cold, it may also be eaten hot.
FERMENT
1 lb uncooked beetroot
STOCK
2 lb uncooked beetroot
1 small head celery
½ lb each of carrots, swede, onions, cabbage, tomatoes
3 pints water
3 chicken stock cubes
1 clove garlic
1 clove garlic, crushed
Few peppercorns
1 bay leaf, pinch of dill seeds
CLARIFYING
2 whisked egg whites
FLAVOUR AND SET
¼ pint white wine
Juice of ½ lemon
1½ oz powdered gelatine (approx.)

Peel the 1 lb of beetroot, slice thinly and cover with water in a bowl. Cover the bowl and leave in a refrigerator or other cool place for about 1–1½ weeks to ferment. (It is this fermented liquor which gives the finished soup its rich red colour and distinctive musky flavour.)

A day or two before the ferment is due to be used, prepare and coarsely chop the vegetables. Place in a large saucepan with the other ingredients for the stock. Cover and simmer gently for about 45 minutes, stirring occasionally, until all the vegetables are very soft. Remove from the heat and strain into a clean saucepan, taking care not to rub as this will make the stock cloudy. Discard the pulp. Bring liquid to a gentle boil, then quickly whisk in the egg white, continuing to whisk over the heat until the egg white is cooked and forms a scum on the surface which entraps all of the particles, leaving the soup clear. Remove from the heat and strain through muslin back into the first saucepan.

Strain the ferment from the raw beetroot into the stock, using muslin to ensure clarity. Then add the wine and lemon juice to taste. Mix the gelatine with a few teaspoons of stock (use ½ oz gelatine for each pint of stock), then stir in to the hot stock and keep on the heat until the gelatine is completely melted. Pour into shallow tins and leave in a cold place until set. Either coarsely chop or cut in cubes and serve ice-cold.
SERVES 6. L.B./C.F.

Smoked salmon soufflé

This soufflé can be prepared in advance and kept in the refrigerator for up to 4 hours before being cooked.

6 eggs
4 tablespoons butter
5 tablespoons plain flour
½ pint milk
6 oz smoked salmon, cut into strips
3 tablespoons soft cream cheese
1½ teaspoons lemon juice
¼ teaspoon salt
¼ teaspoon cream of tartar

Separate the eggs and put them in large bowls. Prepare the 1½ quart soufflé dish in the usual way with a band of butter paper. Make a *roux* by melting the 4 tablespoons of butter, stirring in the flour and, finally, adding the milk. Stir and cook until it begins to leave the sides of the pan, then remove from the heat. Whisk the egg yolks and then beat in the cooked *roux*. Add the salmon, cream cheese and lemon juice and beat until well mixed. Add the cream of tartar and salt to the egg whites, and beat with an electric beater at high speed to the stiff peak stage. Then fold a third of the whipped whites into the warm salmon mixture until well combined and not streaky, then fold in the rest as lightly and quickly as possible. Pour into the prepared dish. If to be refrigerated, set the oven to 350°F (gas 4) for 65 minutes before serving time and bake the soufflé for about 55 minutes. Remove the paper and serve. Or, the soufflé may be baked as soon as it is made at 350 F (gas 4) for about 40 minutes.
SERVES 4. W.G.

Spinach soufflé

Even people who are not mad about spinach often like a soufflé made from it. And, served with a lobster sauce, it is glorious indeed (see page 119).

6 eggs
½ lb spinach
4 tablespoons butter
5 tablespoons plain flour
½ pint milk
1½ oz grated Swiss cheese
1 tablespoon parsley, finely chopped
¼ teaspoon garlic salt
⅛ teaspoon pepper
½ teaspoon salt
¼ teaspoon cream of tartar

Separate the eggs and put the whites in the bowl of the electric mixer and the yolks in another large bowl. Prepare a 1½ quart soufflé dish. Wash the spinach and discard the stalks. Put it into a pan, cover and cook for 5-8 minutes until just tender; drain and chop finely. Melt the

---

Croquettes look appetising and can be served as a first course or a light main course. (Recipes on pages 30, 90 and 106.)

---

butter in a pan, remove from the heat and add the flour and stir until smooth. Then add the milk and put back on the heat. Stir constantly. When thick and leaving the sides of the pan, remove from the heat. Beat the egg yolks with a wooden spoon and beat into the cooked mixture. Add the spinach, cheese, parsley, garlic salt, salt and pepper, and beat until well-blended. Add a little salt and the cream of tartar to the egg whites and beat at high speed until stiff. Fold a third into the warm spinach mixture and blend thoroughly, then fold in the rest of the whites until just blended. Put in prepared dish and bake at 350 F (gas 4) for about 40 minutes.
SERVES 4. W.G.

Mushroom soufflé

2 oz margarine
2 oz flour
½ pint milk
3 eggs, separated
4 oz Cheddar cheese
½ lb mushrooms
1 small onion
Salt and pepper

Make a white sauce with the margarine, flour and milk. Add the 3 egg yolks (beaten), grated cheese, sautéed mushrooms and onion, seasoning. Fold in the stiffly-beaten egg whites; bake in a greased soufflé dish at 375°F (gas 5) for about 40 minutes—until it has risen well. Serve at once.
SERVES 4. V.G.

Cold salmon soufflé

½ pint medium-dry cider
About 12 oz fresh salmon
Aspic jelly powder
About ¼ cucumber
Salt
¼ pint double cream
2 egg whites
GARNISH
Cucumber, parsley

Put the salmon into a fireproof dish with ¼ pint of the cider. Bake at 375°F (gas 5) for 20-30 minutes, until fish is cooked. Leave to cool in cider, then remove skin and bone, and chop. Heat remaining cider; dissolve in it the amount of aspic jelly recommended to make ¼ pint. Cool.

Next, remove skin and seeds from cucumber and chop enough to give 2 heaped tablespoonfuls. Put in nylon sieve, sprinkle with salt and leave until excess liquid has drained off. Stiffly whisk both cream and whites. When the aspic begins to thicken, fold in the salmon and cucumber, then the cream and egg whites. Pour into a soufflé dish (about 4½-inches diameter) with a band of greasproof paper tied to extend 2-inches above its top. When set, remove paper, using knife dipped in hot water.

Decorate top with cucumber slices and chopped parsley.
SERVES 6-8. P.M. (1)

Roux d'églefin fumé
Smoked haddock

1½ lb smoked haddock
3 eggs
Handful parsley, chopped
¼ lb butter
¼ pint milk
Seasoning and pinch basil
1 cup instant mashed potato
1 teaspoon French mustard

Cook haddock in pan on stove, with butter, seasoning and milk, until the fish is soft and flaky. Add the ready-mixed instant potato to the fish, plus the eggs, parsley and mustard. Consistency should enable you to mould it into small fish cakes (if further thickening is necessary, use another egg). Can be served hot or cold, with squares of fried bread and parsley to decorate.
SERVES 6. J.C. (1)

Seafood mousse

½ pint packet aspic powder
8 oz cooked lobster, crab or scampi
1 dessertspoon white wine vinegar
¼ pint double cream
Salt and cayenne pepper

Make up the aspic as directed on the packet, but with only ¼ pint water. Leave until cold. Pound together the shellfish and wine, and put the mixture through a sieve (or whirl it in a blender). Gradually add the aspic, a little at a time. Whip the cream to a soft peak and gradually fold into the crab mixture. It is best if this is done with the crab mixture in a bowl on crushed ice. Add salt and cayenne pepper to taste. Put into a soufflé dish, and garnish with a little chopped parsley.
SERVES 4. M.N.

Papillote de saumon fumé Claudine
Smoked salmon rolls

1 lb smoked salmon
1 smoked trout
½ pint cream
½ oz gelatine
3 tablespoons warm water

Cut four wafer-thin slices of the smoked salmon into large squares. Take the remaining salmon and the smoked trout, beat them both together with the gelatine (dissolved in the warm water).

To make a very fine purée, put them through a very fine sieve. Add the cream slowly and gently in the bowl which should be set on ice. With a spoon, garnish the slices of the smoked salmon and roll it together to make a papillote.

Glaze in aspic and serve very cold.
SERVES 4. M.R.

29

Crab vahine

1 × 4 lb king crab
½ avocado pear
2 tomatoes
¼ red pepper
1 hard-boiled egg
½ onion
1 sprig of parsley
Chervil
A few drops of tabasco sauce
1 lemon
Salt and pepper

Cook crab for 25 minutes in *court bouillon* (stock made with herbs, onions, peppercorns and carrots). Leave to cool. Remove flesh and keep in a cool place. Peel and remove seeds from tomatoes, then chop into cubes, and add finely chopped onion, chopped egg, parsley and chervil, tabasco and lemon juice. Then add salt and pepper to taste. Rinse crab shell with cold water and put mixture into shell. Then add crab meat and decorate.
SERVES 4.   M.R.

Mousse de crabe
Crab mousse

1 large cooked crab
Salt and pepper
Tomato juice
1 tablespoon parmesan cheese
2 drops Worcestershire sauce
¼ pint aspic jelly
¼ pint thick cream
2 egg whites

Take all the meat from the crab and pound it smooth in a mortar with the cheese and seasonings. Melt the aspic and stir in the mixture with the slightly beaten cream. Allow to stand in a cool place until dish has begun to set, then fold in the stiffly beaten egg whites. Turn into a soufflé dish and serve garnished with thinly-sliced cucumber.
SERVES 4-6.   J.E.

Mock caviar mousse

1 tin consommé
3½-oz jar lump fish roe
Chives, chopped
¼ pint double cream
2 large tablespoons mayonnaise
Juice of 1 lemon
¼ oz gelatine
Salt and pepper
Watercress to garnish

Pour consommé into a mould to fill it about ⅓ full. Chill until reset. Meanwhile, mix lump fish roe, chives (plenty), cream, mayonnaise and lemon juice. Dissolve gelatine in a little hot water and add to rest. Season to taste and pour over consommé in the mould. Chill again until set. Unmould and serve decorated with watercress.
SERVES 6-8.   C.W.

Shrimp pâté

4 oz shrimps
3 oz butter
4 oz cod or haddock
¼ teaspoon anchovy essence
Pinch of mace
Pinch of cayenne pepper

For this recipe, fresh shrimps should be used, but frozen ones which have been thawed can be substituted. Shell fresh shrimps and put the shells in a little water. Simmer for 10 minutes and strain this fish stock. Cook the cod or haddock for 5 minutes in the stock, or in plain water if frozen shrimps are used. Drain the haddock or cod, and mash with the mace, cayenne pepper and anchovy essence. Leave to cool, and meanwhile chop the shrimps into small pieces. Melt the butter and reserve 1 tablespoonful. Mash the butter with the cooked haddock or cod, add the shrimps, and press into a small bowl, or two individual bowls. When completely cold, pour on the remaining butter and leave until set.
SERVES 4.   M.N.

Prawn croquettes

1 small onion, minced
2 cloves garlic, crushed
2 tablespoons olive oil
1 tomato, finely chopped
½ green pepper, minced
1½ tablespoons chopped parsley
Pinch dried oregano
Salt and pepper
3 slices dry white bread (crusts removed)
½ pint milk
1½ oz flour
8 oz prawns, chopped
1 tablespoon Madeira
Breadcrumbs
2 eggs, beaten
Fat for frying

Sauté onion and garlic in oil until tender. Add tomato and green pepper, cook for about 10 minutes until soft. Stir in parsley, oregano, salt and pepper to taste. Remove from heat. Cover bread with about ⅖ of the milk; soak until soft. Squeeze dry and add onion mixture. Stir well. Make béchamel with butter and flour and remaining ⅗ of the milk. cook slowly, stirring frequently, for about 10 minutes, until thick and smooth. Remove from heat and stir in onion-tomato mixture, prawns and Madeira. Season. Spread out on flat dish and chill. Shape into croquettes. Coat with breadcrumbs. Dip in beaten egg. Roll again in breadcrumbs. Chill. Then leave at room temperature for an hour before deep-frying.
SERVES 4-6.   L.H./K.S.N.

French beans with prawns

¾-1 lb French beans
French dressing (made with good olive oil and lemon juice)
3-4 oz prawns
2 hard-boiled eggs
Salt and black pepper

Cook beans in boiling salted water until just tender. Drain and, while still warm, season with dressing. Cool. Pile on plate and dot with prawns and quartered hard-boiled eggs.
SERVES 4.   L.H. (2)

Marinated prawns

7 oz button mushrooms
8 oz fresh, peeled prawns
Juice of 1 lemon
3½ fl oz olive oil
Salt, black pepper
Parsley

Slice or chop the mushrooms if they are large. Mix with the prawns and finely-chopped parsley. Season with salt and freshly-ground black pepper. Add lemon juice and olive oil. Stir gently and leave to marinate for a good hour. Serve with hot French bread.
SERVES 4.   A.R. (2)

Prawns are the basis of some of the most decorative of first courses. This simple-to-prepare dish is Marinated Prawns. (Recipe above.)

STARTERS

Pickled prawns

8 oz peeled prawns
2 oz onions
2 bay leaves
⅛ pint salad oil
1½ tablespoons white wine vinegar
1 tablespoon capers
½ teaspoon celery seed
¼ teaspoon salt
Few drops of tabasco sauce

If the prawns are frozen, thaw and drain them well. Arrange prawns, thinly-sliced onions and bay leaves in a dish. Mix together the remaining ingredients and pour into the dish. Cover and refrigerate for 24 hours, spooning the liquid over the fish occasionally. Drain and serve the prawns on lettuce hearts or a bed of watercress, with thin brown bread and butter.
SERVES 4.   M.N.

Mixed seafood salad

10 cooked mussels
10 large shelled prawns
6 oz crabmeat
1 dessertspoon white wine vinegar
1½ tablespoons olive oil
¼ teaspoon made mustard
Salt and pepper
1 tablespoon chopped green pepper
2 tablespoons thick mayonnaise

Put mussels, prawns and crabmeat into a bowl. Mix the vinegar, oil, mustard, salt and pepper and pour over the seafood. Leave for 2 hours. Just before serving, mix in the green pepper and mayonnaise. Serve with crisp, shredded lettuce.
SERVES 4.   M.N.

Gambas al ajillo
Spanish-style prawns in garlic sauce

9 oz prawns (approx 18 to 20)
3 oz butter
2 cloves garlic
3 fl oz dry white wine
Salt, parsley and fresh lemon

Fry prawns in butter. When fried, add chopped garlic, salt, parsley and wine and stir until well-mixed. Serve hot with lemon
SERVES 3-4.   J.S.C.

Prawn-stuffed courgettes

4-6 courgettes
1 small onion
2 teaspoons tomato purée
¼ pint white wine
1 tablespoon chopped parsley
Juice ½ lemon
1 clove garlic
3-4 oz prawns
2 tomatoes, skinned and seeded
Olive oil

Cook whole courgettes in boiling salted water until tender—just. Drain, and

when cool, split in half lengthwise. With a small spoon scrape out and discard seeds so that each half-courgette now has a 'channel' along it. Arrange, skin-side down, on a serving-dish.

Gently fry in oil the finely chopped onion and garlic (if liked) until soft but not brown. Stir in tomato purée. Cook briefly, then add wine to thin, plus chopped tomatoes. Cook a few minutes longer. Remove from heat. Allow to cool slightly. Add prawns, chopped parsley, lemon juice, salt and pepper to taste. Spoon this sauce over each courgette half. Decorate dish with shredded lettuce or watercrêss.
SERVES 4.   L.H. (2)

Curried egg ring with prawns

12 hard-boiled eggs
½ pint jellied stock or tinned consommé
8 fl oz double cream
½ oz gelatine
Salt
FOR THE CURRY SAUCE
2 tablespoons olive oil
1 tablespoon curry powder
1 onion, chopped
1 clove garlic, crushed
1 tablespoon apricot jam
2 tablespoons tomato purée
2 slices lemon
¼ pint water
GARNISH
½ lb prawns
2 tablespoons vinaigrette dressing
Parsley
½ cucumber, sliced

To make the curry sauce, first soften the onion in oil with the garlic. Put in the curry powder and mix well with the onion. Cook all together for a few minutes, stirring well. Put in the tomato purée and the water with the lemon slices. Cook together for 7-10 minutes, and when well mixed, stir in the jam. Bring to the boil. When cool, strain the sauce into a jam-jar with an air-tight lid. It will keep in a fridge for several days.

Chop the hard-boiled eggs coarsely and add salt. Heat the consommé with the gelatine, stirring well. Pour it into a

shallow dish and put in the freezer part of the fridge. When nearly set, remove it, then whip the cream lightly and add the consommé, blending well together. Stir in the chopped eggs and then the curry sauce.

Grease a 9½-inch ring mould and spoon in the mixture. Leave to set in the fridge, overnight if you wish.

To unmould, lay the ring upside down on a plate and cover with a hot wet towel. It helps to loosen the sides first with a spatula knife. Toss the prawns in the dressing and fill the centre. Sprinkle with chopped parsley, and decorate with slices of cucumber.
SERVES 8-10.   A.R. (1)

Hors d'oeuvre roll

A roulade filled with cream and salmon or lump fish roe, which can be made in advance and frozen.
2½ oz butter
2 oz plain flour
Pinch salt
¾ pint milk
3 eggs (separated)
8 fl oz double cream
Juice of ½ lemon
3½ oz pot of salmon or lump fish roe

Line a swiss-role tin 11¾ by 7¾ inches with oiled greasproof paper and dust lightly with flour. Make a white sauce with the butter, flour and milk and season to taste. Remove from the heat and beat in the egg yolks. Beat the egg whites stiffly, fold in and spread the mixture evenly into the prepared tin. Bake 35-40 minutes or until golden brown and firm to the touch at 324°F (gas 3). Turn out onto a greased and floured greaseproof paper and leave to cool.

To prepare the filling, whip the cream until fairly stiff, stir in the lemon juice and the lump fish roe (some of the cream may be replaced by cream cheese if liked). Peel off the paper from the baked slab, trim the edges and spread with the filling. Roll up carefully but firmly. To serve, cut into eight slices.
SERVES 4-6.   L.B./N.C.

Kipper pâté

This is a subtle blend of smoked fish and lemon. It is best made at least a day in advance and stored in the fridge.

8 oz kipper fillets
3 tablespoons milk
3 oz unsalted butter, melted
1 clove garlic
Thinly-pared rind plus the juice of 1
  large lemon
3 tablespoons double cream
Freshly-ground black pepper

Poach the kippers in the milk for about 15 minutes or until they flake with a fork. Drain, remove the skin and bones, then cool. Put the fish into an electric liquidizer with the melted butter, garlic, lemon rind and juice and the cream. Blend until smooth then season to taste with pepper and more lemon juice if liked. Pile into a serving dish, cover firmly with foil or food film and store in the refrigerator for 24 hours. If pre-ferred, turn the pâté into individual dishes and cover with melted butter.

Decorate with sprigs of parsley and thin slices of lemon, then serve with brown bread and butter or melba toast.
SERVES 4.   L.B./J.D. (1)

Mackerel pâté

3 fillets smoked mackerel
10 oz butter, melted
6 oz Philadelphia cream cheese
Juice of ½ lemon
Salt and pepper
A little extra butter
Watercress or parsley to garnish

Have ready a 1 lb terrine or dish. Remove the skin and any odd bones from the mackerel. Purée in a blender in two batches. With the butter, cream cheese, lemon juice and seasoning blend until

smooth. This may be slightly curdled-looking but it doesn't matter one bit and doesn't affect the texture. Turn into the terrine, smooth the top and pour melted butter to cover. Leave in a refrigerator or cool place for several hours. Garnish with a sprig of watercress or parsley. Serve with hot toast and butter. (NOTE: this pâté freezes well.)
SERVES 8.   M.B. (1)

La mousse de maquereaux fumés à l'orange
Smoked mackerel and orange mousse

4 smoked mackerel
¾ pint double cream
3 egg whites
½ kernel nutmeg, grated
Rind and juice of 1 orange
¾ cup bechamel sauce (made with 1 oz
  flour, 1 oz butter, ½ pint cold milk)
1 tablespoon aspic
1 tablespoon tomato purée (optional)

Flake mackerel, removing all skin and bones. Grate orange over and add juice to the mackerel, then mix in grated nutmeg. Make the bechamel by melting butter in a heavy pan, sprinkle in flour, add a little grated nutmeg, a few drops of orange juice and cook slightly. Do not let the flour thicken yet, but allow to develop a strong colour. Take off the heat and slowly add ¼ pint of cold milk, stirring continually. Return to heat and boil gently, allowing to thicken gradu-ally. Season with salt and white pepper. At this point you may add 1 tablespoon of tomato purée if you like. Stir in 1 tablespoon of dissolved aspic and allow to cool. Add the bechamel to the mackerel and put in the blender, allow-ing to blend well. Whip cream to a semi-stiff consistency. Put the contents of the blender in a large mixing-bowl and fold in the cream. Beat the egg

whites until they are very stiff, and fold them in carefully.

Butter a 2½-pint terrine thoroughly, fill with the mixture and place in the refrigerator for 3 hours or more.

Turn out the mousse by placing the bottom of the terrine in boiling water for 10 seconds. If you then pass a knife round the edges, the mousse should come out without any difficulty.
SERVES 6-8.   N.L.

Buttered crab

7½-8 oz white crabmeat, fresh, frozen or
  canned
2 oz butter
1 oz flour
1 tablespoon white wine
2 tablespoons strong consommé
  (can be canned)
1 orange
1 lemon
Salt
A few grains of cayenne pepper
A pinch of grated nutmeg
Cooked shrimps to garnish

Thaw and drain the shellfish if neces-sary. Cut the meat into dice or flake it. Mix the butter and flour to a smooth paste. Mix together the vinegar and consommé. Cut some thin round slices of orange and lemon to garnish the dish. Cut them in half, and keep aside.

Cut the butter mixture into small pieces and mix them with the shellfish in a sauté pan. Heat gently, stirring, until the butter melts and coats the fish. Stir in the vinegar mixture and seasoning slowly, toss the shellfish and sauce together until the fish is well heated through and the sauce is thick. Keep the heat low, but keep the cooking time as short as possible. Put the mixture into warmed crab or scallop shells. Arrange the half-slices of orange and lemon round the edges of the shells, and scatter the shrimps over the sauced crab. Squeeze a few drops of orange juice or lemon juice over them, and serve at once, as hot as possible.
SERVES 4.   M.B. (2)

Quick crab pâté

1 large crab, 2 small ones or 8 oz good
  crab meat
2½ oz double cream
1 tablespoon grated parmesan cheese
Cayenne pepper
Lemon juice
Salt

Extract all the meat from the body and claws of the crab and mash very well with a fork, or pound in a mortar if you have one. Add the thickened cream, lemon juice, cayenne pepper and par-mesan cheese to taste. Pack the mixture into a pot and put it in the fridge for at least an hour before serving.
SERVES 6-8.   V.D./V.W.

Smoked trout mousse with smoked salmon

6 smoked trout
½ pint thick cream
1 tablespoon lemon juice
1 teaspoon horseradish
Black pepper
4 oz smoked salmon, thinly sliced
1 lemon, cut into segments
1 sprig parsley
Brown bread and butter

Take the bones and skin from the trout and put the flesh in a bowl. Pick through it carefully to make sure all the bones have been removed. Add the horse-radish, lemon juice and pepper to taste. Whip the cream and stir in: you should have a moist, but not sloppy paste; if it is too wet, add a tablespoon of fresh white breadcrumbs. Form the mousse into a flat mound on a plate and lay the smoked salmon slices over it, trimming the edges neatly. Decorate with lemon segments and a sprig of parsley. Serve with toast or brown bread and butter. The mousse can be eaten either with a fork or on toast.
SERVES 6-8. P.L.

Taramasalata
Cod's roe pâté

4 oz jar of fish roe
1 small onion
Juice of 3 lemons
¼-½ pint olive oil
4-5 slices white bread, trimmed

Mash the fish roe and add the grated onion. Add a little olive oil and beat thoroughly to a smooth paste. Moisten the bread and squeeze out all excess water. Continue beating the fish roe mixture and add alternately small pieces of the damp bread, olive oil and lemon juice. The mixture should be beaten until smooth and a creamy pink colour. If preferred, this recipe may be made in a blender at medium speed.
SERVES 4. D.V.

Smoked salmon lemons

4 oz smoked salmon pieces
1 oz butter, softened
1 pint double cream
Lemon juice to taste (approx. ½ lemon)
4 lemon shells

Pulverize the smoked salmon in a coffee-grinder or a food-mincer. Cream the butter into the salmon and when quite smooth beat in the cream gradually. Add lemon juice to taste.

Spoon the mixture into lemon shells and decorate with sprigs of parsley.
SERVES 4. L.B. C.P.

Snails with garlic butter is a classic combination. Less well known—in Britain, at least—are Escargots à la Poulette. (Recipe on page 47.)

Salmon and egg mousse

16 oz can consommé
½ oz powdered gelatine
8 hard-boiled eggs
7 oz can salmon
½ pint mayonnaise
¼ pint soured cream
Salt and freshly-ground black pepper
8 stuffed green olives

Put 5 tablespoons liquid consommé in a cup and add the gelatine. Soak for 5 minutes and then stand the cup in a pan of simmering water. Stir until the gelatine has dissolved and add to the remaining consommé. Chop the eggs finely (the easiest way is with a potato masher). Remove bones and skin from the salmon and mash the fish. Mix together the eggs, salmon, mayonnaise, soured cream and three-quarters of the consommé. Season carefully and pour into a 2-pint soufflé dish. Chill until set and then arrange sliced olives over the top. Pour over the remaining consommé which should be cold and almost setting. Chill for 30 minutes before serving. This could also be a light luncheon dish.
SERVES 6. M.N.

Salade Niçoise

3 tins tuna fish
4 hard-boiled eggs
4 tomatoes
1 large red pepper
1 green pepper
1 tin anchovies
Vinaigrette dressing, with chives and
*   parsley added*
Black olives
Ground black pepper

Cover the bottom of a shallow dish with tuna, draining off any surplus oil first. Put the pimentos into boiling water and boil for about five minutes, drain and leave to cool. Pour the vinaigrette over the fish and grind black pepper over it all. De-seed peppers, and with scissors cut them into thin strips. Lay these in an alternate green and red lattice pattern over the tuna. Fill the open spaces with slices of tomatoes and on them slices of eggs, then decorate with strips of anchovies. Dot with stoned black olives.
SERVES 6. A.R. (1)

Sardine eggs

8 hard-boiled eggs
8 sardines
1 tablespoon anchovy essence
2 tablespoons white sauce
A little oil and vinegar
Cayenne pepper

Shell the cold hard-boiled eggs and cut in half. Remove all the yolk. Skin and bone the sardines and then chop them and pound together with the egg yolks, anchovy essence and white sauce until

the whole becomes a smooth moist paste; season with vinegar and pepper. Put the mixture through a sieve and then pile into the egg cases (which should be overfilled). Garnish with parsley.
SERVES 8. J.T.

Calamares fritos
Squid Spanish-style

7 oz squid
3 oz flour
3 eggs
Salt
Lemon
Olive oil

Clean and cut squid crosswise to form rings and sprinkle with salt. Dip into flour and into beaten eggs. Fry until golden and serve hot with lemon. (Remember to cover pan when frying.)
SERVES 3-4. J.S.C.

Pirozhkis
Polish salmon puffs

½ lb cooked salmon
2 oz cream
1 tablespoon well chopped parsley
Seasoning
Lemon wedges
Puff pastry

Mash the salmon well and mix with the cream, parsley and seasoning. Roll out pastry and cut into rounds. Place a little of the salmon mixture on to each round, covering with another, damping the edges slightly and pressing together firmly to ensure that none of the filling escapes. Fry in deep fat until golden. Drain on paper and serve with lemon.
SERVES 4. M.D.

Melon and fish cocktail

1 small melon
¼ lb white grapes
6 oz cooked cod fillet
3 tablespoons mayonnaise
1 tablespoon double cream
Salt and pepper
TO GARNISH
Lettuce leaves
Paprika
A few peeled prawns (optional)
A few peeled grapes

Cut the melon in half, and scoop out the seeds. Cut out the flesh, without damaging the skin, and dice. Peel and seed the grapes and flake the fish into pieces, then add both to the melon. Mix the mayonnaise with the cream and season lightly. Fold the fish and fruit into the dressing, and pile it into the two melon cases. Garnish with peeled halved grapes and prawns; dust with paprika and serve on the lettuce. (It may be necessary to cut a thin slice off the bottom of each melon case so that it remains upright.)
SERVES 2. S.G.

Blinis au caviar rouge suédois
Pancakes with 'caviar'

10½ oz buckwheat flour
5¼ oz plain flour
1¾ oz baker's yeast
1 pint milk, lukewarm
⅓ pint beer
3 egg yolks
3 egg whites, stiffly beaten
Butter
Sour cream
Jar of lump fish roe

Dissolve the yeast in the lukewarm milk and then beat in the flour (sieved), beer, egg yolks, a few tablespoons of sour cream and a pinch of salt. Leave the mixture to stand for about 2 hours, then stir in the stiffly-beaten egg white. Pour a sufficient amount of the mixture, to make a 'pancake' about 5-inches across, into a greased iron pan or griddle and cook in the same way as drop scones, turning them as bubbles rise.

To serve, put a large spoonful of lump fish roe on the blini, plus some finely chopped onion or chives, a spoonful of melted butter and a spoonful of ice-cold sour cream.

(You can substitute smoked eel or herring, or Russian caviar, for the lump fish roe.)
SERVES 6. W.V.

Potted seafood

12 oz cooked lobster, crab, scampi,
  prawns or shrimps (peeled weight)
2 oz melted butter
¼ teaspoon pepper
Pinch of cayenne pepper
¼ teaspoon ground mace
¼ teaspoon salt

Pound large pieces of seafood, but leave small shrimps whole. Put the fish into a saucepan with half the butter and the seasonings, and toss lightly until heated through but not fried. Put into four small pots and leave to cool slightly. Cover with the remaining butter which has been melted but not browned. Store in a cool larder or refrigerator. Serve with hot toast or brown bread and butter. (Potted shellfish can also be used as a sandwich filling, or heated as a sauce with plainly cooked white fish.)
SERVES 4. M.N.

Gruyère savoury flan

This is a type of quiche to which the good melting qualities of Swiss gruyère give an extra appeal.
PASTRY
6 oz plain flour
4 oz softened margarine
1 tablespoon water, cold
Pinch of salt
FILLING
½ pint milk
1 oz butter
½ oz plain flour
3 oz grated gruyère cheese
Grated nutmeg
Salt and pepper
2 tablespoons single cream
4 oz chopped streaky bacon
GARNISH
4 triangles gruyère cheese

To make the pastry (which is very simple), blend together in a bowl 4 rounded tablespoons of the flour with the margarine, water and salt. Add the remaining flour and work together well with the hand until a smooth paste is produced. Roll out on a lightly-floured board and use to line a 7-inch flan ring or dish.

For the filling, put the milk, butter, and flour into a small saucepan and whisk vigorously over a moderate heat until the mixture thickens. Stir in the cheese, seasoning to taste, the cream, and the chopped bacon. Pour into the flan case and bake in the centre of the oven at 375°F (gas 5) for 35-45 minutes.

Ten minutes before the end of the baking time, arrange thin strips of bacon and triangles of cheese on top of the flan. Bake until brown and firm.
SERVES 4-6 L.B./B.S. (2)

Tuna omelette

2 soft herring roes
2 oz drained tuna fish
1 shallot
1 oz butter
3 eggs
Salt and pepper
Chopped parsley and chives
Squeeze of lemon juice

This should really be made with carp roes, but these are rarely obtainable, and the herring roes are a good substitute. Poach the roes lightly in a little water. Chop them with the tuna fish and shallot. Heat the butter and cook gently until the shallot is soft and golden. Break the eggs into a bowl and mix them lightly with a fork. Add to the pan, stir and cook until just set. Turn on to a hot dish and pour over a little more hot butter, chopped herbs and lemon juice.
SERVES 2. M.N.

Asparagus quiche

PASTRY
6 oz plain flour
1½ oz margarine
1½ oz lard
FILLING
Asparagus
½ pint milk
2 eggs
Salt and pepper

Make short-crust pastry in the usual way and line a 7½-inch flan dish or ring, then bake blind and cool. Arrange fresh, cooked asparagus, (tinned asparagus could be substituted) over the bottom of the pastry and pour over a mixture of milk, eggs and seasoning. Bake at 350°F (gas 4) for 40-45 minutes until just set. Serve hot or cold.
SERVES 4. L.B./S.P. (2)

Anchovy cream

6 oz plain flour
2 cloves garlic
7 oz can anchovy fillets
8 oz butter, softened
Juice of ½ lemon

Crush garlic and place in a basin with the drained anchovy fillets. Beat together well, preferably with an electric whisk, to form a smooth paste, then gradually whisk in softened butter and the lemon juice. Serve with toast.
SERVES 4. L.B./G.W. (2)

Dolmades
Stuffed vine leaves

1 cup olive oil
1 lb onions, chopped
1 cup uncooked rice
2 tablespoons chopped mint
1 cup hot water
8 oz minced meat
4 tomatoes, finely chopped
Vine leaves or cabbage leaves
1 lemon
Salt and pepper

Heat half a cup of olive oil and fry the onions until they are opaque. Add the rice and cook on medium heat for 5 minutes. Add all the remaining ingredients, except for the rest of the oil, the lemon and vine or cabbage leaves. Simmer for another 5 minutes; put on one side to cool. Rinse the leaves in cold water. They must be fresh and young, about the size of the palm of the hand. Drop them into boiling water and cook for 3 minutes, drain and rinse in cold water. Place the leaves, rib sides up, on a flat surface, and in the centre place a heaped teaspoonful of the filling. Fold both ends of the leaves inwards and then roll into a small parcel. Don't fold too tightly. Line the bottom of a shallow casserole with foil and place the dolmades side by side in layers. Sprinkle with lemon juice, add half a cup of olive oil and 1½ cups of hot water. Cover with foil and then cook in the middle of the oven at 350 F (gas 4) for about an hour. Serve hot, or cold with yoghurt.
SERVES 6. D.V.

Bacon spread

10 oz cooked bacon
3 teaspoons horseradish sauce
¼ teaspoon ground black pepper
3 tablespoons white sauce
½ teaspoon curry powder

Mince the bacon finely and add the other ingredients, blending them thoroughly. Serve with toast or crispbread.
SERVES 4. A.C. (1)

Bacon mousse

8 oz cooked bacon
4 tablespoons horseradish sauce
2 tablespoons mayonnaise
½ teaspoon mustard powder
½ oz gelatine
¼ pint water
¼ pint single cream

Mince the bacon finely. Melt the gelatine in water and put the bowl into a saucepan of hot water until the gelatine is syrup. Cool slightly and mix with the mayonnaise and cream. Add the remaining ingredients, mixing thoroughly. Pour into a moistened mould and chill until set.
SERVES 4. A.C. (1)

Melon mit Geflügel Salat
Melon with curried chicken

1 small Ogen melon per person
2 oz breast of boiled chicken, chopped
½ shallot, chopped
1 heaped tablespoon diced cucumber
6 banana slices
¼ apple, diced
Orange in wedges
2-3 tablespoons curry-flavoured mayonnaise

Mix all these ingredients together with curry-flavoured mayonnaise. (Quantities can be varied to taste.) Fill an ogen melon and garnish with parsley and radishes.
K.L.

Apple and cucumber salad

1 large cucumber
Equal quantity of sliced apples
Lemon juice
Salt and pepper
Whipped cream

Slice the cucumber, mix with the sliced apples and season with salt and pepper. Sprinkle with lemon juice. Stir in a little whipped cream and serve piled in a salad bowl.
SERVES 8. J.E. (1)

Apple salad

4 red dessert apples, cored
1 lemon
4 sticks celery
2 oz raisins
2 oz shelled walnuts
½ pint mayonnaise
Lettuce

Chop the apples without peeling, sprinkle well with lemon juice. Chop the nuts and celery roughly. Cut the raisins in half. Toss all ingredients in mayonnaise and serve on lettuce leaves.
SERVES 4. J.E. (1)

Savoury apple starter

4 large dessert apples
1 tablespoon lemon juice
1 oz walnuts, chopped
3 oz stilton cheese
2 tablespoons natural yogurt
1-2 sticks celery, chopped
Lettuce ; watercress

Remove the core from each apple. Cut in half horizontally. Sprinkle lemon juice over cut surfaces. Place walnuts, cheese, yogurt and celery into a basin. Mix thoroughly. Pile mixture into the cavities in apple halves. Stand apples on lettuce, decorated with watercress.
SERVES 6-8.

Orange salad

2 large oranges
1 tablespoon salad oil
1 teaspoon vinegar
Salt and pepper
1 teaspoon caster sugar

Cut the oranges in halves across, carefully remove the fruit from the skins without breaking the peel. Remove the pith and pips from the fruit and cut the fruit in small pieces. Mix together the oil, vinegar, sugar and lemon juice, salt and pepper. Mix with the fruit and serve in the orange-peel cups.
SERVES 4. J.E. (1)

In this under-the-eaves kitchen/dining-room, dinner begins with artichokes.

Artichoke hearts with chestnuts

12 cooked artichoke hearts, drained
2 oz lean bacon, diced
2 oz mushrooms, diced
1 oz butter
½ teaspoon thyme
½ teaspoon marjoram
Salt and freshly-ground black pepper
4 oz unsweetened chestnut purée
1 oz cheese, grated
1 oz fresh breadcrumbs
2 tablespoons sherry

Preheat the oven to 350°F (gas 4). Place the artichoke hearts in an ovenproof dish. Gently cook the bacon and mush-rooms in the butter until soft but not browned. Beat the herbs and seasonings into the chestnut purée and mix in the bacon and mushrooms and any juices in the pan. Fill the artichoke hearts—if there is any surplus, spoon it evenly over the dish. Combine the cheese and breadcrumbs and sprinkle over the arti-choke hearts. Pour over the sherry and cook for 30-40 minutes.
SERVES 4-6.   H.W.

Globe artichokes

Allow one artichoke for each person (the large French ones are the best buy).
Wash the artichoke well in salted water and cut off any stalk to level the base.
Cook them in boiling salted water for about 45 minutes or until a leaf can be easily pulled out. Drain well, and serve hot.

Serve hot with melted butter or soured cream and mustard sauce, or cold with French dressing.

SOURED CREAM AND MUSTARD SAUCE
2 level teaspoons dry mustard
1 teaspoon oil
2 teaspoons cider vinegar
Pinch caster sugar
Salt and pepper
¼ pint soured cream

Place the mustard in a small bowl and

blend in the oil, vinegar, sugar and seasoning. Add the soured cream and mix well, pour into a sauce-boat or bowl for serving and leave for at least an hour to allow the flavour to develop. M.B. (1)

Artichokes à la greque

12 small artichokes or 4-6 large ones
2 oz streaky bacon, fried and chopped
COURT BOUILLON
1 pint white wine
1 pint chicken stock
¼ pint olive oil
¼ pint lemon juice
Twist of lemon peel
2 sticks celery
1 large onion
2 carrots
1 leek
4 oz fat bacon
Small bunch parsley
2 sprigs fresh thyme
2 teaspoons black peppercorns, crushed
1 teaspoon coriander seeds, crushed
1 teaspoon salt

Wash, peel, and coarsely chop all the vegetables, and cut the fat bacon in chunks. Put all the bouillon ingredients into a large covered pan and simmer for 10 minutes. Wash the artichokes, break off the stalks at the base then place into the simmering stock and cook covered for 30-40 minutes (it may be necessary to cook a few at a time, depending on their size). The artichokes will be ready when the leaves can be pulled out easily, and the bases feel tender if tested with a skewer. Keep the heat down, and add water only if necessary to prevent boiling dry.

Remove from the pan, then strain and reserve the liquor. Pull off all the leaves, pull out the inner core of yellow leaves, and scoop out the thistle-like hairy choke. (The bases of the outer leaves may be scraped with a knife and the flesh collected added to soup if liked).

Pile the fleshy artichoke bottoms into a serving dish and pour over the liquor. Serve garnished with fried bacon pieces.
SERVES 4-6. L.B. C.T.

Artichoke hearts à la parisienne

4 artichokes
1 lb mushrooms
1 tin of poultry forcemeat balls
   (Quenelles de volaille)
1 or 2 carrots

Cook the artichoke hearts in boiling salted water. Simmer the quartered mushrooms and the forcemeat balls in a Bordelaise Sauce (see page 119). Fill the cooked hearts with this mixture and garnish with strips of cooked carrot.
SERVES 4. S.W. (3)

Oeufs froids Carème
Eggs carème

4 artichokes
6 oz smoked salmon
3 tablespoons mayonnaise
½ truffle
A dash of ketchup
4 eggs
1 lemon
1 sprig of tarragon
Salt and pepper

Cut off stalk and artichoke leaves as necessary to obtain an even base. Cook in salted water to which the lemon juice has been added. Leave to cool. Remove flower. Fill in the space with cubes of smoked salmon mixed with mayonnaise, ketchup and chopped truffle. Poach eggs. When cold, arrange on top of mixture; top with a slice of salmon.

Glaze with aspic and decorate with tarragon leaves.
SERVES 4. M.R.

Piperade

6 eggs
2 peppers
2 onions
2 tomatoes
2 tablespoons olive oil
Salt and pepper
2 slices jambon de Bayonne (optional)

Clean and slice the vegetables, removing seeds from the peppers. Heat the oil and gently fry the peppers and onions until the latter are yellow. Add the tomatoes, cook a few more minutes and add the crumbs to absorb the surplus liquid. Well beat the eggs with the seasoning and add to the pan, stirring all the time as for scrambled eggs, removing as soon as they begin to solidify. If jambon de Bayonne is served, fry quickly in butter in a separate pan.
SERVES 4. M.D.

Bruges eggs

8 eggs
1 teaspoon minced chives
2 oz butter
1 teaspoon French mustard
½ pint cream
4 oz prawns, cut lengthways (or shrimps)
Salt and pepper
1 teaspoon minced parsley
Grated cheese

Hardboil eggs. Shell and chop into small pieces. Place in a saucepan with butter, chives, parsley, mustard, prawns, salt, and pepper and cream. Mix well over a low heat, but don't allow the cream to boil. Remove to a fireproof serving dish and cover with grated cheese. Dot with butter and bake or grill until the cheese melts and becomes brown. Serve with toast.
SERVES 6. C.W.

Oeufs benedictine
Eggs hollandaise

For each person you require:
1 egg
1 crumpet
1 slice of tongue
Hollandaise sauce

Put the slice of tongue on to a toasted unbuttered crumpet, and on top of this put a poached egg. Over the whole pour hollandaise sauce until the egg and crumpet is completely covered. Serve immediately. J.T.

Danish egg-cake

½ lb Danish bacon rashers (back or streaky
1 tablespoon flour
6 tablespoons milk
4 eggs
Salt and pepper
½ oz butter
GARNISH
Chopped chives and tomato quarters

Remove the rinds from the bacon rashers. Cook on grill until golden brown and crisp. Remove and keep warm. Meantime, blend flour and milk. Beat in eggs and season. (If you have any whites over from other cooking, you can add them, but use a little less milk.) Melt butter in pan, heat until just turning brown. Pour in egg mixture and cook over fairly brisk heat until set, lifting the edges occasionally.

When ready, place bacon rashers in star pattern on top, garnish with tomato quarters and chopped chives. Serve immediately in the pan. (Can also be eaten cold.)
SERVES 3-4. I.M.

Huevos à la flamenca
Flamenco eggs

1 small onion
4 tomatoes
8 stuffed green olives
2 canned red peppers
4 oz button mushrooms
A little butter
Salt and freshly ground black pepper
4 eggs

Chop onion very finely. Peel and slice the tomatoes. Slice the olives, pepper and mushrooms and mix with the tomatoes and onion.

Divide mixture between 4 well-buttered individual ovenproof dishes. Dot with butter and season. Stand dishes on a baking tray or meat tin.

Bake at 400°F (gas 6) for about 10 minutes, until vegetables are barely soft. Make a hollow in the vegetable mixture in each dish. Crack eggs into the centres and bake for a further 4-5 minutes, until eggs are just set. Serve at once.
SERVES 4. M.B. (1)

STARTERS

Tortilla Espanola
Traditional Spanish omelette

6 oz potatoes
2 oz onion
3 eggs
Olive oil

Can be served hot or, as a cocktail aperitif, cold and chopped into small cubes. Peel and cut potatoes into small cubes and fry until half-cooked. Add chopped onions. Continue to fry until almost cooked, then add beaten eggs and mix together with a fork. Continue to fry, turning omelette once, until golden.
SERVES 2.   J.S.C.

Egg fricassee

6 hard-boiled eggs
3 anchovy fillets, drained
½ small onion
1 oz butter
½ pint dry white wine
1 tablespoon finely chopped herbs, such as parsley, thyme and marjoram, fresh if possible
1 teaspoon grated lemon rind
6 egg yolks
Sprinkling of grated nutmeg
Salt and pepper if needed

Slice the hard-boiled eggs. Chop the anchovy fillets and onion finely. Heat the butter gently in a deep frying pan or skillet, put in the egg slices, and turn them in the butter until they are well heated through and beginning to colour. Pour off any remaining butter. Add the wine with the chopped anchovy fillets, onions, herbs and lemon rind. Bring gently to simmering point, and cook for 3-4 minutes to reduce the liquid slightly. Take the pan off the heat, and allow to cool a little. While cooling, beat the egg yolks with the sprinkling of nutmeg. Whisk slowly into the yolks 3 table-spoons of hot wine from the pan. When well mixed in, return the pan to the lowest possible heat, and stir until the mixture thickens. Taste, and add any pepper and salt needed. Serve at once.
SERVES 6.   M.B. (2)

Convent eggs

3 hard-boiled eggs
4 medium onions
1 pint milk
2 oz butter
1 oz plain flour
Salt and pepper

Slice the eggs thickly. Peel the onions and boil them until half-cooked. Cut them in slices and fry them until golden in half the butter. Melt the remaining butter, work in the flour and add the milk. Cook gently and stir until the sauce is creamy. Add the onions, and simmer for 15 minutes. Season well; add egg. Simmer for 5 minutes; serve hot.
SERVES 4.   M.N.

Spinach and cheese quiche

WHOLEWHEAT PASTRY
8 oz wholewheat flour
5 oz butter
2 tablespoons water

There is no need to bake the case blind for this dish, just line your flan tin with the paste.
FILLING
2 lb fresh spinach or 8 oz frozen spinach
4 oz mozarella or cream cheese
1 oz butter
Nutmeg
1 onion
A little garlic
Juice of half a lemon
Salt and pepper

Melt butter, gently cook chopped onion, add cooked, drained and squeezed spinach, heat through, adding season-ings. A few herbs may be added if desired, but use sparingly so as not to overpower the spinach. Stir in the cheese. Pack into flan case. Dot top with butter. (A mixture of white breadcrumbs and parmesan cheese can be sprinkled on top, to give a gratin finish.) Bake at oven 350 F-375 F (gas 4-5) for half an hour, until pastry is browned.
SERVES 4.   J.V-Z.

Rillettes

An interesting and easy-to-make alterna-tive to the better-known pate. The secret is prolonged cooking in wine with lots of herbs, to produce meat of a soft, melting quality which keeps well (covered) in the fridge for up to two months.
3 lb pork, half fat and half lean
2 cloves of garlic, crushed
Bay leaf
Sprig each of fresh thyme and fresh sage
½ small onion, chopped
¼ pint white wine
Salt and black pepper

Cut the meat into cubes, place into an ovenproof dish with all the other in-gredients and season well with lots of salt and pepper. Cover and cook at 300°F (gas 2) for about 3 hours or until the meat pulls apart in shreds when tested with two forks. During cooking, keep pressing the meat down below the surface so that is doesn't dry out.

When cooked, drain off the fat and juices and reserve. Discard any large pieces of fat or gristle, then tear the meat apart into shreds with the prongs of the forks, and finally mash well. Pack into six small jars and pour the reserved juices over. Cool and, if necessary, pour over more melted lard so that the entire surface is covered to a depth of a good ¼-inch. Serve with toast.
SERVES 6.   L.B./C.R. (1)

Duck terrine

For this recipe you need a 1-pint size terrine dish.
BASIC INGREDIENT
2 lb duckling
8 oz streaky bacon
MARINADE
Juice of 1 large orange
2 tablespoons brandy
1 chicken stock cube
1 small onion, finely chopped
pinch of rosemary
PÂTÉ
8 oz belly pork fat, cut in small cubes
8 oz chicken livers
1 Spanish onion, coarsely chopped
1 clove garlic
2 oz breadcrumbs
DECORATION AND ASPIC
2-3 small bay leaves
3 orange segments
1 chicken stock cube
¼ oz gelatine
½ pint less 2 tablespoons water
2 tablespoons orange juice

Remove 4-5 slices of breast from the duckling and place in a marinade made by mixing all the listed ingredients together. Allow to stand overnight in the refrigerator to develop the flavour. Put aside remaining duck flesh.

Cut the rind from the bacon and flatten the slices with the back of a knife until they become translucent, then place across the base and sides of a 1-pint terrine dish. Mince together all the pâté ingredients, plus the remaining duck flesh, and mix to a soft moist paste with the marinade drained from the duck. Place half the mixture into the terrine, add the pieces of duck breast, then cover with the rest of the pâté mixture. Set in a pan of hot water, cover, and bake about 2¼ hours at 350°F (gas 4) or until a skewer inserted into the centre comes out clean. Allow to cool for a few minutes, then pour off as much of the collected juices as possible.

Leave the pâté to cool for a further 1 hour then set heavy weights (such as tinned foods, etc.) on top to compress. When completely cold, decorate with orange segments and bay leaves and cover with aspic, made by mixing the ingredients together in a small saucepan over a low heat and stir until the gelatine is completely melted; then strain over top of the pâté. Leave in the refrigerator to set, and serve cold from the terrine with slices of hot toast.
SERVES 6-8.   L.B./S.B.

Mexican-style dips are ideal for buffet and drinks parties. The dish in the foreground is Salsa Mexicana, a hot tomato sauce (page 119). Behind that, at left, is Guacomole, a purée of avocado, highly seasoned with garlic, salt, black pepper and lemon, and, at right, is Ceviche, raw fish marinated in fresh lemon juice (page 68).

Liver and pork pâté
of the 'rough' variety

1 lb of liver
6 oz belly of pork
10 peppercorns
10 juniper berries
2 tablespoons brandy
2 cloves garlic
4 rashers streaky bacon
Salt

Mince together liver, pork, peppercorns, juniper berries and garlic. Stir in the brandy and a little salt. Put the mixture into a terrine, cover with strips of bacon. Place terrine, with lid, in a baking-tin of hot water. Cook for one hour and remove the lid. Continue for half an hour. Keep for two days in the fridge and then serve with hot toast.
SERVES 6-8. U.S.

Chicken cheese and chive terrine

3 lb roasting chicken
2 lb leg of pork or veal
8 oz extra pork fat
8-oz packet of Philadelphia cheese (or 3 3-oz packs)
1 tablespoon finely chopped chives (or green tops of spring onions)
1 tablespoon chopped fresh parsley
Large clove garlic, finely crushed
Finely shredded rind of half lemon
¼ pint cream
4 tablespoons brandy
2 eggs
Salt and pepper

Skin the chicken, leaving breasts whole. Cut meat from legs and wings, etc. Cut pork and fat into mincer-size pieces, and together with leg meat, put twice through mincer. Place boned breasts in shallow dish with garlic and half the parsley. Season lightly. Leave to marinate for 2 hours. Mix cheese with cream, eggs and lemon rind. Mix with mince-meat thoroughly. Add parsley and season well. Mix again to ensure a thorough blend. Pour in marinade liquid and mix yet again.

In the mind's eye, divide the mixture into two or three equal portions (depending whether your terrine is short, fat and deep, or long and narrow, as to whether you make a two- or three-layer affair). Lay the first portion of the forcemeat in the bottom of the dish, pressing well down. Lay the first breast (or both according to shape of dish) on top of

Pâtés and terrines are practical starters for a party as they can be made well in advance. Several variations are given in this chapter—but the one in the photograph is the authentic Pâté de Fois Gras de Strasbourg, available (at a price) from good delicatessens.

this. Now put the second (or final) layer of forcemeat on. Press well down. Cover and cook in a hot-water bath in the oven at 400°F (gas 6) for 1½ hours. Cool, then press with a foil-covered piece of board and a weight. Refrigerate for at least a day. Depending on the state of your household budget, the terrine can be bacon-lined or not!
SERVES 8. M.S.

Swedish pâté

½ tablespoon chives
6 pieces streaky bacon
2 tablespoons chopped onion
1½ tablespoons minced shallots
2 lb pork sausage meat
4 eggs
8 oz fine white breadcrumbs
1 tablespoon black pepper
1 tablespoon salt
Pinch thyme
Pâté crust (see below)

Cook the pieces of streaky bacon over low heat with the chopped onion. When the bacon is crisp and brown, lift it out of the pan and chop it coarsely with the minced chives and shallots. Take the pork sausage meat (preferably that made by your butcher), break it up with a fork and add to the first ingredients. When blended knead the mixture. Now add the whole eggs and fine white breadcrumbs, black pepper, salt and thyme. Again mix well and press into a greased loaf tin or mould lined with the pastry given below. Bake at 350 F (gas 4) for 35-40 minutes. Take out of the oven, invert the tin and leave it to stand all night in a cool place. When cold the contents will slide out of the tin. It may be served garnished with tomato slices, quartered hard-boiled eggs, gherkins and curls of celery and carrot.
SERVES 6. W.G.

French-style pâté crust

1 lb sifted flour
½ teaspoon salt
3 egg yolks
4 fl oz water, cold
12 oz butter

Sift the flour and salt into a bowl, make a well in it and put in the blended egg yolks, cold water and 4 oz of the butter. Work from the centre using a pastry blender or two knives; cut and mix until the mixture looks like fine breadcrumbs. Leave in a cool place for ten minutes to rest, then roll out an inch thick on a floured surface. Dot with the rest of the butter and roll out with a rolling-pin. Fold in four parts, envelope fashion, cover with a damp cloth and put into the refrigerator for about one hour. Roll out again to 1 inch thickness and fold as before and put back into the refrigerator. Repeat this five times in all with an

hour in the refrigerator between each rolling. This paste may encircle the charms of any pâté mixture such as this.
SERVES 6. W.G.

Marbled veal

As the name suggests, this eighteenth-century dish has the appearance of marble when sliced. Serve it straight from the pot in which you cook it, or turn it onto a platter with a clean white napkin. It is better for being made a day or two in advance and should be accompanied by a spoonful of delicate home-made mint jelly or Cumberland Sauce.

12 oz leg of veal
12 oz fat loin of pork
4 oz additional pork fat from loin or back
Thick slice of cooked ox tongue weighing about 4 oz
2 whole raw chicken breasts
2 eggs
1 tablespoon chopped chives or green tops of young spring onions
2 teaspoons finely shredded lemon zest
½ pint water
1 teaspoon gelatine crystals
Salt and freshly ground black pepper

Bring ¼ pint of water to the boil. Remove from the heat, add the gelatine and stir until completely dissolved. Add the remaining ¼ pint of cold water. Put on one side until needed.

Trim the meats of any skin or gristle. Put the veal, pork and fat through the fine blade of the mincer twice. Add all the seasonings and herbs. Bind with the eggs and beat in the cooled gelatine.

Cut the tongue and chicken breasts into ½-inch cubes. Mix together with the prepared forcemeat.

Butter a seamless loaf tin or ovenproof pot that is just large enough to contain the mixture. Fill the receptacle and cover with a lid or foil. Stand this in a meat or dish large enough to hold enough hot water to come half way up the sides of the pot.

Cook in a pre-heated oven at 350°F (gas 4) for 1½ hours or until the juices are clear. Remove the lid or foil for the last 20 minutes of the cooking time.

When cooked, remove the pot from the hot water 'bath' and leave to cool before arranging a foil-covered piece of board and a kitchen weight to press the meat. Put the weighted pot into the refrigerator to set.

NOTES: (1) To arrive at finely-shredded lemon zest, remove the zest with a potato peeler and shred with a large sharp cook's knife. (2) Allow the Marbled Veal to cool completely before refrigerating. (3) Wet the hands with cold water to aid the filling and pressing of the raw forcemeat into the mould.
SERVES 6-8. M.S.

STARTERS

Chicken liver pâté

½ lb chicken livers
½ teaspoon salt
Pinch cayenne
2 oz soft butter or chicken fat or clarified
    goose fat (dripping)
2 pinches ground cloves
1 teaspoon dry mustard
2 teaspoons minced onion
1 pinch nutmeg

Cover the livers with warm water in a pan, bring to the boil and simmer for 15-20 minutes. Strain and put the livers through the mincer, using the finest blade, twice. Mix with the salt, cayenne, butter or fat, nutmeg, mustard, cloves and onion. Blend thoroughly. Pack the mixture into a stone jar and put into the refrigerator. (A truffle mixed with the mixture enhances it.)
SERVES 3-4.   W.G.

Pâté froid de volaille
Chicken pâté

This pâté takes time to prepare but the result is excellent.
5 lb chicken
½ lb lean veal
4 oz ham
½ lb lean pork
4 oz fresh mushrooms
4 fl oz cream
¼ teaspoon salt
⅛ teaspoon black pepper
Pinch cayenne pepper
Dash nutmeg
1 good pinch each of thyme, powdered
    cloves and allspice
4 oz dry breadcrumbs
2 tablespoons grated onion
3½ oz cream cracker crumbs
Pâté crust (see page 43 for recipe)

Bone the chicken and remove the skin. Mince the veal, ham and pork. Put the chicken in a cold place and make the following stuffing. Mix the minced meats, minced mushrooms and add the cream, salt, peppers, herbs and spices. Moisten the crumbs with a little milk, then squeeze them dry, add the bread and the onion to the first mixture. Put all through the mincer and then divide into three parts. Put the boned chicken on a damp surface and spread one part of the stuffing on it and reshape the bird into as near as possible its original shape and lard it with ¼ lb fat pork cut in strips. Line an oval mould with a ⅛-inch layer of pastry crust and spread the second third of the stuffing on it, pressing it firmly into place. Put the stuffed chicken on top and spread the rest of the stuffing on top and into any crevices. Put the mould into the oven pre-heated to 350°F (gas 4) and bake for 2½ hours. If the top begins to get too brown, cover it with paper or cooking foil. When done, take out of the oven, stand for 20

Although these dishes were prepared for a summer picnic, the Asparagus Quiche, served hot, would make an equally good starter for a more formal meal indoors.
1 *Danish sandwiches, made with different types of bread—pumpernickel, Vienna, wholemeal, etc—plus a variety of fish and meat toppings* **2** *British Raised Pie (page 87)* **3** *Irish Spiced Beef (page 83)* **4** *Asparagus Quiche (page 36).*

minutes, then let it slip gradually from the carefully upturned mould on to a baking-tin. The crust will be on top if all has gone well, so brush it with beaten egg and milk and return to the oven with the heat increased to 525°F (gas 7) for a few minutes until the crust is golden-brown and crisp. Cool before eating.
SERVES 8.   W.G.

Spinach nests

2 lb spinach
2 oz butter
2 oz parmesan cheese
¼ pint cream
4 eggs
1 tablespoon flour
Salt and pepper

Clean the spinach by washing under cold running water. Do not drain but put straight in a large, heavy saucepan, without adding any more water, and cook for ten minutes. Drain and squeeze out all excess moisture, using your hands if necessary. Put butter in the saucepan and add spinach. Cook for a few minutes over a high flame. Add salt and pepper and then the flour and the cream. Leave to cook for a few minutes, stir and then put into a large baking-tin. Level the surface and then make four 'nests'. Break an egg into each of these nests. Sprinkle with parmesan cheese and put in a preheated oven and leave until the whites are set.
SERVES 4.   J.B. (1)

Cheese pudding

This is easy to make and is a good way to use leftover bread and scraps of cheese. It is also suitable for a light main course.

6 oz bread
1 pint milk
Pinch of salt
Pinch of mustard
3 large eggs
4-5 oz grated cheddar cheese

Break the bread into small chunks and mix well with the milk, egg yolks and seasonings. Leave for ½ hour for the bread to soften and absorb some of the liquid, then stir in the cheese. Beat the egg whites stiffly and fold lightly into the bread mixture. Turn into a greased 3-pint oven dish and bake for about 45 minutes at 350°F (gas 4) until well risen and golden. Serve the Cheese Pudding at once.
SERVES 4.   L.B.

Mushroom and cauliflower vinaigrette

1 firm cauliflower
½ lb small white button mushrooms
4 fl oz olive oil
Juice of a lemon
Salt and pepper
2 tablespoons split almonds

Break the cauliflower carefully into its smallest florets. Bring a pan of lightly-salted water to the boil and cook the florets for no longer than 2 minutes. Drain and run cold water through them until quite cool. Drain again. Cut the mushrooms into quarters. Make a dressing with the oil, lemon juice, salt and pepper. Toss the mushrooms, florets and almonds in this dressing. Chill before serving.
SERVES 6-8.   M.S.

Mushroom cups

Little bite-sized savouries of pâté and mushrooms in containing cups of bread, served hot or cold.
6 thin slices of brown bread
Butter
3-4 oz pâté
3 tablespoons cream
3 tablespoons cider
12 button mushrooms

Cut the bread into rounds with scone cutters, 2 per slice, then butter well on one side. Press the bread into small patty tins butter side down. Blend the pâté with the cream and cider, then use to fill the bread-lined tins. Sauté the mushrooms in a little butter and place one on top of each filled case. Bake at 350°F (gas 4) for 5-7 minutes until set.
MAKES 12 CUPS   L.B./S.N.

Savoury orange cups

This colourful dish is best made in advance to allow the flavours time to develop. Leftover cooked chicken and cooked rice may be used, and ingredients adjusted to taste.

1 oz American rice
1 oz oil or butter
1 small onion, finely chopped
4 oz button mushrooms, thinly sliced
4-6 oz cooked chicken
2 oz shelled prawns
4 large oranges
2 tablespoons mayonnaise
Salt and pepper

Cook the rice in boiling salted water according to the instructions on the pack. Then leave to cool.

Sauté the onion and mushrooms in the butter until tender and the onion becomes translucent. Remove from the heat and lightly mix with the prawns, chicken cut into small pieces, and the cooled rice.

Cut the oranges in half and carefully remove the half segments, then add these to the other ingredients. Stir in mayonnaise to moisten, season to taste, and pile into the orange shells. Cover to prevent drying-out, and chill well before serving on a bed of lettuce leaves.
SERVES 8. L.B./T.F.

Ryz z szynka
Rice with ham

2 slices smoked ham
4 tablespoons long-grain rice
½ pint sour cream
2 egg yolks
Seasoning

Boil the rice fast (preferably in stock) until just cooked, then drain well. Mix with the cream and egg yolks, seasoning and chopped ham. Put in a well-greased, oven-proof dish and bake for 20 minutes in a moderate oven.
SERVES 4. M.D.

Escargots à la Poulette

24 snails
1 oz butter
1 onion, finely chopped
¼ pint dry white wine
2 egg yolks
1 tablespoon cream
Juice of ½ lemon
Parsley, finely chopped

Melt butter, add finely-chopped onion and gradually stir in wine. Then add egg yolks, cream, lemon juice and parsley. Add the snails and heat through.
SERVES 4. M.D.

Seafood, unadorned, is a luxurious way to begin a summer buffet. For the prawns, a separate bowl of mayonnaise (page 120) should be provided.

Asparagus hollandaise

2 bundles cooked fresh asparagus
6 oz butter
4 tablespoons wine vinegar
6 peppercorns
1 blade of mace
1 slice of onion
Small bay leaf
3 egg yolks
2 tablespoons double cream
Squeeze lemon juice

Gently heat the butter in a small saucepan, until it is completely melted and the bubbling ceases. Skin the froth from the surface, then carefully pour the clear liquid butter into a basin and leave until set. Discard the residue in the pan.

Boil the vinegar with the spices and onion until reduced to about 1 tablespoon. Cream the egg yolks in a basin over hot but not boiling water and add the strained vinegar. Gradually, a small piece at a time, beat in the prepared butter until it is all used and the sauce has thickened. Stir in the cream and lemon juice to taste. The sauce should be served lukewarm with the asparagus (if it is allowed to become too hot and curdles, whisk in a small ice cube until it becomes smooth again).
SERVES 6. L.B./A.C. (2)

Avocado salad

1 large avocado pear
2 lettuce hearts
2 sticks celery
1 green eating apple
½ small green pepper
¼ lb green grapes
DRESSING
6 tablespoons corn or vegetable oil
2 tablespoons lemon juice
Salt and pepper
½ level teaspoon dry mustard
½ level teaspoon caster sugar
A little freshly chopped parsley

Cut the avocado in half lengthwise, remove the stone and the peel, then cut into thin slices, brush with a little lemon juice. Wash and drain the lettuce and break into small pieces. Slice the celery and peel, core and slice the apple.

Remove the seeds and white pith from the pepper and cut into thin strips. Remove any pips from the grapes. Place all the salad ingredients together in a large bowl.

Mix all the dressing ingredients together and pour over the salad, toss well and pile the salad into a bowl or dish, sprinkle with chopped parsley.
SERVES 6-8. M.B. (1)

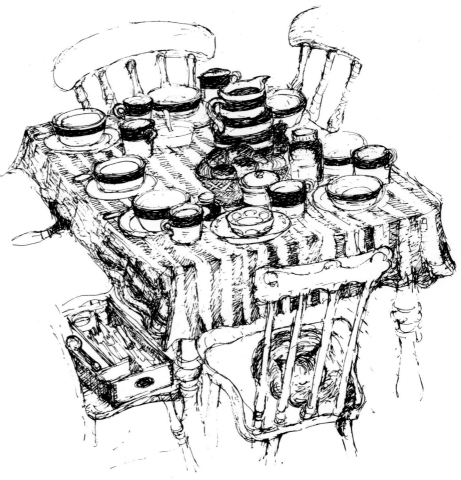

Scampi in cream fondue

2 lb shelled scampi (if frozen, they must
be completely thawed before cooking)
½ pint dry white wine
1 lb mushrooms, ready prepared and
roughly chopped
1 pint double cream
Salt and pepper to taste
A wedge of lemon per person

Heat up the wine to simmering, then
spoon in the mushrooms and cook on at
the same temperature for 5 minutes.
Now add the cream, seasoned rather
lightly, and stir until it boils and thickens.
Then dip in the scampi and cook on for
5 minutes or so, but don't overdo them
or they will toughen. Serve with French
bread.

SERVES 8.   L.B.

Party dips

3 oz English or Welsh butter
6 oz Blue Stilton cheese (grated)
½ teaspoon caster sugar
Pinch cayenne pepper
3 tablespoons port
1 (11 oz) can mandarin oranges
(chopped)

Surround dish with pieces of raw carrot,
celery, fleurets of cauliflower, biscuits or
potato crisps. Cream the butter and beat
in the grated cheese. Stir in port and
season to taste. Stir in chopped oranges,
reserving some for garnish. Serve in
small dish surrounded by vegetables or
biscuits. Garnish with orange segments.

SERVES 12.   P.M. (1)

Olive and anchovy tartlets

6 oz plain flour
1½ oz lard
1½ oz butter
1 egg yolk
Pinch of salt
2 tablespoons finely chopped onion
1 oz butter
2 anchovy fillets
3 eggs
½ pint milk
4 oz olives
6 oz grated cheese
½ teaspoon mustard
Salt and pepper
Paprika

Soak the anchovy fillets for 15 minutes
in cold water. Make the pastry with
flour, lard, butter, egg yolk, water to mix
and a pinch of salt. Roll out thinly and
line small deep tartlet tins. Bake blind
at 400°F (gas 6) for 8 minutes. Drain the
anchovy fillets and chop them into very
small pieces. Cook the onion in the butter
until soft but not brown. Beat the eggs
and milk well together and stir in the
anchovy fillets, the sliced olives, grated

*Three dishes cooked with cheese : **1** Swiss*
*fondue (see this page) **2** Gruyère*
*Savoury Flan (page 36) **3** Surprise*
Soufflé (page 123).

cheese, mustard and seasonings, and
softened onion. Pour into pastry cases
and bake at 350°F (gas 4) for 15 minutes.
Serve hot or cold with sherry, as the
preliminary to a meal.

SERVES 6.   M.N.

Stilton fondue

½ oz butter
½ pint cider or dry white wine
12 oz Stilton (grated)
1 tablespoon cornflour
Black pepper
2 tablespoons kirsch (optional)
1 crusty French loaf (cut into small
cubes)

Place butter, cider, grated cheese, cornflour, pepper and kirsch in a fondue
dish, flameproof casserole or saucepan.
Stir over gentle heat until fondue is
smooth. Keep warm while it is being
served, either using a special fondue set
or a table-warmer. Eat by dipping cubes
of bread on long-handled forks into
fondue.

SERVES 6.   P.M. (1)

Fluffy cheese ramekins

1 oz butter
1 onion, finely chopped
2 oz streaky bacon, chopped
2 tomatoes, chopped
2 oz mushrooms, chopped
Salt and pepper
2½ fl oz milk
2 eggs, separated
6 oz Stilton cheese, grated

Preheat oven to 375°F (gas 5). Melt the
butter in saucepan and gently fry onion.
Add bacon, tomatoes and mushrooms.
Season well and place in 6 buttered
ramekin dishes. Place milk, egg yolks
and cheese in a saucepan. Heat gently
until cheese has melted. Whisk egg

whites until stiff. Fold carefully into the
cheese mixture. Pour into the ramekin
dishes. Bake for 10-15 minutes until well
risen and golden brown. Serve immediately.

SERVES 6.   P.M. (1)

Swiss fondue

A creamy mixture of cheese and wine
into which guests dip cubes of bread.

1 clove garlic
1¼ lb grated gruyère or emmenthal cheese
½ bottle of white wine
Squeeze of lemon juice
Little grated nutmeg
Salt and pepper
Miniature bottle of kirsch

Peel the garlic, cut in half and rub well
around the inside of a fireproof dish of
about 2½ pint capacity. Discard the
remains of the garlic.

Place the cheese, the wine and the
lemon juice in the dish then bring to the
boil over a brisk heat, stirring continuously in a 'figure of eight' motion. When
all the cheese is melted and the mixture
of a smooth, creamy consistency, add
nutmeg and seasonings to taste. Finally
stir in the kirsch.

Remove the dish to a fondue stand or
other spirit warmer at the table to keep
hot. The dish will retain its consistency
for ½ hour or more and should be eaten by
dipping cubes of bread speared on forks
into the mixture. Sesame seed sticks also
make a happy accompaniment.

SERVES 4-6.   L.B./B.S. (1)

Dutch fondue

14 oz Dutch gouda cheese, grated
½ clove garlic
¼ pint medium dry white wine
1 teaspoon lemon juice
1 tablespoon cornflour
1½ tablespoons gin
Freshly ground black pepper
Pinch nutmeg
1 loaf of French bread cut into small
cubes

Rub the inside of an earthenware pan
with the cut garlic and place a little
finely chopped garlic in the pan. Pour
in the wine and lemon juice and heat
slowly until the wine is nearly boiling.
Gradually add the grated cheese, a little
at a time, stirring continuously with a
fork, until all the cheese has melted.
When the mixture is boiling, blend the
cornflour with the gin until smooth and
add to the fondue, stirring well. Add the
seasoning. Serve the cheese fondue in
the earthenware pan, placed over a
spirit heater. There should be a fondue
fork for each person and the cubes of
French bread are speared with the fork
and dipped into the fondue.

SERVES 4.   L.B.

Savoury puffs

An excellent type of snack to serve with drinks can be made from tiny choux pastry buns which can be made in advance and kept stored in the freezer. They thaw quite quickly and are good served cold or heated in the oven.

HOT FILLINGS: shell fish, cooked chicken, or cooked mushrooms in a rich cream sauce. Fill the buns after they are thawed, brush the top with beaten egg and sprinkle grated cheese over before heating in the oven or under the grill.

COLD FILLINGS: mashed well-seasoned sardines in a little thick cream and a touch of lemon rind and juice. Grated cheese mixed with whipped cream and chopped walnuts. Cream cheese mixed with anchovy essence, or tomato paste and a touch of Worcestershire sauce.

L.B./G.W. (1)

Smoked salmon bites

1 large loaf bread, sliced
2 oz butter
4 oz smoked salmon

Cut thinly-sliced brown bread into fish shapes (or triangles or fingers), spread with softened butter, and lay on each a slice of smoked salmon cut to shape. A piece of olive, or a caper, will serve for the 'eye'. L.B./S.A.

Parma ham batons

4 oz parma ham
2 large pears, peeled, cored and quartered

Wrap a slice of ham around each pear quarter. L.B./S.A.

Chicken pick-ups

8 oz raw chicken flesh
3 oz fine white breadcrumbs
1 beaten egg

Cut the chicken flesh into finger-sized pieces. Dip each into the beaten egg, then coat in the breadcrumbs. Fry in deep oil heated to 360°F for about 3 minutes or until crisp and golden. For those who like cheese, 1 oz grated parmesan cheese may be mixed with the crumbs before coating.

Serve hot or cold.
MAKES 30-35. L.B./L.H. (1)

Pâté croûtons

These delicious little pick-up-and-eat morsels are as easy to make as they are to eat. Simply cut out small rounds of stale bread with a small biscuit cutter, then fry until crisp and golden in a mixture of butter and oil. Drain on kitchen paper and, when cool, spread with pâté, then decorate with slices of olives or gherkins, or small whole pickled onions. L.B. E.S.

*New Year's Eve buffet of three courses, all of which are easy to eat standing up: **1** A dish of starters, including Smoked Salmon Bites, Mussel Turnovers, Parma Ham Batons, Taramasalata Boats, miniature sweetcorn (available in jars and tins) and, in the centre, Chicken Pick-ups (recipes on this page) **2** Angel's Hair Gâteau (page 149) **3** Lang Syne Stew (page 100), served in a bowl and needing no additional accompaniments **4** Petits Fours (page 156).*

Nut creams

Beat together until very pliable cream cheese and grated orange peel to taste. Form into small balls and sandwich between walnut or pecan halves. Alternatively, roll the cheese balls in finely-chopped nuts, or if you feel really ambitious, coat the shapes in beaten egg crumbs and cover well with fine breadcrumbs before frying in deep fat.

L.B./E.T.

Mussel turnovers

Flaky pastry made with 8 oz flour
3¾ oz can smoked mussels

Drain the oil from the mussels and thinly roll out the pastry. With a 1½ inch plain cutter, stamp out one round for each mussel. Place a mussel on each pastry circle, moisten the edges with water and seal to form small turnover shapes. Fry in deep oil heated to 360°F for about six minutes or until crisp and golden.

They may be served cold but are even better hot.
MAKES 22 TURNOVERS. L.B./L.H. (1)

Taramasalata boats

PASTRY
6 oz plain flour
3½ oz butter
1 oz grated parmesan cheese
FILLING
4 oz smoked cod's roe
2 oz soft breadcrumbs
2 fl oz milk
4 tablespoons double cream
1 clove garlic, crushed
Juice of 1 lemon
A little grated lemon rind
Seasoning to taste

To make the pastry, rub the butter into the flour in the usual way, then stir in the cheese before mixing to a dough with water. Roll out thinly and line boat-shaped moulds. Prick and bake blind.

For the filling, put all the ingredients into the electric liquidizer and blend until light and creamy. Spoon the filling into the pastry shells. Decorate with sprigs of parsley.
MAKES 24 BOATS. L.B./G.L.

Imps of darkness

12 prunes
1 small onion, finely chopped
2 oz butter
½ teaspoon mixed dried herbs
1 oz breadcrumbs
6 rashers streaky bacon

Carefully stone the prunes which have been soaked overnight; keep the prunes whole. Sauté the onion in the butter until soft, then add herbs and breadcrumbs. Mix well, season to taste and use to stuff the prunes.

De-rind and stretch rashers of bacon, then cut each in half across. Wrap a piece of bacon around each stuffed prune and thread on to skewers. Grill until bacon is cooked, turning as necessary. Remove from the skewers and place on cocktail sticks. Serve hot. L.B./J.W.

Celery slices

4 oz cream cheese
3 tablespoons cream
Paprika
Head of celery

These crisp celery slices are especially appealing with drinks, and they slice conveniently into bite-sized pieces. They are quick to prepare and add a nice touch of colour to the table.

Cream together well cream cheese, cream, and paprika to taste. Wash the celery and divide into its individual stems, discarding any coarse or scarred sticks. Fill the sticks with the cheese mixture (using either a forcing pipe and bag for speed if you are doing a lot, or a knife) then press the stems around one another, starting with the smallest and ending with the large outside stalks. Chill well and cut in slices. (One head makes about 20 good slices.) L.B./S.W. (2)

PASTA

Pepper pasta

3 red peppers
3-4 cloves garlic
4 tablespoons olive oil
Fresh rosemary
1 lb pasta shells
4 large tomatoes
½ lb pecorino or similar Italian cheese
Salt and pepper

Remove the seeds from the peppers and dice. Heat the olive oil in a frying-pan and add peppers. Sauté 10-15 minutes or until cooked through. Add the crushed garlic and rosemary and cook for another 5 minutes. Meanwhile, cook the pasta in a large pan of fast-boiling water. Drain the pasta and put in a large bowl. Pour over the peppers, garlic, rosemary and oil. Mix together thoroughly. Leave to cool. De-seed the tomatoes and dice. Dice the cheese. Combine tomatoes and cheese with the cold pasta mixture. Season with salt and freshly-ground pepper. Serve as a starter or, as a main course, with a green salad.

SERVES 8. B.B.

Scallopini verdi

Veal with green pasta

2 tablespoons plain white flour
1 teaspoon salt
Dash cayenne pepper
6 veal cutlets
2 tablespoons vegetable oil
4 oz chopped onion
16 oz tin tomatoes
3 oz button mushrooms, sliced
1 tablespoon chopped parsley
1 tablespoon capers
¼ teaspoon garlic salt
¼ teaspoon dried oregano
6 oz green fettucini
2 teaspoons cornflour

Mix the flour, salt and pepper and dip each cutlet in it. Heat the oil in a frying-pan and brown the veal in it, then lift out and add the onion and cook until it 'falls' but is not brown. Put the veal back in the pan and stir in the tomatoes, mushrooms, parsley, capers, garlic salt and oregano. Cover and simmer for 20-25 minutes until the meat is tender, stir now and then. Cook the fettucini in boiling salted water until only just tender, drain off the water.

Put the noodles in a dish and arrange the veal on top and keep all warm. Slake the cornflour with cold water and add to the pan and cook and stir until thickened. Then spoon some over the veal and serve the rest in a sauce-boat.

SERVES 6. W.G.

Pepper Pasta is a colourful salad of 'shells', red peppers and Pecorino cheese, which can be served as a starter or a main course for a casual, summer lunch. (Recipe above).

Tuna conchiglioni

4 oz giant cochiglioni (20 shells)
7 oz tin tuna, drained and flaked
3 oz white breadcrumbs
3 tablespoons minced onion
1 beaten egg
2 tablespoons chopped parsley
1 teaspoon lemon juice
1 tin condensed cream of celery soup
¼ pint milk
2 tablespoons snipped parsley
Paprika

Cook the shells in boiling salted water for 15-20 minutes, or until just tender. Drain off the water and rinse the shells in cold water and leave to drain. Mix the tuna, breadcrumbs, egg, first lot of parsley and lemon juice and fill each shell with some: each will take about 1 dessertspoonful. Put the shells in a fire-proof dish as above. In a saucepan, heat the soup, milk and rest of the parsley, pour over the shells and dust with paprika. Cover the dish and bake at 350°F (gas 4) for 20 minutes.

SERVES 4-5. W.G.

Pasta with pork chops

1 lb uncooked farfalle pasta (butterfly)
16 oz-tin tomatoes
½ teaspoon salt
¼ teaspoon dried thyme
6 × ½-inch-thick pork chops
3 oz onion, chopped
1 beef cube
¼ teaspoon salt
¼ teaspoon dried marjoram
Dash cayenne pepper
½ green pepper, de-seeded and cut in rings

Cook the farfalle in boiling salted water for 12 minutes, then drain. Drain the juice from the tomatoes and reserve. Cut the tomatoes into quarters and stir with the ½ teaspoon of salt and the thyme into the pasta. Put in a dish measuring 12 by 7½-inches with 1½-inch deep sides. Trim most of the fat from the chops and cut it up and fry in a frying-pan until there are 2 tablespoons of dripping, then lift out frizzled fat. Brown the chops in the dripping and then arrange on the pasta. Sprinkle the onion on top and dash with pepper and salt. Put the reserved tomato juice into a saucepan, add the crumbled beef cube, the second lot of salt, the marjoram and a dash of black pepper.

Cook the sauce and stir until the mixture is blended, then pour over the pork chops. Then cover the dish and bake at 350°F (gas 4) for 1 hour. Remove the cover and put the thinly-sliced green pepper on top of the chops. Cover again and cook for 15 minutes longer. Dash with paprika if liked.

SERVES 6. W.G.

Ravioli with mushroom sauce

1 lb ready-prepared, fresh ravioli
½ lb mushrooms
2 oz butter
4 tablespoons dry white wine
½ pint soured cream
Salt and freshly-ground black pepper

Put ravioli into boiling water or chicken bouillon. When they rise to the top, they are done. Take out with a strainer, keep hot in a covered bowl set over a pan of boiling water.

To make sauce, wash and chop mushrooms. Heat butter and sauté mushrooms gently with salt and pepper. When all liquid given out by mushrooms has evaporated, add wine and simmer on for a few minutes. Now stir in soured cream, raise heat slightly and bring slowly to the boil while you scrape round the inside of the pan to release all residue stuck to it. Let the sauce reduce and thicken, then pour it over the ravioli. NOTE: this sauce is also excellent to accompany almost any white fish.

SERVES 4. W.G.

Manicotti with meat sauce

Manicotti are large tube-like shapes of pasta.

1 lb best-quality raw minced beef
¾ pint water
6 oz tomato purée
4 tablespoons chopped onion
3 oz tin mushrooms
2 tablespoons parsley
1 level teaspoon dried oregano, crushed
1 teaspoon salt
½ teaspoon sugar
1 large clove garlic, chopped
1½ lb cottage cheese
2 heaped tablespoons grated parmesan cheese
2 eggs
4 tablespoons minced parsley
Little salt
4 oz manicotti (8 pieces)

Brown the meat and drain off the excess fat, add the water, tomato purée, onion, mushrooms, first lot of chopped parsley, the oregano, 1 teaspoon salt and the garlic. Simmer, uncovered, for half an hour. Stir now and then. Mix the cottage cheese, parmesan, the lightly beaten eggs and ½ teaspoon salt. Cook the manicotti in boiling salted water for about 20 minutes until only just tender, then rinse in cold water and drain.

With a small teaspoon, stuff each piece of manicotti with the cheese mixture. Pour half the meat-tomato sauce into an ovenware dish measuring 14 by 9 by 1½-inches (approximately) and arrange the stuffed manicotti on top, then pour the rest of the sauce over them. Bake at 350°F (gas 4) for 30-35 minutes and then leave to stand for a few minutes before serving.

SERVES 6. W.G.

Orange and pasta salad

This is a particularly good accompaniment to serve with roast pork, poultry and game.

6 oz pasta shapes or shortcut macaroni
Salt and pepper
2 oranges, peeled and divided into segments
3 spring onions, chopped
DRESSING
¼ pint soured cream
4 tablespoons orange juice
2 tablespoons oil
1 tablespoon chopped fresh mint

Cook the pasta in a large pan of boiling salted water until just tender. Drain well and season. Mix all the ingredients for the dressing together thoroughly and stir into the warm pasta. Add the orange segments and spring onions and mix lightly together.
SERVES 4. M.O.

Chicken and spinach ravioli

4 oz cooked chicken, finely minced
8 oz spinach when cooked and chopped (not sieved)
2 tablespoons butter, melted
2 tablespoons parmesan cheese, grated
⅛ teaspoon salt
Dash nutmeg
Cayenne pepper
Spicy tomato sauce (see page 119)
RAVIOLI PASTE
4 eggs
½ pint water
½ lb plain flour, plus 7 oz plain flour
1 teaspoon salt

To make the paste, beat the eggs well and mix them with the water in a large bowl, add the ½ lb of flour and the salt and beat well. Then stir in the rest of the flour very slowly to make a firm dough. Turn out on to a floured surface and knead until smooth and elastic, about 10-12 minutes. Divide into two equal parts, cover and leave for 10 minutes. Then roll each piece of dough to measure about 16 by 12 inches and cut into 2-inch squares with a ravioli cutter.
FILLING
Mix the chicken, spinach and melted butter, add the cheese, salt, pepper and nutmeg. Put a teaspoonful on a square of dough, moisten the edges with water and put another square on top and seal carefully with the prongs of a fork. Repeat with the rest of the filling and squares. Put aside for one hour to dry, turn at half-time. The ravioli must be cooked in a large pan of rapidly boiling salted water until tender—about 7-8 minutes. Rinse in cold water and drain well. Arrange in a dish 13½ by 8¾ by 1¾ inches. Pour the spicy tomato sauce (see page 119) over and cover the dish. Bake at 350 F (gas 4) for 30 minutes.
SERVES 4. W.G.

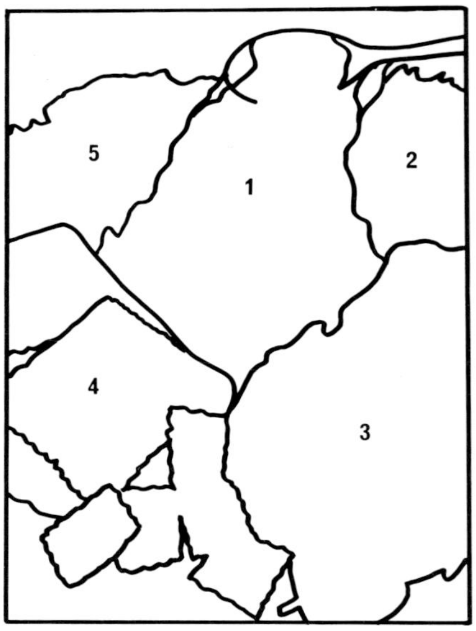

Pasta in subtle colours and intricate patterns: **1** *Tagliarini verde* **2** *Tagliarini* **3** *Tagliatelle* **4** *Ravioli* **5** *Tagliatelle verde. The Ravioli are stuffed with a meat mixture; the green pasta is coloured with spinach juice.*

Fettucini alfredo
Noodles with mushrooms and cream

2 oz butter or margarine
¼ pint double cream
1 oz parmesan cheese, grated
1 lb fettucini (noodles)
6 oz tin button mushrooms

Cream the fat and beat in the cream. When well mixed, add the cheese. Cook the noodles in boiling salted water until they are *al dente*, then drain. Put into a warm dish, add the creamed mixture. Season with cayenne and salt and stir in the mushrooms.
SERVES 6-8. W.G.

Malfada Caruso
Pasta with chicken livers

2 oz onion, minced
1 clove garlic, minced
4 tablespoons olive oil
1 × 29 oz tin tomatoes, cut up
1 × 6 oz tin tomato purée
½ pint water
2 level tablespoons parmesan cheese, grated
3 oz mushrooms, tinned or fresh
1 teaspoon sugar
½ teaspoon salt
¼ teaspoon dried tarragon
Good dash black pepper
1 bay leaf
½ teaspoon oregano
1 lb chicken livers, cut up
8 oz malfada (curly noodles)

Put 2 tablespoons of the oil into a large pan and cook the onion and garlic in it until tender but not brown. Add the tomatoes, tomato purée, water, sliced mushrooms, cheese, sugar and salt. Mix and then add the oregano, pepper, and bay leaf and mix again. Simmer, uncovered over very low heat for ¾ of an hour. Stir occasionally. Cook the malfada in plenty of boiling water, salted until tender, then drain it. Heat the rest of the oil in a frying pan and cook the chicken livers in it for 5 minutes. Add the livers to the sauce and bring just to boiling point. Remove the bay leaf. Dish the malfada; spoon the sauce over it.
SERVES 4. W.G.

Salata di pasta e spinaci
Spinach and pasta salad

6 oz pasta shapes or shortcut macaroni
Salt and pepper
½ lb young spinach leaves
DRESSING
2 tablespoons wine vinegar
6 tablespoons oil
1 clove garlic, crushed
Pinch dry mustard
2 hard-boiled eggs, finely chopped
Pinch grated nutmeg
GARNISH
Grated lemon rind

Cook the pasta in a large pan of boiling salted water until just tender. Drain well. Season. Mix all ingredients for the dressing together thoroughly, and stir into the warm pasta. Allow to cool. Wash the spinach leaves, discarding any wilted ones, and pat dry. Tear the spinach into pieces, and toss lightly through the pasta. Transfer the pasta salad to a bowl and sprinkle with grated lemon rind.
SERVES 4. M.O.

Sweet-sour pasta and chicken salad

1 aubergine, cubed
Salt and pepper
4 tablespoons oil
6 oz pasta shapes or shortcut macaroni
8 oz cooked chicken, chopped
DRESSING
3 tablespoons wine vinegar
6 tablespoons tomato juice
4 tablespoons oil
Juice ½ lemon
1 tablespoon sugar
1 small onion, chopped

Sprinkle the aubergine generously with salt and leave in a colander for ½ hour to drain. Pat the aubergine dry and fry gently in the oil until lightly golden. Add a little extra oil if necessary. Cook the pasta in a large pan of boiling salted water until just tender. Drain well and season. Mix all the ingredients for the dressing together thoroughly, and stir into the warm pasta. Add the aubergine and chicken and mix lightly together. Chill.
SERVES 4. M.O.

Pasta and bean salad

4 oz red kidney beans, soaked overnight
4 oz pasta shapes or shortcut macaroni
Salt and pepper
DRESSING
2 tablespoons wine vinegar
6 tablespoons oil
½ lemon rind, grated
1 tablespoon chopped fresh basil
2 tablespoons chopped parsley
GARNISH
1 tablespooon toasted sesame seeds

Simmer the red kidney beans until just tender, and drain. Cook the pasta in a large pan of boiling salted water until just tender—*al dente*. Drain well and season. Try to time the cooking of the beans and the pasta so that they are both ready at the same time. Meanwhile, make up the dressing by mixing all the ingredients together. Toss the warm pasta in the dressing, and transfer to a bowl. Sprinkle with sesame. Cool.
SERVES 4.   M.O.

Green noodle and bacon salad

6 oz green noodles
Salt and pepper
3 oz button mushrooms, sliced
6 rashers bacon, chopped
DRESSING
2 tablespoons wine vinegar
2 tablespoons oil
2 tablespoons chopped parsley
GARNISH
Crumbled blue cheese

Cook the noodles in a large pan of boiling salted water. Drain well and season to taste. Mix all the ingredients for the dressing together thoroughly and stir into the warm pasta. Add the mushrooms and mix lightly together. Fry the chopped bacon until it gives off its own

All the ingredients for a truly Italian meal: pasta, Proscuitto di Parma, Parmesan cheese and spicy sausages.

fat and becomes crisp. Pour the bacon and its hot fat over the salad, stir to mix, sprinkle with blue cheese.
SERVES 4.   M.O.

Garden pasta salad

6 oz pasta shapes or shortcut macaroni
Salt and pepper
2 courgettes, thinly sliced
1 carrot, thinly sliced
1 onion, cut into rings
1 small leek, cut into matchstick strips
4 radishes, thinly sliced
DRESSING
3 tablespoons lemon juice
6 tablespoons oil
1 tablespoon chopped parsley
1 tablespoon chopped fresh basil
1 tablespoon tomato purée
2 teaspoons sugar
TO SERVE
Grated parmesan cheese

Cook the pasta in a large pan of boiling water until just tender. Drain well and season. Mix all the ingredients for the dressing together thoroughly, and stir into the warm pasta. Cool. Add the prepared vegetables and mix lightly together. Serve with grated parmesan cheese.
SERVES 4-6.   M.O.

Ham-stuffed manicotti

4 oz manicotti (8 shells or tubes)
1 oz onion, chopped
2 tablespoons olive oil
8 oz cooked ham, finely minced
1 × 6 oz tin mushrooms, chopped
2½ tablespoons parmesan cheese, grated
1 oz green pepper, chopped
2 tablespoons butter
2½ tablespoons plain flour
1 pint milk
4 oz processed Swiss cheese, shredded

Cook the manicotti in boiling, salted water for 15 to 20 minutes, not longer,

then drain it. Heat the oil in a frying-pan and cook the onion until tender, add the ham and mushrooms. Stir and remove from the heat to cool, then stir in the parmesan and put to one side. Cook the deseeded green peppers in a small pan in the butter until just softened, then blend in the flour and add the milk, all at once. Cook and stir until bubbling and thickened. Over low heat, stir in the Swiss cheese until it melts. Mix some of this sauce with the ham-mushroom mixture, use about 3-4 tablespoons, then fill each tube with some of the filling. Arrange the tubes in a greased dish measuring 12 by 7 by 3 inches. Pour the rest of the sauce over the manicotti and dust with paprika. Cover the dish and bake at 350°F (gas 4) for 30 minutes.
SERVES 4.   W.G.

Pasta tonnato salad

6 oz pasta shapes or shortcut macaroni
Salt and pepper
French dressing
4 oz prawns, peeled
TONNATO SAUCE
Can tuna fish
4 anchovy fillets
¼ pint mayonnaise
Juice 1 lemon
1 tablespoon capers
1 clove garlic
2 tablespoons chopped parsley
GARNISH
Extra capers and lemon wedges

Cook the pasta in a large pan of boiling salted water until just tender. Drain well. Season. Stir in sufficient French dressing to moisten the warm pasta. Allow to cool. Put all the ingredients for the tonnato sauce into the liquidizer and blend until smooth. Stir the prawns into the pasta and transfer to a serving dish. Spoon over the sauce and garnish with extra capers and lemon wedges.
SERVES 4.   M.O.

FISH

Lobster glazed with white wine

2 lobsters, cooked and halved
1 lettuce
5 tomatoes
Cucumber (piece about 2 inches long)
French dressing
$\frac{1}{4}$ oz gelatine
1 tablespoon water
$\frac{1}{4}$ pint white wine

Dissolve the gelatine in one tablespoon boiling water and add the white wine. Cool until almost set. Meanwhile remove the roes from the lobster halves and replace with alternate slices of tomato and cucumber.

Prepare the salad. When the gelatine is ready, coat the lobster halves with the glaze and leave for $\frac{1}{4}$ hour to set firmly. Serve surrounded by the mixed salad and the dressing poured over or separately.

SERVES 4. S.G.

Coral lobster

$2\frac{1}{2}$ lb cooked lobster (about 14 oz flesh)
$\frac{1}{2}$ pint mixed milk and fish stock
1 medium-sized onion
4-5 peppercorns
Sprig of thyme or fennel
2 oz unsalted butter
1 oz plain flour
1 teaspoon Dijon mustard
$\frac{1}{4}$ pint dry white wine
1 egg yolk
$\frac{1}{4}$ pint single cream
Lemon juice and seasoning to taste

Clean the cooked lobster with a damp cloth, remove the pincers and claws, then cut carefully the length of the underside with a sharp knife, taking care not to cut through top shell. Remove and discard the stomach, 'lungs', and the black vein. Remove the flesh from the lobster shell and from the claws and cut into 1-inch cubes. Sieve the coral and set aside.

Gently infuse the onion, peppercorns and thyme in the milk/stock. Lightly sauté the lobster flesh in the butter, then spoon into the prepared shell. Add the flour to the butter remaining in the pan and cook, stirring gently but constantly, for 2-3 minutes. Then add the mustard, half the coral and the wine and cook for a further minute or two. Make a liaison with the egg yolk and cream, stir into the hot sauce and warm gently. Adjust the flavouring with lemon, salt and pepper.

Spoon the sauce over the lobster flesh in the shell. Carefully place the filled shell inside a giant-size cookbag and support in an upright position with pads of crumpled foil. Seal the bag

Cold lobster, warm sun—a perfect combination for a deliciously extravagant summer luncheon.

and make five or six slashes in the top. Set on a baking tray and bake for 30 minutes at 350°F (gas 4).

To serve, cut open the bag and carefully lift out the lobster. Set on a bed of boiled rice, and garnish with the rest of the coral.

SERVES 4. L.B./D.M.

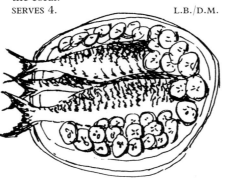

Prawns à l'harissa

Harissa is made from hot chilles and is very popular in North African cooking. It is available at good delicatessens.

1 clove garlic
Oil and butter for cooking
1-2 teaspoons harissa
7 oz prawns
Juice of 1 lemon
Pepper and salt
2 teaspoons parsley

Chop garlic finely and fry gently in equal quantities of oil and butter for a minute or so. Add harissa (not too much the first time you try this), then prawns, lots of lemon juice, parsley, black pepper and, maybe, salt. Stir well, and heat gently. Serve with rice.

SERVES 2 (or 4 as a starter). L.H. (2)

Curried prawns

1 medium onion
2 oz butter
$\frac{1}{2}$ garlic clove
1 tablespoon curry powder
Salt
8 oz tomatoes, peeled and quartered
8 oz cooked prawns

Cut onions in very thin slices. Fry in butter with the crushed garlic until soft. Stir in the curry powder and continue cooking gently for 5 minutes. Add tomatoes and salt and just a little water, to make a thickish sauce. Simmer for 5 minutes. Put in the prawns and continue simmering for 15 minutes. Serve with plain boiled rice.

SERVES 3-4. M.N.

Prawn patties

1 lb peeled prawns
$\frac{1}{4}$ pint sherry
1 tablespoon lemon juice
8 oz puff pastry
2 oz olives
$\frac{1}{2}$ teaspoon anchovy essence

Leave prawns to stand in sherry and lemon juice for an hour. Line small patty tins with pastry (about 12) and divide prawns between them. Add a few pieces of olive to each and a drop of anchovy essence. Moisten with about a teaspoon of the sherry mixture. Cover with pastry lids. Bake at 425°F (gas 7) for 15 minutes, until golden. Serve hot or cold. (NOTE: if patties are cooked too slowly, they may become a little dry.)

SERVES 6. M.N.

FISH

Crab au gratin

This makes a delicious starter for a dinner party but is equally good as a supper dish—served, instead, on hot buttered toast and browned under the grill.

1 freshly-boiled crab weighing 1-1½ lb
dressed
¾ lb potatoes, cooked and mashed
4 scallop shells
SAUCE
¼ oz butter
¼ oz flour
¼ pint milk
1 egg yolk
1 tablespoon Martini extra-dry vermouth
1 tablespoon cream
Salt and pepper
GARNISH
1½ oz parmesan and cheddar cheese,
grated
Finely chopped parsley
Beaten egg

Have ready the scallop shells piped with potato round the edge, using a 6-cut vegetable rose pipe. Make the sauce by melting the butter, adding the flour, off the heat, and then stirring in the milk. Bring to the boil, stirring all the time. Take off the heat and add the egg yolk, Martini and cream. Heat gently, adding the crab meat and season to taste. Place the mixture in the centre of the scallop shells. Sprinkle with grated cheese and brush the potato with a little beaten egg. Brown under a hot grill. Garnish with parsley.

SERVES 4. V.J.

Devilled crab

A well-seasoned dish, served hot in its shell—an interesting change from the more usual cold-dressed crab.

3 lb crab (about 1¾ lb flesh)
4 oz butter
6 tablespoons finely chopped celery
4 tablespoons finely chopped green pepper
3 tablespoons finely chopped parsley
6 tablespoons sliced spring onions
½ level teaspoon salt
2 level teaspoons dry mustard
Few drops Tabasco sauce
4 tablespoons cream

Remove the flesh from the claws and shell of the crab, taking care not to break the shell. Discard the body, stomach sac, and the 'dead men's fingers', but keep the legs for decoration.

Lightly sauté the vegetables in a little of the butter until the celery becomes tender. Add the rest of the butter and stir until completely melted, then add to the crab flesh and the remainder of the ingredients. Mix together well and pile into the prepared shell (any mixture which will not go into the shell should be placed into a small ovenproof dish,

Some decorative-looking dishes based on shell-fish: **1** *Sauce Verte, to accompany cooked prawns (page 120)* **2** *Devilled Crab (recipe on this page)* **3** *Coquille St Jacques au gratin (page 68)* **4** *Oysters with lemon butter (page 67)* **5** *Coral Lobster (page 59).*

covered and heated separately to use as a refill if necessary).

Place the filled shell into a giant-size cookbag, seal and make five or six slashes in the top to allow the steam to escape. Set on a baking-tray and bake at 350°F (gas 4) for about 45 minutes. Remove from the bag and transfer to a serving-dish. Decorate with the crab legs and serve hot.

SERVES 6. L.B./J.B. (2)

Crab in white wine sauce

Meat from two 1¼ lb crabs
2 oz butter
1 small onion, finely chopped
2 oz mushrooms, chopped
¼ pint white wine
3 tablespoons white sauce
Salt and pepper
1 oz fresh white breadcrumbs
Watercress

Melt 1 oz butter in a pan and fry the onion and mushrooms for 5 minutes, add the wine and continue cooking until tender. Stir in the sauce, crab meat and season to taste with salt and pepper. Simmer gently for 5 minutes. Fill the cleaned shells with the crab mixture. Melt remaining butter, toss in the breadcrumbs and cover the top of each crab. Brown quickly under a hot grill and serve the crab at once, garnished with watercress.

SERVES 2. J.E. (1)

Cold devilled crab

6 oz crabmeat
2 hard-boiled eggs
2 tablespoons thick cream
Juice of ½ lemon
Salt and cayenne pepper
3 oz fine breadcrumbs
1 oz butter

Mix together the crabmeat, finely-chopped eggs, cream, lemon, salt and pepper to taste, and nearly all the breadcrumbs. Put into four individual oven-proof dishes and cover with remaining breadcrumbs. Flake on the butter. Bake at 350°F (gas 4) for 15 minutes. Serve very cold with tartare sauce.

SERVES 4. M.N.

Crab cakes

1 lb crabmeat
1 teaspoon salt
1 teaspoon pepper
1 teaspoon dry mustard
2 teaspoons Worcestershire sauce
1 egg yolk
1 tablespoon mayonnaise
1 teaspoon chopped parsley
1 egg beaten with 1 tablespoon water
Flour
Breadcrumbs

Mix together crabmeat, seasoning, egg yolk, mayonnaise and parsley. Form the mixture into four flat round cakes. Dip in flour, then in egg/water mixture and then in breadcrumbs. Fry quickly on both sides. Serve very hot with lemon wedges and a coleslaw salad.

SERVES 4. M.N.

Almejas à la marinera
Cockles à la marinera

17 oz cooked and shelled cockles (frozen
cockles can be used when thawed)
1 large onion
1 clove garlic
2 tablespoons olive oil
1 oz fresh white breadcrumbs
¼ pint water
¼ pint white wine
Juice ½ lemon
Salt and pepper
4 stuffed green olives, thinly sliced
A little chopped parsley

Thoroughly rinse the cockles in cold water to remove any sand and drain well.

Peel and finely chop the onion and crush the garlic. Heat the oil in a frying-pan, add the onion and garlic and fry gently for about 5 minutes until a pale golden brown. Add the breadcrumbs and stir until they have absorbed the oil. Add the water, wine, lemon juice and cockles to the pan, bring to the boil and simmer for 5 minutes. Season and stir in the thinly sliced olives. Spoon into a warm serving dish, sprinkle with parsley and serve with chunks of French bread.

SERVES 4. M.B. (1)

FISH

Stuffed plaice with prawns

2 small whole plaice
1 oz brown breadcrumbs
1 stick celery
3 tablespoons lemon juice
4 tablespoons tomato juice
1-2 oz prawns
Grated rind ½ lemon
Lemon to garnish

Ask your fishmonger to clean and trim the fish. Wash them well and place on a board, with the white skin side uppermost. With a sharp knife ease the flesh away from the backbone to make a small 'pocket' either side.

Mix the breadcrumbs with the finely chopped celery, the lemon juice, tomato juice and the rind and fill this stuffing into the fish, allowing it to fill out generously. Cover the fish loosely with a piece of greaseproof paper and cook at 400°F (gas 6) for 20 minutes. Remove fish from the oven and garnish with prawns and quarters of lemon segments.
SERVES 2.   S.G.

Baked fillets of plaice

4 fillets of plaice, 4 oz each
Salt and pepper
1 oz butter
½ pint milk
2 oz mushrooms, sliced
1 oz flour
2 tomatoes, skinned, seeded and diced
2 level teaspoons almonds

Skin the fillets, season and roll up with skinned side inside. Place in an ovenproof dish, pour the milk over and bake on the centre shelf at 400°F (gas 6) for 15 minutes. Melt the butter and cook mushrooms gently until tender. Add the flour and cook for 2-3 minutes. When the fish is cooked, strain off liquor and arrange the fillets on a hot serving-dish. Add the liquor to the mushrooms, stir well, add the tomatoes and re-heat, stirring well. Simmer for 3-4 minutes, adjust seasoning if necessary, and pour the sauce over the fillets. Sprinkle with shredded and browned almonds and serve.
SERVES 2.   J.E. (1)

Plaice à l'orange

2 plaice
Flour
3 oz butter
2 oranges
1 lemon
1 tablespoon chopped parsley
Juice 1 lemon
Salt and pepper

Skin and fillet the fish. Wash and dry and dust with seasoned flour. Melt 2 oz butter in a heavy pan and, as soon as it begins to foam, fry the plaice in it until golden brown, turning once. Arrange them on a serving dish, garnished with wedges of lemon and carefully skinned orange sections, warmed gently in a little butter. Melt the rest of the butter in a clean pan and when melted and frothy stir in the chopped parsley, lemon juice, salt and pepper. When golden, pour over the fish and serve.
SERVES 2.   J.E. (1)

Plaice gruyère
Plaice in choux pastry

PASTRY
¼ pint water
2 oz butter
2½ oz plain flour
2 small eggs
2 oz cheddar cheese, diced
FILLING
4 plaice fillets
½ oz butter
Salt and pepper
SAUCE
1 oz margarine
1 oz flour
½ pint milk
3 oz gruyère cheese, grated
Salt and pepper
Parmesan cheese

Wash and skin the fish fillets. Roll them up and place in an ovenproof dish. Dot with butter, season and cook in a moderate oven for about 20 minutes. Meanwhile, prepare the cheese sauce. Melt the margarine, stir in the flour and cook for a few moments. Add the milk, stirring all the time. Simmer for 5 minutes, then remove from the heat and add the gruyère cheese. Set aside, cover with a piece of buttered paper to prevent the formation of a skin.

To make the pastry, put the water and butter to heat in a fairly large saucepan. When the mixture boils, remove it from the heat, and add the sifted flour all at once. Beat the paste until smooth. Allow the mixture to cool for a few minutes, then add the beaten eggs one at a time, beating well between each addition. Add the cheese. Pipe or spoon the paste to form a border in a well-oiled ovenproof dish, leaving a hollow in the centre.

Carefully lift the plaice fillets into the centre of the dish and spoon the sauce over them, being careful not to cover the choux pastry. Sprinkle parmesan cheese over the sauce and cook in a hot oven at 425°F (gas 7) for about 30 minutes until the pastry is well risen and golden brown.
SERVES 4.   S.G.

Plaice with prawns

4 fillets plaice, white-skinned
3-4 oz prawns
2 oz button mushrooms
1 small onion, finely chopped
Salt and black pepper
¼ pint white wine
Flour
Butter
Parsley
Juice ½ lemon

In a small saucepan, fry onion in butter until soft but not brown. Add chopped or sliced mushrooms (caps and stalks), plus salt and pepper. Cook gently. Meanwhile, flour the plaice fillets and, in another pan, fry gently on both sides. This only takes a few minutes. When cooked, remove and keep warm. Add prawns to the mixture in the saucepan, a tablespoon finely-chopped parsley, juice of ½ lemon and the wine. Warm through thoroughly but do not cook too hard or this may toughen the prawns. Pour over plaice fillets.
SERVES 2.   I.H. (2)

Sole au gratin

2 plump soles
2 tablespoons breadcrumbs
2 tablespoons finely chopped mushrooms
2 teaspoons finely chopped parsley
1 teaspoon finely chopped fat bacon
2 shallots, finely chopped
½ pint white wine
½ pint good stock
Butter
Brown breadcrumbs
Salt and pepper

Trim and skin the sole. Mix the breadcrumbs, mushrooms, parsley, bacon, shallots and a good seasoning of salt and pepper well together. Cover the bottom of a large, shallow, fireproof dish with a generous amount of butter, over which sprinkle half the prepared mixture and place the fish on the top of it. Cover with the remainder of the seasoning, sprinkle lightly with brown breadcrumbs and add a few drops of melted butter. Pour the wine and stock round the fish, and bake in a moderate oven for 15-20 minutes.

SERVES 2.   J.E. (1)

Filets de Sole

2 soles, skinned and filleted
Salt and pepper
Lemon juice
¼ pint white wine
¼ pint water
Bunch of herbs
¾ oz flour
6 tablespoons cream
1 oz butter
½ lb white grapes

Butter a fireproof dish, lay the fillets of sole, which have been seasoned with salt, pepper and lemon juice, on top and pour over the wine and water. Add the bunch of herbs and poach in a moderate oven at 350°F (gas 4) for 15 minutes. Meanwhile, dip the grapes for a minute in boiling water, peel, seed and set aside. Remove the cooked fillets to a serving-dish and keep them hot. Reduce the cooking liquor by fast boiling for a minute or two. In a separate pan, melt the butter, stir in the flour and gradually stir in the strained fish liquor and the cream. Stir until the sauce is smooth and thick. Season and pour over the fish. Brown under a hot grill. Lightly toss the prepared grapes in melted butter until warmed through. Arrange the grapes around fish and serve hot.

SERVES 2.   J.E. (1)

Filets de sole Desirée

Fillets of sole weighing 2 lb 4 oz
Fish bones
Dry white wine
Shallots
Double cream
Butter
Lemon
Parsley, dill, chervil and tarragon
STUFFING
Pike or whiting (very fresh) weighing
*   about 10½ oz when filleted*
1-2 egg whites
¼ pint double cream
¼ lb peeled shrimps

First, make the stuffing. Put the un-cooked pike or whiting meat through the finest mincer three times, then chill the minced fish. When chilled, stir the fish with a wooden spoon and add the egg whites (also chilled, but not beaten) one

at a time. Dilute with the ice-cold double cream, a little at a time, working the mixture vigorously. Finally, mix in finely chopped shrimps and some cayenne pepper—no salt, as the shrimps are salt enough.

Make some stock, using the fish bones, water, dry white wine, shallots and herbs. Simmer for 20 minutes. Strain the stock through a cloth or fine sieve. Add a little salt.

To stuff the sole with the pike-shrimp mixture, separate top and bottom fillets (top fillets are always thicker). Flatten the fillets and put on a flat board covered with moistened grease-proof paper—first, a top fillet with the skin-side downwards. Put a layer of stuffing 1½ inches thick and cover with the bottom fillet. Press on top so that the stuffing is spread out equally and trim the edges with a knife from all super-fluous stuffing. Put the double fillets in a buttered fireproof dish on a bed of finely chopped shallots. Cover with a greased paper and put in a cool place until the fish is to be baked, preferably at the very last minute. Then squeeze some lemon juice on the fish and pour over boiling stock. Cover with grease-proof paper and bring to the boil on top of the cooker. Then put the dish in a hot oven at 425°F (gas 7) and let the fish simmer for about 10 minutes. Then the fish is ready. Remove fish from stock and set aside. Strain the stock and put in a saucepan. Boil until reduced to the amount you want. (Do not forget that double cream will also be added.) Thicken the boiling stock with *beurre manié* (butter and flour mixed in equal quantities and made into a paste). The sauce should not be too thick. Add about three tablespoons double cream, simmer for some minutes and season to taste with lemon juice, more finely chopped herbs and, if needed, salt and cayenne pepper. Finish with a knob of cold butter to taste.

Transfer the sole fillets to a hot serving-dish and cover with hot sauce. Any sauce which is left over can be served separately. Serve with rice.

SERVES 4.   W.V.

Mackerel in cider

4 mackerel
3 shallots
1 pint dry cider
Flour
Butter
Thyme and bay leaf
Peppercorns and salt

Put the mackerel in a fire-proof dish, add the herbs, salt and peppercorns, sprinkle with chopped shallots, and pour the cider over them. Cook in a moderate oven for about 15-20 minutes

or until fish is tender. When done, put the cider in a small saucepan, add 4 tablespoons of butter, a little flour mixed to a smooth paste. Stir well until it begins to thicken and is perfectly smooth, add 1 teaspoon of chopped parsley and pour over the fish.

SERVES 4.   s.w. (1)

Maquereaux Bretonne
Mackerel with mustard

3 medium-sized mackerel
2 egg yolks
1 tablespoon French mustard
1 tablespoon mixed chopped herbs
*   (parsley, tarragon and chervil)*
1 tablespoon white wine
2 oz butter softened

Clean the fish and poach very gently in stock until tender. Allow to cool in the fish stock. Lift out and carefully remove the fillets from the bone and arrange on a serving-dish. Blend the mustard and the egg yolk and mix in the herbs and wine. Gradually blend in the softened butter until the sauce has the consis-tency of a mayonnaise. Pour it over the fish. Sprinkle with chopped parsley and serve cold with salad of new potatoes, and an oil-and-cider dressing.

SERVES 3.   J.E. (1)

Mackerel niçoise

2 small mackerel
¼ pint water
¼ pint white wine vinegar
1 bay leaf
2 peppercorns
Salt
DRESSING
3 tablespoons oil
1 tablespoon wine vinegar
Salt and pepper
Mustard
SALAD
Small lettuce leaves
2-3 tomatoes
3 oz cooked French beans
6 stoned black olives
Lemon to garnish

Ask the fishmonger to remove the back-bones of the fish. Wash and dry the fish and place in an ovenproof dish. Pour over the water and vinegar and add the bay leaf, peppercorns and salt. Cover, cook in a moderate oven at 350°F (gas 4) for 30 minutes, or until cooked. Put aside to cool in the liquor, then skin. Wash and dry the lettuce. Make the dressing and toss the lettuce; the rest of the dressing should be served separately. Arrange the lettuce on a serving-dish and lay the cold fish carefully on top. Garnish with quartered tomatoes, beans, olives and lemon.

SERVES 2.   S.G.

Grilled mackerel

4 mackerel
2 tablespoons salad oil
Juice 1 lemon
Salt and pepper
1 teaspoon caraway seeds

Clean the fish, which should be very fresh, and slash the flesh diagonally on each side about three times. Brush with olive oil and lemon juice, season with salt and pepper and dust with caraway seeds. Grill or barbecue on both sides over a good heat. Serve with lettuce and cucumber salad.

SERVES 4. M.N.

Brill braised with vermouth

2¼ lb brill
1 teaspoon salt
Pinch white pepper
2½ oz butter
2 tablespoons bread raspings or soft white breadcrumbs (6 tablespoons)
2 shallots, finely chopped
1½ teaspoons chopped parsley
6 tablespoons dry French vermouth

Ask the fishmonger to fillet the fish. Season the fillets with salt and pepper. Melt about 1 oz butter and dip the fillets into it, then toss them in bread raspings.

Put the shallots and parsley into a greased baking-dish. Put in the brill fillets and pour over the rest of the melted butter. Pour in the vermouth carefully, at the side of the dish. Bake at 450 F (gas 8) for 10-15 minutes. Transfer the fish to a hot serving-dish. Pour the cooking juices into a small saucepan. Bring to the boil and reduce the volume by about half by boiling. Lift off the heat and add the rest of the butter in pats. Whisk constantly. Pour some of the sauce around the fish. Serve the rest in a hot sauce-boat.

SERVES 4. S.G.

Fish au gratin

1½ lb firm white fish (mixed hake, halibut, haddock, monk fish, cod)
3 hard-boiled eggs
2 Arbroath smokies
1 pint milk
10 fl oz cream
1 large onion, halved
1 onion, sliced
2 oz cheddar cheese
2 tablespoons flour
2 oz butter
Pinch saffron
3½ oz prawns (optional)
Breadcrumbs
Bay leaf

Simmer the fish in milk with a bay leaf, the halved onion, saffron and seasoning. Meanwhile dip the smokies in boiling water so they skin more easily, then take them off the bone. Gently cook the chopped onion in butter without browning by keeping the lid on the saucepan: when ready, add the flour mixing well with the butter and onion, then gradually put in the strained milk from the fish, until you have a smooth béchamel sauce. Grate in the cheese and when well dissolved, add the cream and bring to the boil. Take the sauce off the heat while deboning the fish. Put the fish and quartered hard-boiled eggs in the sauce and turn out into a fire-proof dish.

If tomatoes are plentiful, cover the surface with thin slices, then sprinkle breadcrumbs and dots of butter.

Brown under the grill or in an oven.

SERVES 6-8. A.R. (1)

Spanish cooking is essentially peasant cooking, but none the less good for that. Grilled sardines are popular in every coastal village. **1** *Pierno de Cordero a la Española (roast leg of lamb, page 89)* **2** *Arroz con pescado (fish paella, page 68)* **3** *Flan con Platanos (banana caramel custard, page 135)* **4** *Fried sardines* **5** *Tapenade (a dip of tuna fish beaten with lemon, cream, salt and pepper to taste)* **6** *Gazpacho andaluz (page 25)* **7** *Pollo Sevilla (Sevillian chicken, page 97)* **8** *Huevos à la flamenca (Flamenco eggs, page 39).*

Cabillaud à la Boulangère
Country-style cod

4 thick cod steaks
1 lb potatoes
½ lb small onions, sliced
Salt and pepper
Butter
Chopped parsley

Parboil the potatoes and cut into thick slices. Blanch the onions for 3 minutes in boiling water. Put the cod steaks in a shallow buttered fireproof dish, surrounded by the potatoes and onions. Season with salt and pepper and brush the fish well with melted butter. Cover with greasproof paper and bake for about 25 minutes in a very moderate oven, basting the fish with melted butter occasionally. Serve sprinkled with chopped parsley.

SERVES 4. J.E. (1)

Cod crayfish-style

1½ to 1¾ lb cod fillet
1 oz butter or margarine
1½ tablespoons bread raspings
¾ teaspoon salt
6 tablespoons cream
3 tablespoons tomato purée (1 small 2¼ oz can)
1½ tablespoons finely chopped dill or 1½ teaspoons dried dill weed

Grease a fireproof baking dish with a knob of butter. Put half the cod fillet, skin-side downwards, into the dish and spread thickly with the tomato purée. Sprinkle dill over the purée. Cover with the rest of the cod fillet, skin-side uppermost. Sprinkle with breadcrumbs and dot with the rest of the butter. Add the salt to the cream and pour the mixture into the dish at one side, keeping the crumbs dry. Bake at 400°F (gas 6) for about 12 minutes until the fish is cooked.
NOTE: If the cod is baked in foil, omit bread raspings and cream.

SERVES 4. S.G.

Fish flan

Rich short crust pastry case, 9 inches across, baked blind
12 oz haddock
1½ oz butter
1 onion, chopped
1½ oz mushrooms, chopped
2-3 tomatoes, peeled, de-seeded and chopped
¾ oz plain flour
½ pint fish stock
Salt and cayenne pepper
1 egg yolk
1 tablespoon cream
1 tablespoon chopped parsley
3 tomatoes sliced
1½ oz button mushrooms

Prepare the onion, mushrooms and tomatoes; simmer in ½ oz of the butter until cooked. Rub through a sieve.

Poach the fish and use the liquor for the sauce. Melt the remaining butter and add the flour, cook for a moment. Gradually stir in the fish stock and add the vegetable purée. Bring to the boil and season to taste. Blend the egg-yolk and cream. Flake the cooked fish and add to the sauce with the cream and yolk. Keep hot. Pour the fish mixture into the cooked pastry case and garnish with slices of tomato and lightly-fried button mushrooms; sprinkle with parsley. Serve hot or cold.

SERVES 4. S.G.

FISH

Skate with prawn cream sauce

2 pieces skate
1 medium-sized onion, sliced
½ pint dry white wine
½ teaspoon tarragon
1 bayleaf
2 oz butter
2 oz button mushrooms, sliced
½ oz flour
2 beaten egg yolks
2 tablespoons single cream
Salt and freshly-ground black pepper
2 oz shelled prawns
8 stuffed green olives, sliced

Put the pieces of skate, a few slices of onion, wine, tarragon and bay leaf in an ovenware dish, cover and cook at 325°F (gas mark 3) for 20 minutes or until the fish is cooked. Remove skin from the fish if necessary. Melt the butter and fry the remaining onion and the mushrooms for 5 minutes. Drain the liquid from the fish and keep it. Take out the bay leaf and add the onions and mushrooms to the fish. Add the flour and the remaining butter in the pan and cook it without browning. Gradually add the fish liquid, stirring all the time. Bring to the boil and cook for 1 minute. Beat the egg yolks and cream together and stir into the sauce. Add the prawns and olives and pour sauce over fish.
SERVES 2.   M.N.

Skate in black butter

The so-called black butter is, of course, only browned, and nothing but new potatoes need be served as accompaniment.

1½ lb wing of skate (approx)
1 large onion, sliced
Parsley
3 tablespoons wine vinegar
4 oz unsalted butter
1½ lb new potatoes

Wash the fish well in salted water to remove the characteristic ammonia odour. Put the whole wing into a wide heavy pan, making sure the fish is flat,

then cover completely with cold water. Add the onion, parsley, and two of the spoons of vinegar. Bring gently to the boil with the pan uncovered and simmer for 15-20 minutes or until the flesh can be separated into strings with two forks. (Turn the fish half-way through the cooking.) When cooked, the skate will be a slightly creamy colour. Remove it from the pan and place on a hot serving dish.

Put the butter into a small pan and heat quickly until it foams and begins to turn brown. At this moment, remove the pan from the heat and pour the hazelnut-coloured butter over the fish. Add the remaining vinegar to the pan, heat and pour this over the fish, then sprinkle with chopped parsley and serve immediately with new potatoes.
SERVES 4. L.B./A.K.

Oysters with lemon butter

6 oysters per person
Lemon butter (see below)

Scrub the oyster shells thoroughly in cold water, then place them in a giant-size cookbag and set on a baking-tray. Slash the top of the bag in five or six places and put into the oven heated to 350 F (gas 4) for about 15 minutes to assist in opening the shells.

Tear open the bag and remove the oysters. To open the oysters, insert the tip of an oyster knife or a strong screw-driver between the two shells and prise open. Discard the free shells and set the oysters in their half shells on appropriate plates. Dot each oyster with butter which has been beaten up with lemon juice, then chilled.

L.B./C.P. (2)

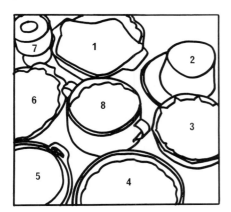

All the dishes shown here are based on typical Normandy recipes, starting with skate. **1** *Skate in black butter (recipe above)* **2** *Mussel timbale (page 73)* **3** *Ratafia cream (page 136)* **4** *Normandy potatoes (page 112)* **5** *Carrot soup (page 20)* **6** *Mangetout peas with mushrooms (page 112)* **7** *Melon with port* **8** *Poulet vallée d'auge (page 98).*

Oyster skewers

2 dozen oysters
4 rashers streaky bacon
4 oz button mushrooms
Butter
Salt and pepper

Cut the bacon into 1-inch squares. Take four long skewers and thread them with alternate oysters, squares of bacon and small mushrooms, ending with a square of bacon. Brush with melted butter, season with salt and freshly-milled pepper, and grill on all sides until brown and tender. Very good served with rice tossed in butter with a hint of curry powder.
SERVES 4. M.N.

Tuna rice ring

A quick, economical dish using store-cupboard supplies.
About 1 oz butter
1 small onion, finely chopped
¼ lb American rice
12 fl oz water
1 chicken stock cube.
QUICK SAUCE
1 oz butter or margarine
1 oz plain flour
¾ pint milk
juice of ½ lemon
3 tablespoons tomato purée
7½ oz can tuna fish
Salt and pepper

Lightly fry the onion and rice in the butter in a medium-sized saucepan until the rice becomes translucent and a light golden colour. Add the water and stock cube, stir, cover tightly and cook over a low heat until all the liquid is absorbed and the rice soft but not tacky (15-20 minutes).

Meanwhile, make the sauce by putting the butter or margarine, flour and milk into a small saucepan and stirring briskly over a moderate heat for 2-3 minutes until the sauce is thickened and smooth. Add the lemon juice and tomato purée and mix well, then gently stir in the drained tuna fish broken into large chunks. Heat to warm the fish through and season to taste.

Turn the cooked rice on to a serving-plate and shape into an oval or round, leaving a well in the centre and building up around the sides. Pour the hot sauce into the centre of the rice and decorate with lemon and parsley. Serve immediately.
SERVES 3-4. L.B./B.P.

Seafood orientale

1 lb onions, finely chopped or sliced
4 tablespoons olive oil
Pinch saffron, soaked in few teaspoons of water
2 tablespoons tomato paste
1 teaspoon paprika
1 clove garlic, crushed
2 bay leaves
Pinch thyme
Juice 1 small lemon
1 lb of any fresh fish fillet, or seafood, or a mixture
Toasted flaked almonds, or whole prawns for decoration

Fry the onions gently in the olive oil until they are soft and beginning to brown. Add the saffron (with its water), the tomato paste, paprika, garlic, the herbs, lemon juice and fish or seafish. Add enough water to prevent the mixture sticking and burning as it cooks very gently for 5-10 minutes, or until the fish is cooked through. Allow to cool in its sauce, then tip into a serving dish and chill well. Before serving sprinkle with a few toasted almonds, or decorate with prawns.
SERVES 4. P.L.

FISH

Arroz con pescado
Fish paella

6 clams or 12 mussels
6 tablespoons white wine
¾ lb monk fish
5-6 scallops
3 scampi in their shells
3 tablespoons olive oil
1 large onion, chopped
2 cloves garlic, crushed
½ lb tomatoes
12 oz long-grained rice
1½ pints fish or chicken stock
Pinch of saffron
1 level teaspoon salt
1 level teaspoon cayenne pepper
4 oz packet frozen peas
2 canned red peppers
1 level tablespoon chopped parsley
8 stuffed green olives
Lemon wedges
4 oz peeled prawns

Wash the clams or mussels, discard those that do not close tightly, place in a saucepan with the wine, cover with a tight-fitting lid and cook quickly until the clams or mussels open. Lift out of the pan, remove from the shells and reserve the cooking liquid.

Wash the monk fish and cut into 1-inch pieces, halve the scallops, remove the shells from the scampi and cut into thick slices.

Heat the oil in a large frying-pan and fry the onion and garlic until lightly brown. Add the monkfish and scallops with the tomatoes that have been skinned, quartered and seeded, and simmer slowly for 5 minutes. Stir in the rice, add the liquor from the clams or mussels, stock, saffron and seasoning. Bring to the boil and reduce heat, simmer for about 20 minutes.

Stir in the peas and the red peppers cut in strips and continue cooking for a further 5-10 minutes or until the rice is cooked and has absorbed all the stock.

Stir in the prawns and olives with the cooked clams or mussels. Pile on to a serving dish, sprinkle with parsley and garnish with lemon wedges.
SERVES 6. M.B. (1)

Ceviche
Mexican marinated fish

2 lb cod fillets, or any firm white fish
⅜ pint fresh lemon juice
2 chopped chillis
2 onions
1 tomato
¼ teaspoon garlic
Salt and pepper

Skin fish and marinate in lemon juice for at least four hours. (If preferred, slightly boil the fish first.) Dice into chunks. Add chopped garlic, chilli and chopped onion. Season to taste and decorate with onion rings and sliced tomato. Ketchup can be added for colour, and a little cream will make the fish taste blander.
SERVES 6. J.D. (2)

Coquille St Jacques au gratin

4 large scallops in their shells
2 oz butter
1 clove garlic, crushed
¼ pint dry white wine
Sprig of fresh fennel
1 oz plain flour
4-5 tablespoons cream
Seasoning
GRATIN
2 oz breadcrumbs
1 oz parmesan cheese, grated
1 oz butter

Prise open the shells with a strong knife and discard the flat part of the shell. With a sharp knife, cut the scallops from the rounded shells and scrub the shells thoroughly. Trim away the membrane and the black vein from the scallops, then wash them well in cold water. Cut the scallop flesh and the coral into bite-sized pieces.

Heat the butter and the garlic in a sauté pan until the butter froths. Add the prepared scallops and sauté lightly for a few minutes. Add the wine and the fennel and simmer until the scallops become opaque and white in appearance. Remove the scallops and place in the prepared shells, and discard the garlic clove and the fennel. Mix the flour smoothly with the cream, then stir into the liquor. Cook, stirring constantly, for 2-3 minutes until thickened and smooth. Season to taste and adjust the consistency with a little more cream if liked. Pour over the scallops. Rub all the gratin ingredients together and sprinkle over. Brown under grill.
SERVES 4. L.B./A.C. (2)

Seafarers' stew

4½ lb mixed white fish
Vegetables and herbs for making stock
½ lb prawns in their shells
1 lb crab claws (leave on the attractive black tips)
¼ lb small prawns
¼ pint white wine
Seasoning

Prepare the white fish by removing the skins and heads and cutting the flesh into large cubes. Make a well-flavoured stock from the heads, skin and bone and, when cool, strain. Put the stock and the white fish pieces into a large saucepan and bring slowly to the boil. Simmer gently for five minutes. Add the other fish and simmer for a further five minutes, taking care not to break up the fish (the large prawns look attractive if their tails are left on). Add wine and seasoning to taste. Serve hot.
SERVES 12. L.B. C.L.

Fish stew

2 oz shelled prawns
1 onion
½ lb tomatoes
½ cucumber
Parsley
2 oz olive oil
¼ pint water
2 teaspoons salt
Pinch mace
Red and black pepper
Bay leaf
Thyme
3 cloves garlic
¼ pint white wine
2 fillets lemon sole
½ lb halibut
½ lb smoked cod fillet

Fry onion gently in the oil, add garlic, herbs, sliced unpeeled cucumber, skinned tomatoes, salt, red and black pepper, mace. Finally, add wine, then water. Simmer for about 20 minutes or until cucumber is quite soft.

Skin and cut into thick slices the fillets of sole, halibut and smoked cod fillet. Put smoked fish into prepared broth, followed by the other fish 5 minutes later. (At this point a few slices of prepared inkfish and/or 1 pint of mussels may be added.) Cook for another five minutes and add 2 oz shelled prawns, cook for a further 3-4 minutes.
SERVES 4. R.J.

Glassblowers' herring

2 large filleted pickled herrings
½ onion, sliced
1 teaspoon peppercorns
½ teaspoon sugar
4 bay leaves
¼ pint vinegar
¼ pint water
4 tablespoons sugar
Dill

Soak herrings in cold water for 12 hours, and then cut in slices about ½-inch thick. Arrange in layers with sliced onion, peppercorns, sugar and bay leaves. A marinade of vinegar, water and the 4 tablespoons sugar is boiled and poured over the fish. Sprinkle with dill and leave for 3 days before use.
SERVES 2. C.W.

Herrings à la Calaisienne

4 herrings
2 shallots, finely chopped
1 tablespoon chopped parsley
2 tablespoons cream
1 slice white bread (crumbs)
Salt and pepper
Lemon juice
2 oz butter
¼ pint milk

Remove the heads of the herrings and the backbones. Make the stuffing for the fish with their own chopped roes,

With its delicate flavour and texture, plaice is a fine dish for entertaining—too often, alas, forgotten. Crisply fried, it is unbeatable.

the shallots, parsley and breadcrumbs soaked in milk. Season with salt, pepper and lemon juice, and bind with the cream and half the softened butter. Stuff the herrings with this mixture and put them in a buttered fireproof dish. Melt the rest of the butter, pour it over them and cover with a piece of buttered paper. Bake in a moderate oven, 350 F (gas 4) for 25 minutes. Serve with *maître d'hôtel* butter which is made by blending salt, pepper, lemon juice and a tablespoon of chopped parsley into 4 oz of softened butter. Garnish with wedges of lemon.

SERVES 4.   J.E. (1)

Herrings with sherry

4 Danish Matjes herrings
7 fl oz vinegar
3 tablespoons sugar
2 bay leaves
10 whole peppercorns
1 tablespoon tomato purée
2 fl oz sherry

Heat the sugar, bay leaves, peppercorns and tomato purée slowly until the sugar has dissolved. Cool marinade, add the sherry and pour over the Matjes herrings and decorate with onion slices. Leave for at least 12 hours before serving.

SERVES 4.   I.M.

Herrings with dill

4 Danish marinated herring fillets
6 heaped tablespoons mayonnaise
2 tablespoons single cream
1 teaspoon vinegar
Fresh chopped dill
Salt and pepper to taste
Strips tomato, seeded and peeled

Mix the mayonnaise, cream, vinegar, salt and pepper and most of the chopped dill. Pour the dressing over the herrings and decorate with the tomato strips and the remainder of the dill. (This can also be served as a starter.)

SERVES 4.   J.G. (1)

Pescada a Maiota
Maia hake

1 lb hake fillets (about ½-inch thick)
Lemon juice
Salt
1 lb potatoes
¼ pint mayonnaise
Chopped onion (optional)

Place prepared fillets in an ovenproof dish sprinkled with lemon juice and salt. Boil potatoes, dice and fry lightly in a little olive oil. Add to fish. Place mayonnaise on top, mixing it in to the fish and potatoes. Then gently smooth over the top with the back of a spoon. Bake, and when it rises like a soufflé on top it is ready—usually about ½ hour in a medium oven. Some finely chopped onion can be added on top of the potatoes and olive oil can be added during baking if necessary.

SERVES 4. C.W.

Cataplana
Portuguese pork and seafood
1 lb lean pork, cubed
2 pints mussels (or clams)
2 onions, sliced
1 green pepper, chopped
4 tomatoes, chopped
Lemon
White wine
Salt and pepper

Wash and scrub the mussels thoroughly and remove beards. Put into boiling water with a piece of lemon to help them open. Discard any that don't. Lightly brown the pork, onions, pepper and tomatoes in oil. Add the mussels, salt and pepper and wine. Cover tightly and cook the mixture in a medium oven or on top of the stove.

SERVES 4. L.H. (2)

Seafood quiche

4 oz short pastry
1 small onion
1 oz butter
6 oz peeled prawns
Salt and black pepper
1 tablespoon chopped parsley
1 egg and 1 egg yolk
¼ pint single cream
1 oz gruyère cheese

Roll out the pastry and line a 6-inch flan ring. Bake the pastry 'blind' at 425°F (gas 7) for 15 minutes, then at 375°F (gas 5) for 5 minutes. Grate the onion and fry it gently in butter until yellow. Add the prawns, salt and pepper, and put the mixture into a pastry case. Sprinkle on the parsley. Lightly beat together the eggs, cream and grated cheese, and pour over the prawns. Bake at 350°F (gas 4) for 40 minutes until just firm.

SERVES 4. M.N.

Salmon croquettes

10 oz flaked salmon
Béchamel sauce
2 oz mushrooms, finely chopped
Butter
Salt and pepper
Dill
Beaten egg yolk
1 teaspoon lemon juice
2 eggs, beaten
Breadcrumbs
Fat for frying

Lightly fry mushrooms in butter. Add salmon, mushrooms, seasoning, egg yolk and lemon juice to béchamel sauce. Spread mixture on flat dish. Chill thoroughly and then shape into croquettes. Coat with egg and breadcrumbs. Chill the croquettes again for about an hour. Then deep fry.

SERVES 4. L.H. (2)

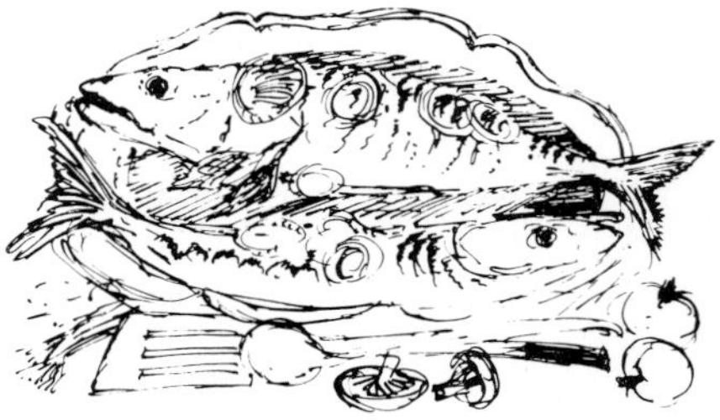

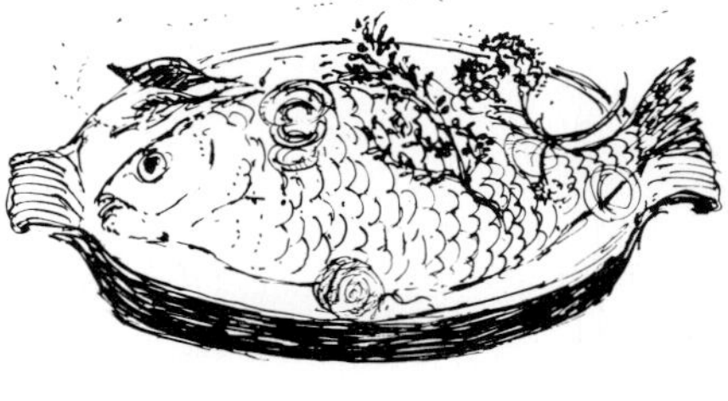

Red mullet à la Niçoise

4 red mullet
Flour
Olive oil
1 lb tomatoes
1 large clove garlic
Salt and pepper
Stuffed olives
Anchovy fillets
Lemon

Wipe the fish and dust with flour seasoned with salt and pepper. Fry in hot olive oil, turning once, and keep warm. Chop the tomatoes roughly and stew them until soft in a little olive oil with the crushed clove of garlic. Season well and rub through a sieve. Arrange fish on a dish bordered with scalloped slices of lemon and pour over the tomato purée. Garnish the fish with sliced stuffed olives and a lattice of anchovy.

SERVES 4. J.E. (1)

Redfish à la crème

2½ lb redfish or whiting fillets
⅜ pint dry white wine
⅜ pint water
1 bouquet garni, consisting of parsley stalks, 1 bay leaf and thyme
1½ oz butter or margarine
1 small onion, finely chopped
1 blade mace
Salt
5 white peppercorns, freshly ground
½ lemon
1 tablespoon plain flour
6 tablespoons top of milk or single cream
1 tablespoon chopped parsley

Clean the redfish, cut off the head and tail. Cook the trimmings with the wine and water for 15 to 20 minutes.

Grease a fireproof dish with half the butter. Sprinkle the onion over the bottom of the dish. Cut the fish into 1½-inch pieces and put them into the dish. Season with the mace, salt to taste and pepper. Sprinkle with the juice from half a lemon. Cover and cook gently over a top heat for about 15 minutes. Drain the fish and keep it hot. Remove the mace. Cook the rest of the butter with the flour. Remove from the heat. Gradually add the strained stock. Bring to the boil and cook for 3 to 5 minutes. Add the cream and parsley. Coat fish with sauce. Pour the mixture into a vol-au-vent case or serve with crisp *croûtons* fried in oil and butter, or with mashed potatoes.

SERVES 6. S.G.

Scallop fritters

4 scallops
2 oz plain flour
Pinch of salt
Pinch of cayenne pepper
⅛ pint milk and water mixed
1 small egg
1 dessertspoon butter, melted
1 dessertspoon brandy or Pernod

Clean the scallops and separate the coral from the white (frozen scallops should be thawed and well drained before use). Cut the white part in two thin rounds. Make a batter with the flour, salt, cayenne pepper, mixed milk and water, and the egg yolk. Leave the batter to stand for an hour, then fold in the melted butter, brandy or Pernod and the stiffly-beaten egg white. Coat the pieces of scallop with the batter and fry them in hot oil for 4-5 minutes. Drain and serve hot with Sauce Tartare, a sprinkling of parsley and lemon slices.

SERVES 4. M.N.

Cataplana is a traditional Portuguese dish of pork and clams. Sometimes, as here, mussels, are used instead. (Recipe on this page.)

Fresh sardines grilled in the open make an inexpensive summer meal—a delicious reminder of holidays in Spain and Portugal.

Barbecued fish in herb marinade

*3 lb salmon, haddock or halibut steaks
  (cut about 1-inch thick)*
2 bay leaves
½ teaspoon thyme
8 fl oz wine vinegar

Put fish into a shallow dish. Combine bay leaves, thyme and vinegar in a saucepan, and heat gently just to boiling point. Cool and pour over fish. Leave fish for 30 minutes, then drain well. Brush fish with a little cooking oil and barbecue over medium heat, about 3-inches from the fire for 12 minutes, turning once. (The same marinade can be used for ordinary grilling.)
SERVES 6-8.   M.N.

Turbot salad

2 lb turbot, cut in ½-inch pieces
1 pint water
1 pint milk
10 tablespoons olive oil
Juice 2 lemons
Salt and pepper
6 oz peeled prawns
3 tablespoons finely chopped parsley
3 tablespoons chopped onion

Poach the fish slowly in the salted water and milk until it can be flaked with a fork. Drain. Remove skin and bones. Dress with olive oil, lemon juice and salt and pepper to taste. Add the prawns, parsley, onion. Serve cold.
SERVES 4-6.   S.G.

Normandy haddock

10 oz haddock fillets
¼ pint white wine
1 onion, quartered
1 bayleaf
3 oz butter
2 oz plain flour
½ pint milk
¼ pint double cream
Salt and pepper
4 oz button mushrooms
4 oz peeled prawns
8 oz shelled mussels

The prawns and mussels may be frozen if necessary, but should be thawed before use. Cut the haddock fillets into six portions. Put them in a saucepan

with wine and ¼ pint water, onion and bay leaf. Bring to the boil, cover and simmer for 15 minutes. Drain the haddock, reserving the cooking liquid, remove the skin, and put the portions into a large serving dish. Keep warm in a cool oven. Melt 2 oz butter in a pan, stir in the flour and cook over a low heat for 2 minutes, stirring all the time. Take off the heat and gradually stir in the cooking liquid and the milk, stirring well until smooth. Return to the heat, bring to the boil, stirring constantly until thickened, and then cook for 3 minutes. Take off the heat and stir in the cream, with salt and pepper to taste. Heat the remaining butter in a frying-pan, add the mushrooms and fry for 2 minutes. Add them to the sauce with the prawns and mussels. Heat through very gently and spoon the sauce over the haddock.
SERVES 4-6.   M.N.

Pancakes with creamed haddock

PANCAKE BATTER
Pancake batter
4 oz plain flour
1 egg
1 egg yolk
½ teaspoon salt
½ pint milk
FILLING
1 lb smoked haddock
1 small onion chopped
¾ pint milk
Salt and pepper
2 oz plain flour
2 oz butter
1 tablespoon lemon juice
2 tablespoons single cream
GRATIN TOP
1 oz melted butter
2 tablespoons grated gruyère
1 tablespoon toasted breadcrumbs

Prepare the batter and fry eight thin pancakes in a 6-inch frying-pan. To make the filling, poach fish and onion in milk (¾ pint of this will be needed to make the sauce), seasoned with salt and pepper, for about 15 minutes. Then set aside.

Prepare sauce in a separate saucepan. Melt the butter and stir in flour. Gradually add the milk that the fish was cooked in, along with the lemon juice. Bring slowly to the boil. Cook for about 3 minutes. Roughly flake the fish and stir into the sauce with the onion. Stir in cream. Place a quantity of filling on each pancake and roll up. Pack the rolled up pancakes tightly together in a greased fireproof dish. Thin the remaining mixture with additional milk to a pouring consistency and pour over the rolled up stuffed pancakes.

Top with the gratin mixture and brown under a hot grill. Serve immediately.
SERVES 4.   S.G.

Mussel timbale

This is a deep case of cheese pastry with a filling of mussels in a well flavoured sauce. It makes an excellent, rich main course.
PASTRY
8 oz plain flour
6 oz butter
1 oz grated parmesan cheese
3 fl oz water
MUSSELS
3 quarts mussels
3 tablespoons water
SAUCE
1 oz butter
1 small carrot, chopped
1 small onion, chopped
1 stick celery, chopped
1 oz flour
¼ pint stock from the mussels
¼ pint white wine
Bay leaf
Few peppercorns
Sprig parsley
3 whole cloves
Pinch of paprika
Pinch of salt
Pinch of ground nutmeg
2 tablespoons tomato paste
3 tablespoons single cream
8 oz whiting, cut into chunks
1 egg, beaten for glaze

Make the pastry by rubbing the butter into the flour to give pieces which look like oat flakes, then stir in the cheese. Stir in the water and gather together into a very soft, pliable dough. Turn out onto a lightly-floured board and knead with the heel of the hand, working with one section of the dough at a time—this is to make a pastry strong enough to hold its shape in a deep mould. Wrap the dough in foil or film and chill in the 'fridge for at least 2 hours. Roll out to a circle about 5 inches diameter and shape over the outside of a straight-sided metal mould about 3½ inches deep. Trim off the excess pastry and chill the pastry mould in an inverted position in the 'fridge while you cook the mussels and make the sauce.

Scrub the mussels thoroughly in cold water to remove all sand and pull off the beards. Put into a large pan with the water, cover and cook gently over a low heat for a few minutes until the shells open. Remove the mussels from the shells with a fork and set aside. Reserve ¼ pint of the cooking liquor.

Cook the vegetables in the butter for about 5 minutes, until the onions become translucent, then stir in the flour and continue cooking for a further minute. Add the stock and wine, the herbs and other flavouring ingredients and cook, stirring frequently, for about 10 minutes to thicken the sauce and until the vegetables are tender. Add the cream and adjust the flavour to taste, then lightly stir in the mussels and the chunks

of raw whiting. Leave to cool.

Ease the pastry shape away from the outside of the mould. Butter the inside of the mould, and gently press the pastry shape into it, fitting well down into the corners. Fill with the cooled mussel mixture and roll out the reserved scraps of pastry to form a lid for the top. Brush the pastry edges with egg, fit the top in place and press firmly around to seal. Brush over the top with the egg glaze, set the mould on a baking tray and bake at 400°F (gas 6) for about 40 minutes or until golden brown.

Invert the mould immediately onto a serving dish but leave the mould in position for about 15 minutes to set, then carefully lift off. The timbale will hold its shape for a good half hour. Cut in slices and serve hot.
SERVES 6.   L.B./A.P.

Moules provençale

2 quarts well-scrubbed mussels in the shell
1 clove garlic, minced
1 large onion, finely chopped
3 tablespoons white wine
2¼ oz can tomato purée
Seasoning
Pinch dried marjoram
1 small red pepper, seeded and sliced
1 small green pepper, seeded and sliced
1 lb tomatoes, quartered
4 oz can anchovy fillets

Put the mussels, garlic, onion and wine into a saucepan or pan suitable for cooking and serving. Cover and cook over a moderate heat for 3-5 minutes or until the mussels open. Remove one half shell from each mussel and return the shells with mussels attached to the pan. Add all the remaining ingredients except the anchovy fillets, cover and simmer gently for a few minutes until the peppers are tender. (This dish may be cooked in the oven if more convenient.)

Before serving, roll up the anchovies and place on top of the sauce and mussels. Serve in the pot.
SERVES 3-4.   L.B./H.C. (1)

Marinated kipper fillets

2-3 boned kipper fillets per person, depending on size
MARINADE
2 tablespoons lemon juice
6 tablespoons oil
Salt and pepper
A little sugar to taste
GARNISH
Watercress

Marinade the kipper fillets for 1½ hours in the fridge, turning once. Drain and serve on dishes garnished with watercress. Serve with hot garlic bread.
V.J.

Veal chops Monique

4 veal chops
4 oz raw minced veal
¼ pint béchamel sauce
1 oz ham
1 oz tongue
1 tablespoon double cream
1 egg, beaten
2 tablespoons grated parmesan cheese
1 egg yolk
Sufficient breadcrumbs to coat chops
1 oz butter
Juice of ½ lemon
1 tablespoon chopped parsley

Slit the veal chops right through to the bone. Combine the minced veal with half the cold béchamel sauce. Add the ham and tongue, cut into very fine strips, the cream and half the beaten egg. Stuff the chops with this mixture. Add the cheese to the egg yolk and the remaining béchamel sauce and use this to coat the veal chops on both sides. Put them into the fridge for ½ hour to set. Coat the prepared chops with the remaining beaten egg and breadcrumbs. Sauté in a little butter until brown on both sides. Put into serving dish and cook at 375°F (gas 5) for 30 minutes. Heat the 1 oz butter until nut brown. Add the lemon juice and the parsley. Pour this over the veal immediately.
SERVES 4.   M.L.

Veal and dill stew

2 lb stewing veal, cut into small pieces
Juice of 1 lemon
1 knob of butter
½ pint sour cream
1 lb mushroom stalks
Salt and pepper
1 tablespoon dried dill

Cook the veal in butter and lemon juice in heavy pan, with lid, until the meat is very tender. Add mushroom stalks and dill. Cook slowly for a quarter of an hour, stir in cream. Heat through and serve with creamed potatoes.
SERVES 6.   U.S.

Ternera al ajillo
Veal in garlic sauce

2 veal escalopes
2 cloves garlic
3 oz butter
2 fl oz dry white wine
Parsley
Salt
Olive oil

Fry veal in oil with chopped garlic. When cooked, add wine, parsley and salt. Serve hot.
SERVES 2.   J.S.C.

Veal with vermouth is a simple, quick dish to prepare and is pleasantly piquant. (Recipe at right.)

Vitello tonnato
Veal with tuna mayonnaise

This recipe should be made with veal, but as this is expensive, pork could be used instead.
2 lb fillet of veal (or 2 lb boned rolled loin of pork)
½ pint white wine
A small handful black peppercorns
Bayleaves
1 onion
2 7-oz tins tuna fish
½ pint thick home-made mayonnaise
Anchovy fillets to garnish

Roast the veal in white wine, with peppercorns, bayleaves, chopped onion and ½ pint of water, at 300°F (gas 2) in a tightly-sealed casserole for about 2 hours, or until cooked. Allow meat to cool, slice very thinly. Liquidize the tuna fish with a cupful of the stock in which you have cooked the meat; add to mayonnaise. Place the sliced meat on a bed of half the mayonnaise mixture, cover with the rest, garnish with anchovy strips. Chill and serve.
SERVES 6-8.   V.D./V.W.

Veal with vermouth

¾ lb veal escalope, cut into small pieces
Flour
Salt and pepper
Butter
4 tablespoons dry vermouth
4 tablespoons beef stock
Fresh rosemary
6-8 spring onions
Parsley
Lemon slices

Dust flattened pieces of veal with well-seasoned flour; sauté quickly in butter. Add dry vermouth and beef stock, and reduce until thickened a little. Sprinkle with fresh rosemary, chopped spring onion and parsley; add wafer-thin slices slices of lemon and cook gently for 2 or 3 minutes more.
SERVES 2.   L.H.

Stuffed veal birds

8 ½-inch-thick slices of veal
8 oz soft liver sausage
1 egg
1 stick celery
1 tablespoon parsley
1 tablespoon chopped green pepper

Beat veal very thin. Mash liver sausage with a fork and add beaten egg, minced celery, parsley and green pepper. Spread mixture evenly on each veal slice and roll up, securing with a skewer. Brush with cooking oil. Grill or roast, turning often and brushing with more oil, for about 25 minutes.
SERVES 4.   M.N.

Barbecued veal chops in foil

4 veal chops
2 tablespoons olive oil
4 garlic cloves
Salt and pepper
1 tablespoon tomato purée
1 teaspoon basil

Brush the chops on both sides with the oil and grill for 2 minutes on each side. Put each chop on a square of foil and scatter on chopped garlic. Add a dab of tomato purée and season with salt, pepper and basil. Form into a parcel and grill for 10 minutes on each side over medium heat. The initial grilling and wrapping in foil may be done well in advance of the barbecue grilling.
NOTE: Pork and lamb chops may also be cooked this way.
SERVES 4.   M.N.

MEAT

Steak tartare 'Mitchell'

A delicious and unconventional version of a classic dish.

1 lb best quality fresh mince
1 medium onion
4 slices of toast (white or brown)
4 egg yolks
2 teaspoons capers
4-6 baby beets, finely chopped
Salt and freshly ground black pepper
Worcestershire sauce

Peel and slice onion, keeping four onion rings of even size aside. Finely chop remainder and place in bowl. Prepare beetroot and place in bowl.

Separate eggs and place the egg yolks in individual egg-cups. Form mince into four cakes, pat them fairly flat (½-inch thick) and score them criss-cross-ways on each side. Sprinkle with salt and pepper.

Make toast and place on dish.

Heat heavy pan over brisk heat until it begins to smoke. Place meat cakes on hot, dry pan—two at a time—and almost immediately turn them with spatula. If the pan is hot enough they will not stick. After a minute, remove quickly to toast slices. The steaks are now brown on both sides but raw inside. Decorate with onion rings and a few capers. Serve with chopped onion, beetroot, more capers and the egg yolks, Worcestershire sauce, pepper and salt. The egg yolk will fit into the onion ring and you can vary the garnishes to include chopped green and red peppers, cucumber, tomatoes, etc.
SERVES 4. I.M.

Spring beef casserole

1½ lb chuck steak
2 tablespoons seasoned flour
3 tablespoons oil
2 medium onions
2 medium carrots
4 sticks celery
14 oz can tomatoes
½ pint beef stock
1 tablespoon Worcestershire sauce
Salt and pepper
Bouquet garni
10 Spanish stuffed green olives

Cut the meat into 1-inch pieces and toss in seasoned flour. Heat the oil and fry the meat until brown. Put into a casserole. Chop the onions, slice the carrots and chop the celery. Cook them in the frying-pan until soft, and add to the meat in the casserole. Mix any remaining seasoned flour into the oil left in the pan, and cook until brown. Stir in the tomatoes and add to the casserole together with stock, sauce, seasoning and bouquet garni. Put on the lid and cook at 325°F (gas 3) for 2½ hours. Add the olives and take out the bouquet garni. Very good with plainly boiled rice and a crisp green salad.
SERVES 4. M.N.

Fillet of beef in any form is delicious, but this unusual presentation is particularly good. Served cold, it is an excellent main course for a summer meal. 1 Marinade of Beef (page 83) 2 Jellied Bortsch (page 26) 3 Iced Prawn Soup (page 22) 4 Duck Terrine (page 40).

Boeuf bourguignon
Beef with red wine

1 lb stewing steak
4 sliced onions
2 diced carrots
½ pint red wine
¼ lb mushrooms
Clove of garlic
Bouquet garni (sprigs of parsley, thyme and a bay leaf tied together)

Cut the steak into cubes and marinate with the onions, carrots and wine for twenty-four hours. Now strain off the liquid, putting it aside. Roll the steak in flour and fry. Put in a saucepan with the wine, carrots and onions. Add the garlic, the bouquet garni and the mushrooms and simmer for 1½ hours. Remove bouquet garni and serve with baked potatoes.
SERVES 4. M.D.

Steak and ale pie

1 oz lard
1½ lb chuck steak
1 onion
4 sticks celery
¾ pint stock
Salt and pepper
1 oz flour
Flaky pastry, made with 12 oz flour
Beaten egg to glaze
½ pint brown ale

Melt lard and fry cubed steak, sliced onion and chopped celery. Stir in the stock and seasoning. Bring to the boil, cover and simmer for 1½ hours until meat is tender. Mix the flour with a little water to form a smooth paste and stir into the pan gradually. Bring to the boil, stirring. Turn meat and vegetables with half the gravy into a 1½-pint ovenware pie dish, and cool. Roll out pastry and cover pie. Brush with beaten egg and bake at 425°F (gas 7) for 10 minutes. Reduce heat to 375°F (gas 5) for 20 minutes. Put ale in a saucepan and boil rapidly to reduce to ¼ pint. Before serving the pie, remove the crust and cut into triangular portions. Stir hot ale into the meat and replace the crust. The surplus gravy may be served separately if liked.
SERVES 4. M.N.

Carpet-bag steak and caramel potatoes

4 rump steaks
½ dozen oysters
¼ lb chopped mushrooms
1 oz butter
4 oz fresh breadcrumbs
Grated rind ½ lemon
Salt and freshly ground black pepper
Paprika
Parsley, finely chopped
Garlic clove
1 egg yolk

Make a large slit in the side of each steak. Cook the oysters, chopped mushrooms and garlic slowly in a little butter for five minutes. Add the breadcrumbs, lemon rind, seasoning and chopped parsley, then stir in the egg yolk to bind the mixture. Pack this stuffing into the steaks. Skewer or sew the openings. Roast in moderate oven for an hour. Serve with caramel potatoes (see page 115.)
SERVES 4. J.M.

Boeuf à la mode
Topside of beef with leeks

4½ lb boned rolled topside
A little oil for browning
½ pint white wine
Spray of fresh rosemary
3 lb leeks

Brown the topside all over its fat covering in the oil in a roaster or meat tin. Add the wine and rosemary, cover and cook in the oven at 425°F (gas 7) for 1¼ hours. This will give a rare interior; for a more well-done joint, cook longer.

Twenty minutes before the end of the cooking time, put freshly-washed and sliced leeks around the meat in the juices in the tin, cover again and cook only until tender. Serve the meat in thin slices with the leeks for garnish and thicken the juices in the pan to make a most delicious gravy, but remove the rosemary first.
SERVES 6 (plus 6 cold meals) L.B./A.G.

Spit-roasted beef

2 lb topside beef
Sprig of rosemary
Olive oil
Salt and pepper

Spit the beef, brush with oil and sprinkle with rosemary. Just before serving, sprinkle with salt and pepper and cut the beef in thick slices. Serve with garlic butter, made by creaming butter with crushed garlic and chopped parsley, forming into a cylinder and cutting into slices.
SERVES 4-6.   M.N.

Barbecued salted steak

2 lb steak, 3 inches thick
6 garlic cloves
Cooking oil
1 tablespoon prepared mustard
Coarse salt

Crush the garlic cloves and spread on both sides of steak. Brush with cooking oil. Spread mustard on both sides of steak. Cover steak completely with coarse salt to form a crust, and leave to stand for 30 minutes. Put salt-coated steak directly on the fire and cook rare (20 minutes each side) or medium (25 minutes each side), turning only once. Break off salt crust, and slice meat across the grain.
SERVES 4.   M.N.

Zigeuner-Spiess
Skewers of mixed meats

Lamb
Pork
Fillet steak
Mushrooms
Onion
Bacon
Green pepper
Bay leaf
Marinade (see below)

Quantities depend on the number of people to be served. Arrange ingredients alternately on skewers. Place in marinade of oil, lemon juice, sweet ground paprika, crushed garlic, crushed white peppercorns, dash of Worcestershire sauce. Leave for 24 hours, turning skewer occasionally. Then grill. To serve, make a fried-bread pillar as shown in the photograph on page 86. Serve with Lyonnaise potatoes, garnish with watercress.

                             K.L.

Meat rarely tastes more delicious than when cooked and eaten outdoors. Here, barbecued steak is served with a variety of summer salads : lettuce, new potatoes, spring onions.

Steak and orange casserole

1 lb stewing steak
1 orange
1 potato
1 carrot
1 onion
A little dripping
Salt and pepper
¼ pint stock

Cut meat into small pieces, roll in flour and fry in dripping. Put in casserole. Slice the unpeeled orange, potato, onion and carrot. Place on top of the meat. Pour over stock and season to taste. Cook in moderate oven for 3 hours.
SERVES 3.   J.E. (1)

Fillet steak in cream sauce

2 oz butter
1 small onion
1 carrot
1 stick celery
1 bay leaf
10 white peppercorns
¾ pint milk
2 oz plain flour
1 tablespoon white wine vinegar
1 egg yolk
¼ pint double cream
Salt and pepper
4 × 6 oz fillet steaks
4 slices bread
Watercress sprigs for garnish

Cut the onion in quarters and slice the carrot and celery. Put into a saucepan with the bay leaf, peppercorns and milk, and bring slowly to the boil. Take off the heat, cover and leave to infuse for 30 minutes. Strain the milk and discard the vegetables. Heat the butter, stir in the flour and cook over a low heat for 3 minutes. Remove from the heat and gradually stir in the flavoured milk, and beat until smooth. Return to the heat and bring to the boil, stirring continuously for about 3 minutes. Take off the heat and stir in the vinegar, egg yolk and cream. Stir over a very low heat to gently cook the egg. Add salt and pepper to taste. While the milk has been infusing, prepare the steaks. Sprinkle with salt and freshly ground black pepper. Heat some butter in a large frying-pan, add the steaks and fry for 4 minutes on each side, turning once, to give medium rare steaks. Cut each piece of bread in a round the same size as the steaks. Fry in a little extra butter until golden brown on each side. Serve each steak on a piece of bread, pour a little sauce over each steak and garnish with watercress. Serve remaining sauce separately.
SERVES 4.   M.N.

Barbecued spare ribs

½ lb sugar
1½ oz salt
10 oz ground bean sauce
1½ oz red bean curd
1 garlic clove, finely sliced
2 oz meikueilu (or sherry)
3 lb spare ribs

Mix the above ingredients (except spare ribs) in a bowl and stir until the sugar and salt have dissolved. Marinate the spare ribs in the above for two hours, during which time stir frequently so that the ribs are thoroughly soaked. Heat the oven to a medium heat. Put the spare ribs in for fifteen minutes. Turn and roast for fifteen more minutes or until the side bones come out.
SERVES 6.   W.L.P.

MEAT

Steak and oyster pudding

1½ lb topside of beef
1 4-oz tin smoked oysters
2 oz plain flour
Pinch of ground nutmeg
Pepper and salt
3 tablespoons chopped parsley
4 oz mushrooms, coarsely chopped
1 medium onion, coarsely chopped
Suet pastry made with 12 oz self-raising
  flour

Cut the meat into cubes about an inch
square and put into a bowl. Rinse the
oysters in cold water, drain well and add
to the meat. Sieve the flour, nutmeg, and
salt and pepper over the meat and toss
together. Stir in the parsley, mushrooms
and onion.

Roll out the pastry to approximately
1½ inches thick in a circle about 14 inches
diameter. With a sharp knife, cut out a
wedge (quarter of the circle) and set this
aside for the top. Grease the inside of a
basin of approximately 2-pint capacity,
then roll the large piece of pastry around
the hand in a cone and insert into the
basin. Neatly shape the pastry to the
basin and fill with the meat mixture.

Roll out the reserved piece of pastry
to a circle the diameter of the top of the
basin and lay over the filling. Dampen
the edges, then roll the edges of the
lining pastry over top, pressing and
pinching into position. Completely wrap
the basin in a piece of foil making sure
there is room for the pastry to rise but
that no water can get into it. Set into a
large saucepan of boiling water, cover
and boil for five hours, topping up with
boiling water as necessary.

Serve in the traditional way with a
napkin tucked around the basin.
SERVES 6.   L.B./J.C. (2)

Barbecued oriental kebabs

1 lb shoulder lamb
1 lb sirloin steak
20-oz can pineapple chunks
8 oz large, green pitted olives
8 fl oz pineapple juice
2 tablespoons soy sauce
2 tablespoons lemon juice
2 chopped garlic cloves
1 bay leaf
Pinch of ground cloves

Mix pineapple juice, soy sauce, lemon
juice, garlic, bay leaf and cloves and
shake well in a jar. Cut lamb and beef
into 1½ inch cubes and leave in pineapple
marinade for 6 hours at room temperature. Drain meat and save the marinade.
Thread meat, pineapple chunks and
olives on skewers and brush with marinade. Grill close to the fire, basting with
marinade and turning frequently for
about 15 minutes until meat is done
medium-rare.
SERVES 6.   M.N.

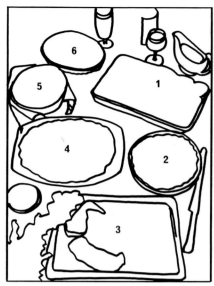

*Traditional British meat dishes are hard
to beat for a winter meal : 1 Silverside
and Dumplings (recipe on this page)
2 Oxtail Stew (page 94) 3 Mixed Fry
(kidneys, bacon, lamb cutlets, sausages,
etc) 4 Bœuf à la Mode (page 76) 5 Steak
and Oyster Pudding (this page) 6 Steak
and Kidney Pie (this page).*

Entrecôte Bordelaise
Steak with wine

4 inch-thick sirloin steaks trimmed of
  most of their fat
4 oz beef marrow (optional but
  authentic)
Oil and butter for frying
Salt and pepper
Garlic clove
Half-bottle red wine
Small onion, very finely chopped (or
  3 shallots if you can get them)
1 oz mushrooms, finely chopped
Level teaspoon flour
1 tablespoon freshly chopped parsley

Reduce the wine by about one-third by
boiling rapidly. Cut marrow (if available)
into four discs and poach in lightly-
salted water. Crush garlic with salt and
milled pepper and rub into steaks.

Heat two tablespoons of oil until
smoking and quickly brown the steaks
on both sides ensuring they remain
saignant (unless you like your steaks
well-cooked, in which case cook longer).
Remove steaks to warm serving dish.
Add an ounce of butter to the pan juices.
Soften the shallots and mushrooms.
Sprinkle with the flour and stir well in.
Add the reduced wine and boil rapidly,
stirring all the time for a further 3 or 4
minutes, or until the sauce looks bright
and a good consistency. Check seasoning
carefully, remembering that the steaks
are already seasoned. Strain over the
waiting steaks topped with a disc of
marrow. Sprinkle with parsley.
SERVES 4.   M.S.

Silverside and dumplings

4½-5 lb salt silverside
Bouquet garni (1 bay leaf, parsley stalks,
  sprig of thyme, few peppercorns)
1 medium onion stuck with a few whole
  cloves
1¼ lb each of onions, carrots, and
  turnips
8 oz flour made into dumplings

Put the meat into a large pan and cover
completely with cold water. Bring slowly
to the boil, skimming off any foam which
rises. Add the bouquet and the onion,
cover the pan and simmer until no pink
juice comes from the joint when pierced
with a skewer—about 2¼ hours for a 5 lb
joint.

Peel the vegetables and leave whole
in cold water until required. About ¾
hour before the end of the total cooking
time, add the vegetables, at the same
time removing the bouquet and skimming the surface again. Make the dumplings, roll into small balls and drop into
the boiling liquid about 15 minutes
before the end, cooking all the time with
the lid on.

Serve the joint on a hot dish surrounded by the vegetables and dumplings, and some of the stock in a sauce-
boat. To keep the joint tightly rolled and
easier to carve, leave the string on and
remove only as you slice the meat.
SERVES 6 (plus 6 cold meals).   L.B./M.C.

Steak and kidney pie

1½ lb braising steak
6 oz kidney
1 oz flour (approx)
Seasoning
1 onion
1 oz butter or oil
2 tablespoons mixed herbs
8 fl oz stock or water
Rough puff pastry made with 1¼ lb flour
Egg wash for glaze

Cut the steak into small pieces. Peel, core
and skin the kidney, then cut into slices.
Coat both the meat and the kidney in
well-seasoned flour by shaking in a
plastic bag. Slice the onion and brown
lightly in the butter in a saucepan, add
the meats and fry further until browned.
Add the herbs and stock, cover and
simmer gently for one hour, then remove from the heat and leave to cool.

When the meat is cooled, turn into a
pie dish of 1½-pint capacity. Roll the
pastry thinly and from the centre cut an
oval the size of the dish. Brush the edges
of the dish with water and use the pastry
trimmings to cut strips which can be
used to place around the dish edges.
Brush again with water and roll the
pastry top into position. Decorate and
brush well with egg beaten with a little
milk or water and chill for an hour. Bake
for about half an hour at 400°F (gas 6).
SERVES 4-6.   L.B./A.E.

Marinade of beef

An unusual way of cooking fillet of beef which, served cold, is an outstanding centrepiece for a luncheon or supper.

2 lb fillet steak in the piece
MARINADE
¼ *pint white wine*
½ *pint olive oil*
1 chicken stock cube
VEGETABLES
1 large aubergine
2 oz butter
Few spring onions
1 small green pepper
1 small red pepper
2 small firm tomatoes
5-6 black olives
DRESSING
1 chicken stock cube
3 tablespoons olive oil
1 tablespoon wine vinegar

Trim away any membrane from the meat, then roll neatly and tie firmly at intervals with string. Put into a bowl, together with the marinade and leave in a cool place for 6 to 12 hours to develop the flavours. Turn as often as possible. Cook under a hot grill (if the grill is large enough), turning to give even browning all over, or in a hot oven at 450°F (gas 8) for 25 to 30 minutes, until well browned on the outside but rare inside. Baste with the marinade throughout the cooking. Leave until quite cold, then cut in 6 thick slices.

Cut the aubergine into 6 slices also, sprinkle on either side with salt and leave for about 5 minutes before blotting

Regional dishes are always best with local wines. Here, Bordeaux wines accompany Entrecôte bordelaise (page 80), served with courgettes, potatoes and Cèpes bordelaise (page 115).

well with paper or a cloth to remove the bitterness. Lightly fry on either side in the butter. Cool, then transfer to a suitable serving plate and set a slice of cooked fillet on top of each slice of aubergine.

Clean the onions and discard the coarser part of the tops. Remove the seeds from the peppers, cut them in strips and blanch for a few minutes in hot water. Cut the tomatoes in quarters and remove the seeds; remove the stones from the olives. Pile the vegetables up in the centre of the serving plate and spoon over the dressing.
SERVES 6.   L.B./J.B. (3)

Una's steak-and-kidney pie

This is a huge pie served in a large flat pie dish.

12 oz shortcrust pastry
1½ lb of stewing steak, cut in small cubes
½ lb kidney, cut in small cubes
1 lb mushroom stalks
3 large onions
Salt, pepper and stock

Toss meat in flour, and brown in a large pan with lid on. Add salt, pepper, onions and stock (enough liquid to cover). Cover and simmer for 2 to 3 hours until tender. Thicken the juice a little with your favourite form of gravy. (Yeast extract with cornflour is excellent for this.) Pour all the ingredients into the large dish and leave to cool. Roll the pastry to size of dish, leaving an inch extra all round. Trim off extra inch of pastry and place under pie crust edge; flute together and decorate. Brush with egg. Cook for quarter of an hour at 425°F (gas 7) then 325°F (gas 3) for half an hour until pastry is golden.
SERVES 8.   U.S.

Poldki befsztyk
Fillet steak Polish-wise

4 fillets of steak
¼ *lb mushrooms*
Redcurrant jelly
¼ *lb flour*
1 oz margarine
¼ *pint milk*
Salt and pepper
Beef stock
3 green tomatoes
1 red and 1 green pepper
Half a firm white cabbage
2 onions
10 slices of cucumber
Oil and vinegar

First make the dumplings by putting the flour in a basin. Make a hole in the centre and pour in the milk, mixing well. Add the margarine and seasoning; mix until it leaves the basin cleanly. Form into balls and roll in flour and boil 8 minutes in beef stock. For the salad, slice the peppers, having first removed the seeds, chop the onions finely, shred the cabbage and add to the sliced tomatoes and cucumber. Season and add oil and vinegar. Now fry the steak, together with the mushrooms and serve with the salad and redcurrant jelly.
SERVES 4.   M.D.

Irish spiced beef

This has almost faded from our cuisine because of the somewhat lengthy process necessary and the high cost of beef. To make it worth the trouble, it is wise to use a fairly large joint, then store it ready-sliced in the freezer. For buffet entertaining or for cold suppers nothing could be more delectable.

3½-4 lb rolled topside
2 oz salt
CURING THE MEAT
*1 level teaspoon each of ground mace,
    cloves, and nutmeg*
¼ *level teaspoon cayenne*
1 oz juniper berries
1 teaspoon black peppercorns
½ *oz saltpetre*
4 oz soft brown sugar

Pound together all the spices, etc, listed for curing the meat. Then rub well into the meat and leave in a covered container in a cool place for 3 days. Rub 2 oz salt into the meat and baste it well with the juices which have collected. Cover, and repeat this process of basting every day for a further 3 weeks.

To cook the topside, discard the juices and rinse the surface of the meat. Put into a large saucepan of cold water with a bay leaf, a coarsely-chopped onion and a carrot, a pinch of thyme, and a sprig of parsley. Bring to the boil, remove the scum, and continue cooking gently for 20 minutes per pound. Cool the meat in the cooking liquor (excellent for soup).
SERVES 6.   L.B.

MEAT

Beef and chestnut casserole

2 lb topside
2 fl oz oil
1 small onion, finely chopped
4 oz smoked, streaky bacon, chopped
½ pint beef stock
3 tablespoons tomato purée
1 tablespoon brown sugar
2 tablespoons orange juice
1 lb chestnuts, peeled
Salt and freshly ground black pepper
MARINADE
1 onion, finely chopped
Grated rind of 1 orange
Salt and freshly ground black pepper
1 teaspoon ground mixed spice
1 teaspoon cinnamon
1 teaspoon ground coriander
6 cloves
½ pint full-bodied red wine
Chopped parsley

Combine all the marinade ingredients in a large bowl or casserole. Add the meat and leave to marinate for 6-8 hours, or overnight, turning if possible.

Remove the meat and dry well. Reserve the marinade. Heat the oil and fry the onion and bacon until just beginning to brown. Transfer to a casserole. Fry the meat in the oil, turning, until evenly browned. Place in the casserole. Pour the stock into the pan which has been used for frying and stir well to dislodge any sediment. Bring to the boil and add the remaining ingredients together with the marinade. Pour over the meat and cook for 3 hours at 325°F (gas 3). Remove the meat and cut into thick slices. Place on a serving dish and keep warm. Boil the liquid rapidly until reduced to almost a half. Pour sufficient over the meat slices to cover, sprinkle with parsley and serve. Serve the remaining sauce separately.
SERVES 4-6.   H.W.

Pepperpot beef

Particularly good with avocado and green salad for one of those not-so-warm summer evenings.
2 lb braising steak
1 oz flour
1 teaspoon salt
⅛ teaspoon pepper
½ teaspoon ground ginger
2 oz lard or dripping
SAUCE
¼ teaspoon Tabasco sauce
8 oz can tomatoes
¼ lb sliced mushrooms
2 tablespoons soft brown sugar
2 tablespoons wine vinegar
2 cloves garlic, crushed
1 bay leaf
1 red pepper
15 oz can red kidney beans

Cut the beef into 1 inch cubes. Mix together the flour, seasonings and ginger

and use to coat the beef. Heat the lard in a large pan, add the beef and fry quickly until browned, turning once, then transfer to a 3-pint ovenproof casserole. Combine all the ingredients for the sauce, except the pepper and beans, and pour over the meat. Cover the casserole and cook in the oven for about 2 hours or until tender at 325°F (gas 3).

Remove the seeds and white pith from the pepper and cut in rings. Drain the kidney beans and add to the casserole with the pepper for the last 30 minutes of the cooking time.
SERVES 6.   M.B. (1)

Beef olives

8 thin slices topside beef
2 tablespoons oil
1 oz butter
1 chopped medium-sized onion
4 oz sliced button mushrooms
1 oz flour
1 pint beef stock
FILLING
2 oz shredded suet
4 oz white breadcrumbs
4 oz finely chopped calves liver
1 teaspoon chopped fresh parsley
1 teaspoon chopped fresh thyme
2 teaspoons lemon juice
1 teaspoon strong horseradish sauce
Salt and freshly ground black pepper
10 halved stuffed green olives
1 beaten egg

Mix together all the ingredients for the filling and bind with the egg. Beat the slices of the topside to flatten and tender-ise them. Spread each slice with filling, roll and tie up with string. Heat the oil and butter and add the onion and mushrooms, and fry gently until brown. Put into a 3-pint ovenware casserole. Fry the beef rolls in the remaining fat until they turn brown on the outside. Put the rolls into the casserole. Stir the flour into the remaining fat and cook until brown, stirring constantly. Gradually pour on the stock, stirring all the time, bring to the boil and boil for 1 minute. Pour over the meat and cover the casserole. Cook at 350°F (gas 4) for 1½ hours. Before serving, check the seasoning and remove the string from the beef rolls.
SERVES 4.   M.N.

Curried beef moulds

About ¾ lb cold beef
4 oz breadcrumbs
2 oz butter
1 egg
Salt and pepper
½ teaspoon curry powder
2 tablespoons gravy
1 tablespoon chutney
Mashed potatoes or rice

Put beef through mincer, mix with it the pepper and salt, curry powder mixed with the gravy, the butter, melted, breadcrumbs and the beaten egg. Press firmly into small buttered moulds and steam gently for three quarters of an hour. Turn out and serve on a hot dish surrounded with well-seasoned mashed potatoes or rice sprinkled with chutney.
SERVES 2-3.   J.E. (1)

Cassoulet

The traditional cassoulet is made from white beans, fat pork, and Toulouse sausages simmered for hours in an earthenware pot, then served with chunks of roast goose. In this recipe roast duck has been substituted for the goose as it is more readily available.

It is important to cook the beans until they begin to form a thick mass. And do try to get good French sausages of the Toulouse type. Really good country pork sausages might be a reasonable alternative, but the standard British banger is not for this dish.

1 lb white beans, soaked overnight
1 lb belly pork
Bouquet garni
1 teaspoon green peppercorns
2 small onions stuck with cloves
3 cloves of garlic, crushed
Salt
¼-½ pint dry white wine
1 lb Toulouse sausages
Buttered crumbs
1 duckling, 2½-3 lb oven-ready weight

Pour away the soaking water and rinse the beans in cold water. Put into a saucepan with 3 pints cold water, cover and bring to the boil. Remove from the heat and leave to stand for 40 minutes (this is important as it makes the beans less gaseous). Meanwhile, remove the skin and bone from the pork and cut into 1-inch cubes.

Drain the beans and put into a large casserole with 2 pints of boiling water, the pork, bouquet garni, peppercorns, onions, garlic and 2 level teaspoons of salt. Cover and cook slowly in the oven at 300°F (gas 2) for about 5 hours. When the beans are nearing the correct consistency, they should begin to lose their shape, become a thickened mass, and bubble up around the edges of the casserole. Do not stop the cooking too soon—too often instructions for cassoulet tend not to give an adequate cooking time and the result is just boiled beans!

Taste, and add extra salt if necessary, stir in the wine and the sausages. If you are using the large fat sausages, you may like to cut them in halves. Cook for a further hour, uncovered, then sprinkle with buttered crumbs and brown at the top of a hot oven. Serve piping hot from the casserole with portions of crisply-roasted duckling arranged on top.
SERVES 6. L.B./C.R. (1)

Gulasz wieprzowy
Polish pork goulash

2 lb pork
1 lb sauerkraut
1 oz paprika
4 large onions
1 oz flour
2 ripe tomatoes
1 oz soured cream
Salt and pepper
2 fl oz olive oil

Cut the pork into cubes and slice the onions and tomatoes. Heat the oil in a pan and add the pork and onions. Cook gently until the onions are yellow, then add the paprika, flour, tomatoes, seasoning and sauerkraut. Add ¼ pint of water and simmer for 1 hour. Stir in the cream and simmer for a further 5 minutes.
SERVES 6. M.D.

Pork with cider cream sauce

1 lb pork fillet or 8 thin pork steaks
2 level teaspoons flour
2 oz butter
1 large onion, finely chopped
6 oz mushrooms, sliced
½ pint dry cider
Salt and pepper
4 tablespoons double cream
Chopped parsley

Cut pork fillet into 8 pieces. Coat with flour. Melt butter and cook pork slowly for five minutes on each side. Drain and keep warm. Add onions and mushrooms to pan, and cook gently until tender but not brown. Stir in remaining flour, and cook for a minute. Remove from heat, and gradually stir in cider. Return to heat, stirring and cook for a minute. Add cooked pork and seasoning, then stir in cream. Heat through, but do not boil. Garnish with chopped parsley.
SERVES 4. S.W. (1)

Orange and lemon pork

2 large pork chops
1 oz butter
1 tablespoon oil
1 finely chopped onion
2 oz back bacon
¼ pint dry white wine
1 teaspoon tomato purée
1 pint stock
2 oz button mushrooms
½ teaspoon mixed herbs
Grated rind ½ orange
Grated rind ½ lemon
Salt and pepper

Heat the butter and oil together and fry the chops for 10 minutes on each side. Remove from the pan and keep warm. Fry the onion and the bacon (cut into strips) lightly until softened, but not coloured. Stir in the wine, tomato purée, stock and sliced mushrooms. Add the herbs and cook uncovered for 10 minutes. Return the chops to the pan and heat through. Stir in the fruit rinds and season to taste.
SERVES 2. M.N.

Pork chop 'Great Dane'

For each person you will need:
1 large pork chop
1 large onion, sliced finely
2 medium-sized apples, sliced
Salt and pepper
Butter

Place the pork chop on a warm, dry frying-pan and cook each side for 2 minutes—this will seal the juices. Then salt and pepper the meat, add butter and fry until cooked. Remove pork chop from pan and keep warm.

Braise the onion and apple slices in the same pan, using the same juices. When cooked pour over the pork chop and serve. Accompany this dish with *pommes sautés* and red cabbage with parsley. J.G.

Costeletas a Moda de Braga
Spanish-style pork

8-12 pork cutlets
1¾ lb potatoes
3½ oz butter
1-2 large onions
3 tablespoons white wine
3½ oz cooking fat
5 oz ham
Salt and pepper

Trim cutlets and season with salt and pepper. Sprinkle with the wine. Fry in butter and fat. In another pan, lightly fry potatoes cut in thin slices. Add chopped ham and onion to the fat in which the cutlets were fried and cook till golden brown. Add the cutlets, the rest of the wine and potatoes to the pan and simmer gently together for ½ hour.
SERVES 4-6. C.W.

Frikadeller
Danish meat balls

½ lb finely minced veal
½ lb finely minced pork
1 medium-sized onion, chopped
3 tablespoons flour
½ pint milk
1 egg, well beaten
Salt and pepper
3-4 oz butter

Mix the meat thoroughly with the onion and then stir in the flour until it is evenly distributed. Gradually beat in the milk, 2 tablespoons at a time, so that the mixture is aerated. Beat in the egg and seasoning until the mixture is puffy. The mixture should be shaped into oblongs with the use of two spoons. Fry the *frikadeller* in hot butter until browned on all sides.

Serve with boiled or caramellized potatoes and red cabbage.

SERVES 4. J.G. (1)

Braised pork Chinese-style

2 lb belly pork cut in 1-inch wide long
    strips
2 tablespoons sugar
2 tablespoons light soy sauce
1 tablespoon dark soy sauce
2 slices fresh ginger root
3 spring onions, cut into half
1 pint stock
Oil for frying

Put the pork into boiling water for ten minutes and drain off all the water. Put two tablespoons of cooking oil into a non-stick pan and heat, add the spring onions and ginger and cook until the onions are lightly browned. Add the pork to the above and keep moving and stirring for a couple of minutes. Add the rest of the ingredients and cover. Simmer on a gentle heat. When the sauce gets nearly dry, test to see if the pork is tender. If not, add ⅓ pint of stock and simmer again. When the pork is tender and the sauce is reduced to about 4 tablespoons, remove from the heat. Remove ginger and onions, cut the pork into small pieces and serve with the sauce in which the meat was cooked.

SERVES 4-6. W.L.P.

Fidget pie

1 lb streaky bacon
8 oz onions
1 lb cooking apples
Salt and pepper
¼ pint cider
Shortcrust pastry, made with 12 oz flour
1 egg, beaten

Remove rind from the bacon and cut the bacon into dice. Peel and chop the onions. Core and chop the apples. Mix well together and season. Put into a 2-

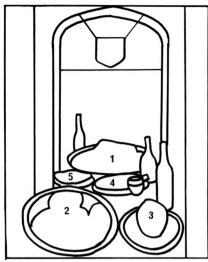

Variations on traditional Austrian dishes : 1 Zigeuner-Spiess (page 79) 2 Kalbsnieren-Bratan (best end of veal, boned and stuffed with a mousse of veal kidney, rolled, tied and roasted) 3 Melon mit Geflügel Salat (page 37) 4 Boiled rice with peas 5 Cucumber salad.

pint pie dish and pour over the cider. Roll out the pastry to cover the pie. Make four cuts out from the centre about 3 inches long, and fold back the triangles of pastry to expose the filling. Roll out any trimmings and cut out crescents, using a fluted cutter. Brush them with beaten egg and arrange round the edge of the pastry lid. Brush all over the pastry with egg and bake at 425°F (gas 7) for 20 minutes. Lower heat to 350°F (gas 4) for 30 minutes.

SERVES 4. A.C. (1)

Bacon in beer

3 lb forehock bacon joint, boned and rolled
1½ oz dripping
12 button onions
12 small carrots
4 leeks
1 pint beer
3 bay leaves
Thyme and parsley

This is a very good way of cooking a cheaper joint of bacon, to serve with jacket potatoes or hunks of French bread. Soak the bacon in cold water for about 6 hours if smoked, or 2 hours if unsmoked. Put in a saucepan, cover with cold water, bring to the boil. Simmer for 40 minutes. Take out the bacon, remove the skin and score the fat into diamonds. Melt the dripping in a large fireproof casserole. Peel the onions and carrots and fry in the dripping until lightly browned. Add the beer. Put the bacon in the casserole with the bay leaves and other herbs. Cover and bake at 350°F (gas 4) for 30 minutes. Take off the lid and cook at 425°F (gas 7) for 15 minutes.

SERVES 6. A.C. (1)

Glazed gammon

4 lb middle or corner gammon
1 large onion
1 bay leaf
6 peppercorns
3 oz soft brown sugar
2 teaspoons mustard powder
Whole cloves

Soak the gammon overnight in cold water. Put into a saucepan with 2 pints water, the onion cut in quarters, bay leaf and peppercorns. Cover and bring to the boil, then reduce the heat and simmer for 1½ hours. Peel off the skin from the gammon, mark the fat into diamond shapes with a sharp knife, and put the bacon into a roasting tin. Mix the sugar and mustard together and press on to the fat. Stick a clove in the centre of each diamond. Bake at 425°F (gas 7) for 15 minutes. The following variations on the glaze are also delicious.

CIDER GLAZE
When the fat has been marked into diamonds, stick a clove in each one, and sprinkle with 2 tablespoons Demerara sugar. Pour over ½ pint medium-sweet cider and baste while cooking in the oven. When the joint is cooked and the fat is golden brown, thicken the juice with cornflour as a sauce.

APPLE AND ORANGE GLAZE
Spread the scored fat with 4 oz thick marmalade. Peel, core and slice a large eating apple and leave to stand in lemon juice for 10 minutes. Drain the apple slices and arrange on the fat, securing with cocktail sticks. Brush with a little more marmalade, and baste during cooking. Remove sticks before serving.

RAISIN GLAZE
Put 4 oz raisins, grated rind and juice of 1 lemon, and ¼ pint water in a pan and cover, and simmer very gently for 10 minutes. Strain and add 4 tablespoons honey and a shake of black pepper to the liquid. Pour over the bacon joint and baste during baking. Return raisins to the liquid round the joint; spoon over bacon until it is completely cooked.

SERVES 8. A.C. (1)

British raised pie

1 lb plain flour
5 oz lard
1 lb minced pork
1 lb minced streaky bacon
Salt and pepper
Beaten egg

Make hot-water crust pastry using the flour and 5 oz lard. Cover the pastry and leave to stand for ½ hour, then use ⅔ of it to line a 6½-inch loose-bottomed deep cake tin. Fill with minced pork and streaky bacon, well seasoned. Cover with the remaining pastry, glaze with beaten egg and bake 1½-2 hours or until well browned at 350°F (gas 4). Cool well.

SERVES 4-6. L.B./E.B. (1)

MEAT

Schinken im Brotteig
Ham baked in bread dough

1½ lb gammon
1 onion
1 bay leaf
2¼ lb plain flour
4 oz fresh breadcrumbs
2 oz yeast
1 teaspoon caraway seeds
Pinch of salt
Cold water

Simmer the gammon in a large pan, together with the onion and bay leaf, plus enough water to cover the joint, for 75 minutes. Remove the gammon from the stock and allow to cool.

Let the yeast rise for 15 minutes in a little warm water. Mix the flour, breadcrumbs, caraway seeds, yeast and pinch of salt with a little cold water until you have a heavy bread dough—the less water you use, the better. Leave the dough to rise for at least 24 hours.

Work the dough just before baking. Divide the dough into two rounds and roll in two circles just large enough to cover the gammon. Place the gammon in the centre of one circle and cover with the other. Join the dough securely. Cook at 350°F (gas 4) for 2½ hours and serve while hot. Serve with potato salad.
SERVES 4.   W.S.

Spanish gammon

4 lb piece of gammon
¾ pint apple juice
1 onion
Freshly ground black pepper
2 tablespoons honey
12 Spanish stuffed green olives

Soak the gammon for 12 hours in cold water, drain. Place in a pan and pour over the apple juice, slice the onion and add with the pepper to the pan, cover and simmer for 20 minutes for each pound plus 20 minutes over. Remove the gammon from the pan and leave to cool slightly. Remove the skin and score the fat diagonally into diamond shapes. Put in a shallow ovenproof dish and brush with honey. Bake in the centre of a hot oven 425°F (gas 7) for about 15 minutes or until a rich golden brown, remove and leave to become quite cold.

Put olives on cocktail sticks and decorate gammon.
SERVES 10.   M.B. (1)

French lamb

2½ lb fillet end leg of lamb
2 garlic cloves
1 tablespoon French mustard

Cut the garlic into thin strips. Insert pieces of garlic into the skin and near the bone. Spread mustard all over the joint and roast at 350°F (gas 4) for 1½ hours.
SERVES 4-6.   M.N.

Lamb scallopini

2 lb leg of lamb, frozen
Flour
Salt and pepper
2 tablespoons oil
8 tablespoons stock
1 lemon, cut in paper-thin slices
4 teaspoons lemon juice
1 oz butter

While the lamb is still slightly frozen, cut thin crosswise slices with an electric carving knife, or very sharp knife. When completely thawed, pound out the lamb slices and dust them with seasoned flour. Brown quickly in hot oil, add the stock and put the lemon slices on top. Cover and simmer gently for 10 minutes. Take out the scallopini and keep them warm. Add the butter and lemon juice to the pan. Check the seasoning, and pour over the scallopini, and garnish with the lemon slices. These thin lamb slices may be cooked in various ways and are a good way of making the meat go a long way. Variations include:

SCALLOPINI WITH CHEESE
Pound the lamb slices and dust with seasoned flour. Dip into a beaten egg mixed with a tablespoon of water. Pass through some fresh white breadcrumbs and brown on both sides in hot oil. Drain and put into a fireproof dish. Sprinkle thickly with grated cheese and put under a hot grill until melted and golden.

SCALLOPINI PROVENÇALE
Pound the lamb slices, dust with seasoned flour and brown quickly in hot oil. For 2 lb lamb, add 2 finely-chopped onions, 1 lb chopped tomatoes (skinned and de-seeded), 1 tablespoon tomato purée, ½ pint white wine and 8 oz thinly sliced mushrooms. Simmer for 15 minutes, season and serve on boiled rice.

SCALLOPINI A LA MARSALA
Pound the lamb slices and dust with seasoned flour. Heat 2 tablespoons oil and add 1 crushed garlic clove. Brown the lamb on both sides. For 2 lb lamb, add 8 oz sliced mushrooms and cook until soft. Add ¼ pint marsala or sherry and 1 tablespoon tomato purée. Simmer for 5 minutes and serve on a bed of rice sprinkled with chopped parsley.
SERVES 8.   M.N.

Lamb steaks with redcurrant jelly

4 1-inch thick lamb steaks cut from
    shoulder
4 oz redcurrant jelly

Melt redcurrant jelly over low heat. Grill steaks about 3 inches from the fire. 10 minutes on each side, brushing frequently with redcurrant jelly. Season with salt and pepper just before serving.
SERVES 4.   M.N.

Lemon and ginger chops

4 chump chops
4 tablespoons oil
Grated rind of 1 lemon
2 tablespoons lemon juice
1 tablespoon brown sugar
1½ tablespoons ground ginger
Salt and pepper

Put the chops in a shallow dish. Mix the other ingredients and pour over them. Leave for 3 hours, turning the chops occasionally. Take out the chops and put under a hot grill. Cook for 15 minutes, turning the chops occasionally and basting them with the marinade. Serve with new potatoes and a green salad.
SERVES 4.   M.N.

Collared roll of lamb

1 or 2 breasts of lamb weighing about
    3½ lb with bone
¼ teaspoon grated nutmeg
¼ teaspoon ground cloves
½ teaspoon ground mace
Salt and pepper
3 teaspoons finely chopped fresh herbs or
    2 teaspoons dried mixed herbs
1 tablespoon chopped parsley
2 teaspoons grated lemon rind
½ shallot, minced
3-4 button mushrooms, finely chopped
1 slice white bread without crusts,
    crumbled
2 tablespoons butter or margarine
Flour for thickening (if serving hot)
1 oz unsalted butter (if serving hot)
A few chopped capers and small gherkins

Bone the meat, taking care not to cut right through it; it should weigh 1¾-2 lb, boned. Lay it flat, skin side down; if using two breasts, place them end to end, overlapping a little. Sprinkle the inside all over with the spices and herbs, lemon rind and shallot, mushrooms and

bread. Roll the meat up tightly from one short end, and tie with string like any rolled joint. Spread the butter or margarine over a piece of foil big enough to enclose the meat. Wrap the meat in it, put it in a baking tin with a little water, and bake at 325°F (gas 3) for 1½-1¾ hours. 15 minutes before the end of this time, take off the foil, baste the meat with the pan juices and let it brown.

Keep the meat hot on a warmed serving dish while making a thickened gravy with the pan juices, flour, and unsalted butter. Add the capers and gherkins to the gravy.

Alternatively, cool the meat quickly, wrap and refrigerate it for serving cold with capers and gherkins as a garnish.
SERVES 6.   M.B. (2)

Lamb and apple breakfast cakes

1 lb minced lean lamb
2 oz breadcrumbs
1 small finely chopped onion
1 egg, beaten
3 teaspoons Worcestershire sauce
2 oz brown sugar
½ teaspoon dry mustard
2 oz butter
2 dessert apples
8 bacon rolls
Salt and pepper

Combine all the ingredients except sugar, mustard, butter, apples and bacon rolls. Shape into eight round cakes. Core apples and cut into half-inch-thick slices. Put in shallow baking-pan with butter, bacon rolls and lamb cakes. Combine sugar and mustard and sprinkle over cakes and apples. Bake for 35 minutes at 375°F (gas 5). Serve with apple rings and bacon rolls on top of lamb cakes.
SERVES 4.   J.M.

Gigot d'agneau provençale
Leg of lamb provençal

1 leg of lamb (4 lb weight)
1 clove garlic
Salt and freshly ground black pepper
2 level teaspoons fresh basil
½ pint white wine
5 tablespoons fresh white breadcrumbs
5 tablespoons chopped parsley
Extra chopped parsley for serving
Small roast potatoes for garnish

Wipe the meat. Peel the garlic and cut it into thin slivers. Insert the slivers of garlic in the lamb, close to the bone. Place the lamb in a roasting-pan, sprinkle with salt, pepper, chopped basil and the wine. Allow the lamb to marinade for 2-3 hours, turning occasionally.

Place the lamb and marinade in a hot oven at 400°F (gas 6) and cook for 1 hour, covered with greaseproof paper or aluminium foil. Mix the breadcrumbs and parsley together in a small bowl.

Remove the paper from the meat and press the breadcrumbs and parsley all over the lamb with a palette knife. Baste the lamb with the juices in the pan. Reduce the temperature of the oven to 300°F (gas 2) and continue cooking the meat, uncovered, for 30 minutes. Baste occasionally.

Place the meat on a heated serving plate, press the extra chopped parsley over the top. Serve garnished with small roast potatoes.
NOTE: Substitute 1 teaspoon of dried herbs if fresh are unobtainable.
SERVES 6-8.   A.B.

Boiled lamb and melted butter

A boiled leg of mutton was very popular in Victorian and Edwardian times. Lamb cooked this way can be just as delicious, and if liked the stock can be made into caper or parsley sauce to serve with it.

1 leg of lamb
1 large onion
1 carrot
1 turnip
Bunch of mixed herbs
6 peppercorns
Pinch of mace
Salt

Put the meat into a saucepan and cover with boiling water. Boil for 5 minutes, then add the vegetables, herbs and spice. Lower the heat and simmer the meat, allowing 20 minutes per lb and 20 minutes over. Remove any scum from time to time. Half an hour before serving, add salt. To serve, drain the meat and put on a serving dish. Chop the vegetables, cut them into small pieces and put round the meat. Melt about 4 oz butter and pour over.
SERVES 6.   M.N.

Pierno de cordero à la Espanola
Roast leg of lamb Spanish-style

1 leg of lamb, about 4 lb in weight
2 cloves of garlic, crushed
1 level teaspoon mixed dried herbs
    including rosemary
4 tablespoons sherry
4 tablespoons water
12 small onions
6 stuffed green olives, sliced
Few sprigs fresh rosemary

Trim any surplus fat from the lamb, place in a roasting-tin. Spread with the crushed garlic and sprinkle with the dried herbs, pour over the sherry and leave to stand for about 3 hours.

Add the water to the tin. Peel the onions but leave whole and place around the lamb. Cook in a moderately hot oven, 365°F (gas 5) for about 1¼ hours, allowing 20 minutes to the lb and 20 over, basting occasionally.

Place the lamb on a serving-dish and arrange the onions around. Stir the olives into the juices in the pan and spoon over the lamb. Garnish with fresh rosemary.
NOTE: If a gravy is liked, add an extra ½ pint of stock to the roasting-tin after removing the lamb and onions. Blend 2 level teaspoons cornflour with a little cold water, add to the pan and bring to the boil stirring, simmer for 2 minutes, add olives, and serve with the joint.
SERVES 6.   M.B. (1)

Lamb with orange sauce

12 oz cooked lamb slices
1 small onion
1 tablespoon oil
2 oranges
1 tablespoon redcurrant jelly
½ pint stock
½ teaspoon mustard powder
½ teaspoon caster sugar
Pinch of cayenne pepper
1 tablespoon cornflour

Chop the onion very finely and fry gently in the oil until soft. Grate the orange rind finely, and cut four slices from one of the oranges. Trim off the pith from the slices and keep them for garnish. Squeeze the juice from the remaining oranges and add to the onion with the orange rind, redcurrant jelly and stock. Bring to the boil, reduce the heat and simmer gently with a lid on for 5 minutes. Blend the mustard, sugar, cayenne pepper and cornflour with 2 tablespoons cold water, and stir into the orange sauce. Season to taste with salt and pepper. Add the lamb slices and bring to the boil. Reduce the heat and simmer gently for 15 minutes. Serve with a garnish of reserved orange slices. This is good with a potato purée.
SERVES 4.   M.N.

MEAT

Stuffed shoulder of lamb

1 boned shoulder of lamb
5 oz cooked rice
2 oz sultanas
Rind of ½ an orange, coarsely chopped
Marjoram
1 clove garlic
Salt and pepper
1 tablespoon flour
2 tablespoons oil
6 tomatoes
4 small oranges
¼ pint stock

To make stuffing, mix rice, sultanas, orange rind, little marjoram, crushed garlic and seasoning together. Spread on inner surface of meat, roll up and tie. Rub surface with flour. Calculate cooking time, allowing 25 minutes for each pound and 20 minutes over. Put lamb in tin with oil, pour on stock, cover with foil and roast at 400°F (gas 6). Baste occasionally, and 25 minutes before end of cooking put in tomatoes and peeled whole oranges.

To serve: remove string, put meat on hot dish with tomatoes and oranges round. Boil remaining liquid in roasting-tin for a few minutes, re-season if necessary and serve as gravy.
SERVES 4-6.   J.E. (1)

Lamb with apple

1½ lb stewing lamb
2 oz dripping or cooking fat
1 large onion, sliced
1-2 sticks celery, chopped
1 tablespoon curry powder
1 teaspoon curry paste
2 tablespoons flour
½ pint stock or water
2 tablespoons sweet chutney
2 large cooking apples

Cut the meat into pieces and trim off surplus fat. Heat the cooking fat and fry the onions and celery gently. Add the meat and fry briskly until nicely coloured. Remove from heat, stir in the curry powder, paste and flour and continue frying gently for 4-5 minutes. Blend in the stock or water and bring to the simmer and add the chutney. Cover and cook gently for 1 hour. Peel and core the apples. Cut into dice and add to the pan. Continue cooking for 30 minutes or until the lamb is tender. Season to taste with salt and lemon juice. Serve with fluffy boiled rice, fried poppadums, and Apple Relish.
APPLE RELISH
3 dessert apples
2 tablespoons caster sugar
2 tablespoons chopped mint
Cider vinegar to moisten

Peel and shred the apples coarsely and mix with sugar and mint. Moisten well with cider vinegar and serve with curry.
SERVES 4.   P.B-P.

Moussaka

2½ lb aubergines
1 medium onion, diced
¼ cup butter
1½ lb minced meat
5 tablespoons white wine
3 peeled and chopped tomatoes
    (or a 16 oz can)
Chopped parsley
3 cups béchamel sauce
Salt and pepper
2 heaped tablespoons toasted
    breadcrumbs
2 egg whites, lightly beaten
Olive oil for frying
Breadcrumbs
2 egg yolks
1 egg
1 lb cheese, grated

Cut the aubergines into slices ½ inch thick, sprinkle with salt and leave on one side for an hour.

Sauté the onion in a little butter until soft and opaque. Add the mince and 4 tablespoons water. Cook over medium heat, stirring with a fork to keep the meat broken up. Add the wine, tomatoes, parsley, salt and pepper and simmer, covered, for about 45 minutes. Remove from the heat to add toasted breadcrumbs and the egg whites and stir well. Rinse and dry the aubergines and fry lightly in olive oil on both sides. Grease an ovenproof dish, about 9 by 13 by 2 inches deep, sprinkle with breadcrumbs and line the bottom with half the aubergines. Spread on the meat mixture and cover with remaining aubergines. Beat the egg yolks with the whole egg and stir into the béchamel sauce. Add most of the cheese, and pour over the aubergines, covering the whole dish. Sprinkle the remaining cheese on top and bake in a moderate oven for about 45 minutes or until the top is golden.
SERVES 6.   D.V.

Alice Springs honey lamb

2¼ lb lean shoulder of lamb
2 oz butter
2 onions
1 clove garlic
½ pint apricot purée
2 tablespoons curry powder
3 tablespoons malt vinegar
10 tablespoons honey
¼ pint dry white wine
Salt and pepper

Cut the meat into small cubes. Melt butter in heavy pan, add chopped onions and garlic, cook until soft. Add apricot purée, salt and pepper to taste, curry powder, vinegar and honey. Simmer for 10 minutes. Add wine, then pour mixture over meat in bowl and leave overnight. Remove meat from sauce and thread on skewers and grill for 15 minutes. Serve with rice, and heated sauce.
SERVES 6.   J.M.

Navarin of lamb
Lamb casserole

2 lb middle neck boned stewing lamb
Seasoned flour
2 oz butter
1 medium onion
1 lb new carrots
Bouquet garni
¾ pint chicken stock
Salt and black pepper
½ lb peas
8-12 small new potatoes

Trim the meat and cut into neat pieces. Dip each piece in seasoned flour, then fry in butter to brown and seal. Transfer the pieces to a casserole dish as they brown, then add the peeled and sliced onion, and the carrots cut in rounds and the herbs.

Add about 1 tablespoon of the seasoned flour to the hot fat remaining in the frying-pan and cook gently to a golden brown. Gradually stir in the hot stock and mix well till boiling. Check the seasoning and strain over the contents in casserole. Cover with lid and place in centre of the oven at 325°F (gas 3) and cook for 1½ hours. About 30 minutes before the end of cooking time, add the shelled peas and new potatoes. Sprinkle with parsley before serving.
SERVES 4-6.   J.T.

Curried croquettes

8 oz minced cooked lamb or chicken
4 oz seasoned cooked long-grained rice
3 tablespoons chopped fresh parsley
1 medium onion, chopped
2 cloves garlic, crushed
3 tablespoons cooking oil
1 tablespoon curry powder
Pinch cayenne
1½ teaspoons ground coriander
Salt and pepper
1½ tablespoons lemon juice
2 tablespoons tomato purée
1 oz flour
½ pint hot water
Fine dry breadcrumbs
2 eggs, beaten
Fat for frying

Combine the lamb or chicken, rice and fresh parsley. Set aside. Sauté onion and garlic in oil until tender. Add the curry powder, cayenne, ground coriander, and salt and pepper to taste. Mix well. Cook, stirring, 1 minute. Stir in the lemon juice and tomato purée. Add the flour and cook, stirring 2 minutes. Slowly add 1½ cups of hot water and cook over low heat, stirring, until it becomes a thick and smooth sauce. Remove from the heat and stir in the lamb-rice mixture. Spread evenly in a flat dish and chill. Shape into croquettes, coat with egg and breadcrumbs. Chill thoroughly, then leave at room temperature 1 hour. Deep fry.
SERVES 6.   L.H. (2)

Tranches de Mouton à la Poitevine is an unusual, highly-flavoured dish, best served with plain vegetables. (Recipe below.)

Tranches de mouton à la poitevine

Mutton or lamb stewed with brandy and garlic

*6 slices (about 1½ inches thick) from a
   leg of mutton or lamb with bone
Butter
4 fl oz brandy
4 fl oz water
12 cloves garlic, peeled
Salt and pepper*

Brown lamb in butter in a heavy, shallow pan, then pour over brandy and add garlic, salt, pepper, then cover tightly with foil, plus the lid. Lower the heat until simmering and leave to cook very slowly for about 2½ hours. Only a little juice should be left. Serve with plain boiled or braised vegetables.
SERVES 6.   B.D.

Pieczen barania

Polish roast lamb

*Boned leg or shoulder of lamb
1 large onion
Chopped parsley
1 egg yolk
1 lb mushrooms
2 oz butter
4 oz margarine
1 tablespoon flour
¼ pint soured cream*

Mince the onion and add to the parsley, egg yolk and seasoning. Stuff the lamb with this and roast 1¾ hours in the margarine. Serve with the mushrooms which should be washed well and then sliced. Simmer in the butter for 10 minutes. Blend flour and cream and add mushrooms. Cook for further 5 minutes.
SERVES 6.   M.D.

Roast lamb and mint sauce salad

*Cooked roast lamb
½ packet aspic jelly
2 tablespoons mint sauce
1 cabbage lettuce
¼ pint mayonnaise*

Cut the lamb into neat slices removing any superfluous fat, and place on a dish and sprinkle with pepper. Melt the aspic and mix the mint sauce with it. When jelly is quite soft and beginning to set, dip each piece of lamb into the jelly so that it is well coated, and put them on a dish in a cold place to set. Wash, dry and break the lettuce in small pieces, and toss in the mayonnaise. Serve in a glass dish with the jellied lamb arranged round in a circle.
SERVES 4.   J.E. (1)

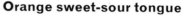

Lamb in wine

1 leg of lamb
¼ pint water
¼ pint red wine
¾ pint stock
1 small onion
Bay leaf, thyme and parsley
Salt and pepper
¼ pint single cream
2 egg yolks

Put the meat in a heavy pan with the water, and cook over high heat until the water has evaporated and the meat coloured. Add the wine, stock, chopped onion, herbs, salt and pepper. Cover very tightly and simmer for 2 hours. The joint may be cooked at 325°F (gas 3) if preferred. Just before serving, put the joint on a serving dish. Strain the liquid and mix with beaten cream and egg yolks. Heat very gently without boiling and pour over the meat.

SERVES 6.   M.N.

Barbecued lamb in mint sauce

8 2-inch-thick lamb chops
8 fl oz vinegar
6 fl oz of cooking oil
4 tablespoons chopped mint
Pinch of sugar
Salt and pepper

Wipe chops. Mix all other ingredients and pour over chops. Cover and leave at room temperature for 2 hours, turning once. Drain chops. Barbecue about 3 inches from fire over medium heat for about fifteen minutes each side.

SERVES 4.   M.N.

Tartelettes Marquis de Caussade
Sweetbread tartlets

PASTRY SHELLS
4 oz self-raising flour
2 whole eggs
1 extra egg white, stiffly beaten
Salt
Milk to mix

Make up the batter in the usual way, adding the egg white just before using.

Heat the tartelette iron in smoking oil (Universal thermometer 375 F). Dip it in the batter, return the iron to the hot fat and fry for about one minute. Remove the tartelette case very carefully and drain on kitchen paper. These will keep in an airtight tin for weeks. When required, just warm them through in a low oven until crisp. Fill cases on the guests' plates, otherwise they go soggy.

A mixture of sweetbreads and kidneys in an Armagnac-flavoured sauce is used to fill small cases of batter or pastry to make Tartelettes Marquis de Caussade (recipe above).

PASTRY SHELLS (alternative)
8 oz plain flour
5 oz butter
1 egg yolk
3 tablespoons ice-cold water
A little salt and pepper

Make up pastry in the usual way; roll out. Line 3-inch diameter loose-bottomed tart tins. Bake blind. Warm through for serving.

FILLING
1 lb calves' sweetbreads
2 calves' kidneys
2 oz button mushrooms
2 oz butter
1 teaspoon flour
6 tablespoons Armagnac
½ pint double cream
1 level teaspoon mild French mustard
Salt and pepper

Prepare the sweetbrads by blanching, refreshing and removing any skin and membranes. Cut into 1-inch pieces.

Skin and slice kidneys in similar pieces. Quarter mushrooms.

Melt the butter in a heavy-bottomed skillet, fry the breads and kidneys quickly (in smallish batches). Sprinkle over the flour (returning all the sweetbreads, etc, to the same pan). Stir well in. Pour over the brandy and flame. Add the cream, mustard and mushrooms. Simmer until just tender. Remove the breads, etc, to a warm serving-dish.

Reduce the sauce by boiling until bright and viscous; season. Pour over the waiting ingredients, and fill the shells.

SERVES 6.   M.S.

Orange sweet-sour tongue

3 lb fresh ox tongue
1 medium onion, sliced
1 carrot, sliced
2 sticks celery, sliced
2 sprigs of parsley
Boiling water
2 teaspoons salt
2 oz butter
1½ oz flour
⅛ teaspoon pepper
1 teaspoon soft brown sugar
¼ pint fresh orange juice
1 orange, segmented
1 tablespoon grated orange peel

Wash the tongue and place in a large saucepan. Add the onion, carrot, celery, parsley and salt. Pour on enough boiling water just to cover the meat. Cover the pan and simmer for 2½ to 3 hours or until tender. Remove the tongue from the liquor, trim off the bone and gristle at the thick end, skin the tongue, slice lengthways and keep warm. Strain off the vegetables and 1 pint of the cooking liquor. Purée the vegetables. Melt the butter in a pan, stir in the flour and cook gently for 1 minute. Stir in the liquor with puréed vegetables. Simmer until thickened. Flavour with the pepper, sugar, orange juice and peel. Stir in the orange segments and heat through. Pour the sauce over the warm tongue.

SERVES 6.   J.E. (1)

Ox tongue in tomato sauce

Cold ox tongue
1 oz butter
1 onion, chopped
1 8 oz tinned tomatoes
Salt and pepper
Pinch of curry powder
1 tablespoon tomato purée
Chopped parsley
8 oz patna rice

Slice ox tongue. Melt butter in a frying-pan and gently cook onion for 5 minutes. Stir in the tomatoes, seasonings, curry powder and tomato purée and simmer for 5 minutes. Sieve or whisk in electric liquidizer, return to pan. Add slices of ox tongue and heat through gently, about 5 minutes. Arrange ox tongue in a dish and pour sauce over. Sprinkle with parsley and serve with plain, boiled rice.
SERVES 4.   J.E. (1)

Tongue in chestnut and raisin sauce

1 oz butter
2 tablespoons flour
10 fl oz stock
2 oz raisins, soaked for 20 minutes in
*   4 tablespoons Madeira*
4 oz chestnuts, cooked and peeled and
*   roughly chopped*
Bouquet garni
Salt and freshly ground black pepper
⅛ teaspoon cayenne pepper
4 thick slices tongue
Parsley

Melt the butter and stir in the flour. Gradually stir in the stock and bring to the boil, still stirring. Add the raisins with the Madeira, the chestnuts and seasonings. Place the tongue in an oven-proof casserole and pour over the sauce. Cover with a lid or foil and leave in a pre-heated moderate oven 350°F (gas 4) for 20-30 minutes until heated through. Garnish with the parsley.
SERVES 4.   H.W.

Kidney risotto

¼ lb American rice
1-2 oz butter
1 small onion, finely chopped
¼ lb button mushrooms, thinly sliced
4 oz frozen peas, cooked
4-oz can red peppers, drained and
*   chopped*
½ lb lambs' kidneys
SAUCE
½ oz plain flour
¼ pint stock or water
¼ pint white wine
3 tablespoons single cream
Seasoning to taste

Cook the rice in boiling, salted water according to the instructions on the pack.

Rice combines well with many meat and fish recipes : **1** *Kebabs (these can be made with a variety of meats and vegetables—an Austrian recipe is on page 79)* **2** *Tuna-rice ring (page 67)* **3** *Kidney Risotto (recipe on this page)* **4** *Savoury Orange Cups (page 47).*

Lightly sauté the onions and mushrooms in the butter in a frying-pan until tender, and the onions become translucent. Transfer to a serving-dish, add the peas and peppers, cover and keep hot. Remove the skin from the kidneys, wash in lightly salted water, then cut in half and remove the cores. Fry in the butter remaining in the frying-pan, adding more butter if required, for 5 minutes or until tender. Add to the vegetables and keep hot while the sauce is being made.

Stir the flour into the pan in which the kidneys have been cooked and cook over a gentle heat to form a roux. Add the stock or water and the wine, then cook for a further 2-3 minutes, stirring constantly. Stir in the cream and seasoning to taste.

Toss together the cooked rice and the hot vegetables and kidneys. Place in one large dish or four individual ones, and spoon the sauce over. Serve hot.
SERVES 4.   L.B./J.A.

Kidneys à la Dubois

8-10 lambs' kidneys
¼ pint stock
1 teaspoon flour
Chopped parsley
2 tomatoes
1 medium onion
2 oz butter
¼ lb button mushrooms
Salt and pepper
Lemon juice

Fry onion in melted butter. Add kidneys,

chopped or finely sliced, plus salt and pepper and fry gently for about 10 minutes. Remove from heat and blend in flour, stock, more seasoning to taste, skinned and chopped tomatoes and chopped mushrooms. Boil gently for about 6 minutes. Add lemon juice and parsley. Reheat and serve. Serve with noodles and a green salad.
SERVES 3-4.   C.W.

Liver with sultana sauce

1 lb best calves liver
3 oz butter
1 oz plain flour
½ pint cold water
2 oz sultanas
⅛ pint dry white wine
Salt and pepper

Wash liver, and season with salt and pepper. Fry gently with half the butter until tender. Meanwhile, melt rest of butter in saucepan and stir in sifted flour. Leave to cook very gently, undisturbed, until flour turns rich golden colour. Then add water, sultanas and white wine. Bring slowly to boil stirring all the while, then simmer for ten minutes or so until sultanas are plumped up and soft. Serve fried liver with this sauce poured over.
SERVES 3-4.   J.M.

Oxtail stew

2 medium onions
1 oz beef dripping
1 stick celery
4 oz peeled carrots
Rind of ½ lemon
Rind of ½ an orange, coarsely chopped
1 oxtail (approx 2-2½ lb)
1 tablespoon lemon juice
1 tablespoon tomato purée
¼ pint red wine
3 oz beef stock
Bouquet garni

Slice the onions and fry in the dripping until golden brown, then drain off and put into an oven dish. Chop the celery and carrots and add to the casserole along with the peel of the orange and lemon.

Trim the oxtail of excess fat, wash and dry, then brown in the fat remaining in the pan. Drain and arrange on top of the vegetables in the casserole. Stir together the lemon juice, tomato purée, wine, stock and bouquet, then pour over the oxtail. Cover and cook in the centre of the oven at 325°F (gas 3) for about 3½ hours. The meat should be tender and falling away from the bones.

Cool the stew, chill thoroughly overnight, then lift off the hardened fat from the surface and reheat the casserole for 30-40 minutes at 350°F (gas 4).
SERVES 3-4.   L.B./P.G.

POULTRY AND GAME

Chicken pimento

This dish is excellent for a cold buffet and may be served with potatoes vinaigrette and a tossed green salad.

3-3½ lb chicken
1 onion
1 carrot
Bay leaf
Salt and pepper
SAUCE
½ pint mayonnaise (made with 2 egg yolks, ½ pint groundnut oil, salt, pepper, mustard and vinegar to taste)
8 oz tinned pimentos
1 tablespoon tomato purée
1 teaspoon sugar
Salt and pepper
1 large clove garlic
GARNISH
4 oz thinly-sliced pimento
Finely chopped parsley
Tomatoes
Watercress

Put the chicken into a large pan with the sliced onion, carrot and bayleaf and enough water to cover. Season well, bring to the boil, cover and simmer until tender. Leave to cool in the liquid and then take out the chicken and remove the meat from the bone, discarding the skin. Shred the meat and arrange on a serving dish. In the meantime, make the mayonnaise. To make the purée, cook the sliced pimentos with a little of the liquid from the tin, adding the tomato purée, sugar, salt and pepper, and simmer for five minutes. When cooked, liquidize or sieve and leave to cool. When cold add the crushed garlic and stir the sauce into the mayonnaise, a little at a time, according to taste. This should be of a coating consistency. If too thick add a little hot water. Coat the chicken and garnish with the pimento and parsley. Decorate the dish with a bunch of watercress and a few sliced tomatoes.
SERVES 4-6. V.J.

Pollo Sevilla

3½ lb chicken
2 tablespoons olive oil
2 onions
1 clove garlic
½ lb tomatoes
1 canned red pepper
¼ lb mushrooms
4 tablespoons sherry
8 stuffed green olives

Heat the oven to 375°F (gas 5). Wash and dry the chicken. Heat the oil in a large frying-pan and fry the chicken

A simple roast chicken, well-flavoured with herbs, seasoning and butter, is light and delicious, but a free-range bird is essential for this. Frozen chicken has little flavour.

until brown all over. Remove and place in a casserole.

Peel and chop the onion, crush the garlic. Peel the tomatoes, cut in quarters and remove the seeds, slice the red pepper, add to the pan and cook for about 5 minutes, or until onion is soft but not brown. Pour over the chicken, cover and cook in the oven for 45 minutes.

Slice the mushrooms and add with the sherry and olives to the casserole and cook for a further 15 minutes or until the chicken is tender. Place on a serving-dish and spoon the sauce over.
SERVES 4-6. M.B. (1)

Chicken à la Suisse

3½ lb roasting chicken
4 thin rashers streaky bacon
1 large onion, thinly sliced
2 large carrots, thinly sliced
1 stick celery, thinly sliced
3 fl oz stock made from chicken giblets
Bouquet garni
½ lb noodles
1 oz butter
Freshly ground pepper
½ oz parmesan cheese
CHEESE SAUCE
1 oz butter
1 oz flour
¾ pint milk
2 oz gouda cheese, grated
Salt and pepper
3 tablespoons double cream

Lay bacon at bottom of deep pan. Cover with the onion, carrots and celery and put the chicken on top. Cover and cook over a very gentle heat for 10-15 minutes. Pour stock over the chicken, put in the bouquet garni, cover pan and put in oven 350°F (gas 4) for 1 hour. While this dish is in the oven, cook noodles until just tender, drain them and put them back into pan with ½ pint lukewarm water. Prepare the cheese sauce in the usual way. Add the cheese and cream and keep warm.

Remove chicken from the pan. Reduce the gravy a little and strain. Skim off as much of the fat as you can and add the strained liquid to the sauce. Drain noodles and heat them in butter. Sprinkle

with freshly ground pepper and put them into a hot ovenproof serving dish. Carve chicken and arrange the joints on top of the noodles. Pour the sauce all over. Dust with the grated parmesan cheese and brown under the grill.
SERVES 6. M.L.

Roast chicken with pineapple

1 roasting chicken, 3-4 lb
2 oz butter
1 tin pineapple slices
Salt and pepper
STUFFING
2 oz butter
4 oz chopped pineapple
1 level teaspoon salt
2 oz dry white breadcrumbs
2 oz chopped walnuts
Grated rind ½ lemon

Sprinkle inside the bird with salt and pre-heat the oven to 375°F (gas 5). Make the stuffing. Melt the 2 oz of butter in a pan and add the breadcrumbs, stir and cook for a minute or two. Then stir in the salt, lemon rind, walnuts and 4 oz chopped pineapple from the tin. Mix well, if it seems rather dry, add a little of the pineapple juice. Pack the stuffing into the body of the chicken. Put the giblets, except the liver, into a baking-tin with the chicken. Spread the soft butter all over the bird and cover with buttered paper. If cooked in a covered roaster, the paper will not be needed. Calculate roasting time from the oven-ready weight, allowing 20 minutes to the lb and 20 over. Put in the oven and 20 minutes before cooking time is up, add the liver and baste the chicken. Leave the lid off and finish cooking. When done, dish the bird and add ½ pint of boiling water to the tin, stir and boil for 5 minutes and strain into a gravy boat. To garnish, surround the chicken with heated pineapple slices, each topped with a walnut half, and decorate with watercress.
SERVES 4. W.G.

Spring chicken in mushroom sauce

1 spring chicken, jointed
½ lb skinned and sliced tomatoes
2 oz sliced mushrooms
¼ pint chicken stock, made from simmered giblets
2 oz butter
4 oz macaroni
Watercress

Put macaroni to cook in boiling water. Heat butter, cook chicken in frying-pan until brown. Put tomatoes and stock into pan with the chicken, add the mushrooms, season and cook until the vegetables and chicken are tender. Serve with border of macaroni, and garnish with watercress.
SERVES 3-4. J.E. (1)

Chicken stuffed with grapes

3½ lb roasting chicken
4 hard-boiled eggs
6 oz green grapes
1 spring onion
1 bunch parsley
2-3 tablespoons softened chicken fat or margarine
Salt and pepper
¼ teaspoon each ground cinnamon and ginger
¼ pint chicken stock
Chicken fat or margarine for basting
Watercress sprigs

Prepare the chicken for stuffing and roasting. Separate the egg whites and yolks. Keep a few perfect grapes for garnishing; halve and pip the rest. Slice the spring onion, both green and white. Put 3-4 small parsley sprigs aside, and chop the rest finely.

Mash the egg yolks thoroughly with the chopped parsley, fat and seasonings. Mix to a fairly smooth paste, then mix in the halved grapes. Stuff the chicken with the mixture, then truss it for roasting.

Put the stock in the bottom of a roasting-tin, and put in the chicken. Roast the bird in your usual way, basting it with a little fat from time to time. When the bird is cooked, keep it hot on a warmed serving-dish while making a thin, pan-juice gravy with the stock and any pan drippings. Garnish the bird with the reserved parsley sprigs and grapes and the watercress sprigs just before serving.

SERVES 4-5. M.B. (2)

Cold lemon chicken with pineapple and walnuts

4 lb cooked chicken
1 small fresh pineapple
Juice of 1 large lemon
½ pint thick home-made mayonnaise
Salt and pepper
1 oz chopped walnuts
Parsley to garnish

Carefully remove the meat from the chicken. Cut the dark meat into neat bite-sized pieces and slice the white meat.

Cut the pineapple across in slices and remove the skin and centre core. Cut two slices in half and reserve for garnish. Chop remaining pineapple.

Stir the lemon juice into the mayonnaise and season to taste. Place 3 to 4 tablespoons of mayonnaise in a bowl, add the dark meat and mix well, place it on a serving dish. Spread the chopped pineapple on top. Carefully arrange the slices of white meat on the pineapple and coat with the remaining mayonnaise.

Sprinkle over the walnuts and garnish with the halved pineapple slices and sprigs of parsley.

SERVES 6-8. M.B. (1)

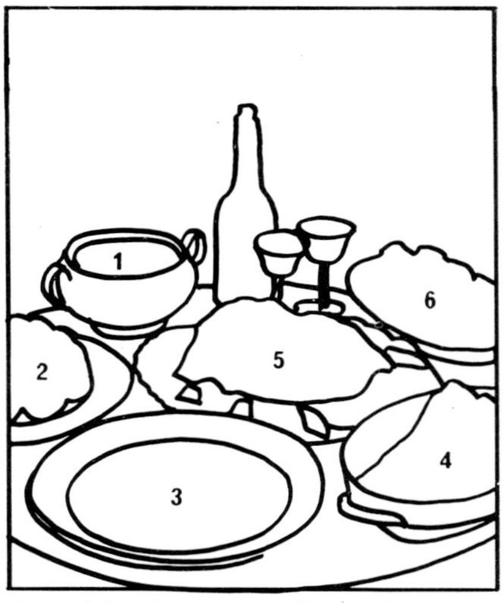

A meal for the great outdoors, with duck pâté en croûte as the centrepiece:
1 *Jellied Consommé Rosé (page 25)*
2 *Smoked Salmon Lemons (page 35)*
3 *Caribbean Cream (page 125)*
4 *Asparagus hollandaise (page 47)*
5 *Pâte de Canard en Croûte (page 103)*
6 *Summer fruit bowl (page 131)*

Poulet sauté vallée d'auge

Chicken with apple sauce

It is difficult to translate the name of this marvellous dish from Normandy without making it sound too pedestrian.

3¼ lb chicken, cut into portions
3 oz butter
2 tablespoons cooking oil
4 tablespoons calvados
1 oz chopped shallots
1 oz chopped celery
Large sprig of fresh thyme
3 fl oz chicken stock
3 fl oz dry cider
6 oz cooking apples, peeled and chopped
¼ pint double cream
Salt and pepper

Skin the chicken and brown in the butter and oil in a large frying-pan. Heat the calvados in a ladle or large spoon, set it alight and pour over the chicken. Keep the pan on the heat until the flames have died out then transfer the chicken to a casserole.

Lightly sauté the onions, celery and thyme in the fat remaining in the pan, then lift out with a drain-spoon and sprinkle over the chicken. Pour off the fat from the pan, and use the pan to simmer the stock, cider and apples until the apples are tender. Stir in the cream and adjust the seasoning to taste. Pour the sauce over the chicken, cover the casserole and cook in the oven at 325°F (gas 3) for 20-30 minutes until the chicken is tender. If you prefer a completely smooth sauce, sieve before adding to the chicken. Sprinkle with chopped parsley.

SERVES 4-6. L.B./D.G.

Coq au vin

Chicken in red wine

1 roasting chicken (4 lb weight)
2 oz butter
1 tablespoon vegetable oil
10 shallots
3 rashers streaky bacon
½ pint full-bodied red wine
¾ pint chicken stock
Freshly ground black pepper
Bouquet garni
2 cloves garlic, crushed
6 oz small button mushrooms
Salt if necessary
Beurre manié: made by creaming 1¼ oz butter with 1 oz plain flour
Garnish: croutons of fried bread, chopped parsley

Divide the chicken into 4 or 6 serving pieces, as required. Place the butter and oil in a large heavy saucepan, heat gently until hot and combined but not browning. Fry the chicken pieces until golden all over. Remove the pan from the heat, drain the chicken on absorbent kitchen paper. Peel the shallots carefully. Remove the rind from the bacon and cut into ½-inch pieces. Fry the shallots and bacon in the oil and butter, stirring frequently until golden. Return the chicken to the pan, add the wine, stock, pepper, bouquet garni, garlic and button mushrooms. Bring to the boil, cover the pan and simmer gently for about 35 minutes or until the chicken is tender when tested with a skewer.

Remove the chicken from the cooking liquor and arrange it in a heated serving-dish. Discard the bouquet garni. Taste and adjust the seasoning. Add the *beurre manié* to the cooking liquor, gradually, in small pieces. Allow the liquid to simmer gently and stir constantly. Add enough *buerre manié* to thicken the liquid slightly, simmer 2-3 minutes. Pour the sauce over chicken and garnish if desired.

SERVES 4-6. A.B.

Barbecued chicken in basting sauce

3 lb chicken pieces
¼ pint wine vinegar
¼ pint lemon juice
¼ pint salad oil
½ teaspoon soy sauce
Salt and pepper

Wash and wipe chicken pieces. Shake together all other ingredients in a jar. Brush chicken pieces with sauce and arrange close to hot fire, searing both sides for 3 minutes each. Move chicken pieces about 3 inches from the fire and continue cooking over medium heat, brushing chicken with more sauce and turning frequently for 25 minutes or until done.

SERVES 6. M.N.

Chicken with avocado

2 oz plain flour
Salt and pepper
1 teaspoon dried marjoram
6 chicken joints
3 oz butter
1 large onion
½ pint white wine
¼ pint chicken stock
¼ pint double cream
2 ripe avocado pears
1 tablespoon lemon juice

Place 1 oz flour on a plate, add salt and pepper to taste and the marjoram. Coat the chicken joints in the seasoned flour, pressing it on with a palette knife. Heat 2 oz butter in a flameproof casserole, add the chicken pieces and fry until browned all over. Heat the remaining butter in a saucepan, add the sliced onion and fry gently for 5 minutes. Stir in the remaining flour and cook for 3 minutes. Take off the heat and blend in the wine and stock. Beat until smooth and return to

the heat. Stir until thickened and cook for 3 minutes. Pour the sauce over the chicken in the casserole, cover and bake at 375°F (gas 5) for 1 hour. Remove from the oven and leave until the liquid is no longer boiling. Stir in the cream. Peel the avocado pears, slice them, sprinkle with lemon juice and put on top of the chicken. Brush with a little oil, cover and return to the oven for a further 10 minutes.
SERVES 6.   M.N.

POULTRY AND GAME

Lang syne stew

Chestnuts and chicken make an excellent
and hearty meal-in-a-bowl for a buffet.
2½-3 lb chicken
Vegetables and herbs for making stock
3 lb fresh chestnuts in the shells
¼ pint single cream
¼ pint white wine
Grated rind and juice of 1 lemon
Salt and pepper

Cook the chicken with vegetables and
herbs to make a well-flavoured stock.
Strain off the stock (2½-3 pints) and cut
the chicken flesh into bite-sized pieces.
Peel the chestnuts and cook until just
tender in the stock. Drain off about half
the nuts and pulverize them. Heat
together the chicken, chestnuts, chestnut
purée and stock. Add cream, wine,
lemon and seasoning to taste. Serve hot.
SERVES 12.   L.B./D.L. (1)

Lemon chicken

4 oz cream cheese
3 lemons
Salt and pepper
3½ lb chicken
2 oz butter
1 carrot
Sprig of thyme
1 bay leaf
¼ oz plain flour
¼ pint stock

Grate the rind from one lemon and mix
with the cream cheese. Season well with
pepper and salt and put inside the
chicken. Brown the chicken in the butter
and put into a casserole. Sprinkle with
salt and pepper and add sliced carrot,
thyme and bay leaf. Cover and cook at
350°F (gas 4) for 45 minutes, basting
with the juice of the lemon. Cut a second
lemon into thin slices and put under the
chicken, and continue cooking without
a lid for 30 minutes, basting occasionally
with pan juices. Put the chicken on a
serving dish and keep warm. Strain the
pan juices into a small pan and remove
surplus fat. Mix the flour and stock and
add to the pan juices. Bring to the boil,
and stir and simmer for a few minutes
until well blended. Garnish the chicken
with the third lemon cut in wedges; the
sauce should be served separately.
SERVES 4-6.   M.N.

Tarragon chicken with cherries and walnuts

1 large roasting chicken
Good handful fresh tarragon
½ lb fresh cherries, preferably red
4 oz halved walnuts
Vinaigrette dressing

Pot-roast the chicken with plenty of
tarragon, butter, salt, pepper and enough
water or stock to make sure that about
¼-½ pint of rich juices are left in the pot
at the end of the cooking time. Take the

lid off the pot before the chicken is
cooked so that its skin is crispy and
brown. Leave the chicken to get quite
cold, then joint it neatly and put it in a
dish. Strain the cooking juices into a
bowl and leave to cool. When it has
jellied, skim off the fat, melt it down to a
liquid again and mix it with about ¼ pint
of vinaigrette dressing. Pour this sauce
over the chicken and decorate all over
with the stoned cherries, walnuts and
tarragon leaves. Put the walnuts on at
the last minute, otherwise they will
blacken.
SERVES 6.   V.D./V.W.

Universal chicken

4 lb chicken, cut in serving pieces
1 pint tomato purée
½ pint port
1 tablespoon brandy
1 shallot
1 clove garlic
½ green pepper, chopped and de-seeded
¼ teaspoon each of coriander seeds finely
    ground
½ teaspoon basil
2 tablespoons butter
2 tablespoons olive oil
½ lb sliced mushrooms
1 large carrot, sliced
1 tablespoon chopped parsley

Arrange chicken pieces in a large casserole. Put the tomato purée and port,
brandy, shallot, garlic, green pepper and
herbs into a saucepan. Cover and simmer
for 15 minutes, then pour over the
chicken. Cover and refrigerate for about
48 hours.

   Then drain the chicken, saving the
marinade and pat the pieces dry with
soft paper. Melt the butter and heat the
oil in a large frying-pan, add the garlic
and the chicken pieces and brown delicately. Put the chicken back in the

casserole with the marinade, mush-
rooms, carrot and parsley, and cover.
Bake at 300°F (gas 2) for 1½ hours.
Serve hot with boiled long-grain rice.

   To serve cold, remove all fat from
the surface. Cut the chicken into small
pieces, discarding all skin and bone and
arrange in a mould. Cook the marinade
for 5 minutes, then pour over the chicken
and chill until set. If a very firm set is
required, add 1 tablespoon of gelatine to
the hot marinade: it will dissolve if it is
sprinkled on the surface.
SERVES 6.   W.G.

Southern chicken

2 tablespoons oil
2 oz butter
4 poussins
2 onions, chopped
2 sticks celery, cut into ½-inch pieces
1 small red pepper, seeded and chopped
4 oz sliced button mushrooms
16 oz can pineapple pieces
½ pint chicken stock
4 tablespoons Madeira
3 teaspoons curry paste
12 halved stuffed green olives
Salt and pepper
2 teaspoons cornflour
2 tablespoons cold water

Heat the oil and butter in a frying-pan,
and brown the poussins. Put them into
a 4-pint casserole. Fry the onion, celery,
pepper and mushrooms in the remaining
fat until soft. Add to the poussins,
together with the pineapple pieces and
Madeira. Stir in the curry paste and
olives, season, and cover with a lid. Cook
at 350°F (gas 4) for 50 minutes. Blend
the cornflour with the water until
smooth, add a little of the boiling juice
from the casserole, and mix well. Return
to the casserole and cook for 5 minutes.
Check seasoning before serving.
SERVES 4.   M.N.

Hereford chicken casserole

¾ *pint dry cider*
3½ *lb chicken*
1 *oz butter*
2 *tablespoons oil*
2 *medium onions*
2 *level teaspoons curry powder*
1 *tablespoon flour*
Large can pineapple slices
2 *tablespoons cream or top-of-the-milk*

Cut the chicken into joints or get your supplier to do so. Melt the butter and oil together and fry the joints until lightly browned. Transfer to a casserole and fry the sliced onions until soft. Stir in the curry powder and flour, and then add the cider, a little at a time, to make a sauce. Pour over the chicken, cover with the lid and cook at 375°F (gas 5) for about 1 hour. Add one drained pineapple slice for each person and return to the oven for a further 10 minutes. Arrange the chicken and pineapple on a heated serving-dish, rub the sauce through a sieve and reheat. Stir in the cream, pour over the chicken and serve hot. (If liked, serve in a ring of cooked rice. Note: this dish can be cooked for a longer time in a cooler oven if more convenient.)
SERVES 6.   P.M. (1)

Chicken delmonico

2 *oz finely chopped mushrooms*
1 *tablespoon butter*
2 *level teaspoons cornflour*
¼ *pint thin cream*
3 *oz grated Swiss cheese*
¼ *teaspoon salt and a dash of pepper*
   (cayenne)
1½ *teaspoons chopped parsley*
1½ *teaspoons chopped pimento*
3 *large chicken breasts, boned*
Flour, egg and breadcrumbs for coating
3 *tablespoons butter, melted*

Sauté mushrooms in a tablespoon of butter and blend in cornflour and cream; cook and stir until smooth and thickened. Add the cheese, salt and pepper and cook just enough to melt the cheese over very low heat, then mix in the parsley and pimento and chill the sauce. Flatten the chicken breasts with a small mallet or the back of a wooden spoon. Spread the sauce on each fillet and roll up to enclose the sauce completely. Chill. Then dust the breasts with flour, dip in egg and then in breadcrumbs. Melt the 3 tablespoons of butter and sauté the breasts for 10-12 minutes. Put in a casserole and bake at 350°F (gas 4) for 20 minutes.
SERVES 3.   W.G.

Savoury brioche

A rich butter yeast dough, baked in a traditional fluted tin and filled, when cool, with creamed chicken-liver pâté. The method is slightly unusual but easy to follow, and the results are excellent.

SPONGE BALL
6 *tablespoons water, lukewarm*
1 *level tablespoon dried yeast*
4 *oz strong plain flour*
Pinch of salt
PASTRY
12 *oz strong plain flour*
4 *eggs, lightly beaten*
6 *oz softened butter*
FILLING
½ *lb chicken-liver pâté*
3-4 *tablespoons cream*

TO MAKE THE SPONGE BALL: Sprinkle the yeast onto the surface of the water and leave for about 10 minutes until dissolved and frothy on the top. Stir this mixture into the flour and salt to form a smooth ball of dough. Half fill a 2-pint basin with lukewarm water. Cut a cross in the top of the dough and drop it cross side down into the bowl of water. Set over a pan of warm water for 15-20 minutes, by which time it will have become very puffy and sloppy.
TO MAKE THE PASTRY: Put the flour into a large mixing bowl, make a well in the centre and stir in the eggs to form a sticky paste. Turn out onto a table or board, flatten, and work in the butter by turning the paste up around it and kneading it with the hand. Eventually the mixture will form a pastry. Drain the yeast ball, place onto the pastry and again work the pastry up around the yeast ball. Continue working for 5-10 minutes to form a smooth, slack mixture which is slightly sticky. Return to the bowl, place inside a large plastic bag and leave to rise for about 3½ hours. At this stage, the dough is fluffy and well risen although a little sticky. Knead for a few minutes and it will become very smooth.

Replace dough in bowl and put into the bag, but leave in the refrigerator overnight, by which time the dough will be quite firm. Work it down and divide into two pieces—in proportions of ¾ and ¼. Shape each piece into a smooth ball. Cut a cross into the top of the larger, and pull out an extension of the smaller to make a pear shape. Place the large piece in a greased large brioche mould and set the small piece on top with the prong of dough wedged into the cross. Put into a large plastic bag and leave to rise in a warm place but away from direct heat—about 2 hours—until the dough rises to about double in bulk.

Brush with beaten egg and bake at 375°F (gas 5) for approximately 1 hour or until the brioche has risen well, browned all over, and looks baked around the join. Cool on a wire rack. To fill, lift off the top ball and scoop out some of the centre from each ball. Whip up the pâté with cream to make a soft consistency, then pile into the cavity. Set the top back in place.
SERVES 6.   L.B./J.E. (2)

Chicken provençe

¾ *lb finely chopped cooked chicken*
6 *oz quick-cooking macaroni*
Small tin anchovy fillets
Small bottle black olives
2 *tablespoons tomato purée*
2 *tablespoons olive oil*
Salt and cayenne pepper

Stone the olives and cut them up, then chop the anchovies. Mix the oil and chopped chicken and cook in a pan over low heat until delicately browned, then add the olives and anchovies. Stir and add the tomato purée and season with salt and pepper. (Be sparing with the salt.) Heat all together. Cook the macaroni according to the directions on the packet, then strain and put on a hot plate. Pile the chicken mixture on top and serve at once.
SERVES 3.   W.G.

Giblet pie

Shortcrust pastry, made with 12 oz flour
1 lb poultry giblets
Salt and pepper
8 oz stewing steak
1 large onion
2 cloves
2 hard-boiled eggs

Put the giblets into a pan, cover with cold water and let them come to the boil. Skim well, add salt and pepper and simmer for 2 hours. Cut the giblets into small pieces and put them into a pie dish, sprinkling lightly with a little flour. Add steak cut in very small pieces, sliced onion, cloves and quartered eggs. Cover with giblet stock and with pastry. Bake at 375°F (gas 5) for 45 minutes.

SERVES 4. M.N.

Canard 'la bonne vie' en croûte

Duck in pastry

1 duck
1 chicken
1 woodpigeon
1 grouse
½ lb sliced ham
Puff pastry

STUFFING
½ lb veal
¼ lb chicken liver
1 lemon
2 eggs
½ loaf rye bread, crumbed
¼ lb walnuts
1 onion
1 carrot
¼ pint Madeira
¼ lb stewed prunes
Salt and pepper
Thyme
Parsley

Start with the stuffing. Chop veal and liver, turn in butter gently until firm; add vegetables, seasoning and juice of lemon and gratings from peel. Cook until tender. Add all rest of ingredients, put in liquidiser. Blend until smooth. Return to pan, cook for 10 minutes, then allow to cool.

Bone whole duck, chicken, woodpigeon and grouse, leaving duck leg bones intact only. This is a lengthy and difficult task, so be sure to allow enough time.

Mould stuffing into a ball and wrap the grouse over it. Then cover with a layer of ham, then the woodpigeon, a layer of ham, then the chicken, a layer of ham. Then comes the difficult bit—easing all this into the duck. Once achieved, use string and a large darning needle to sew down each end of duck and string legs into position. In other words, try to mould the bird into its normal shape.

Place bird in a large pot, cover with water and half a bottle of wine, seasoning to taste. Simmer slowly in the oven for three hours. (Use judgement on size of duck). Take out and cool. Cool stock in fridge until jellified. Scrape off excess fat.

Roll out pastry, wrap carefully around the duck and seal, then glaze with egg. Cook in the oven for about 25-35 minutes until the pastry is brown and golden.

The *canard* can be served hot or cold.

SERVES 12. J.C. (1)

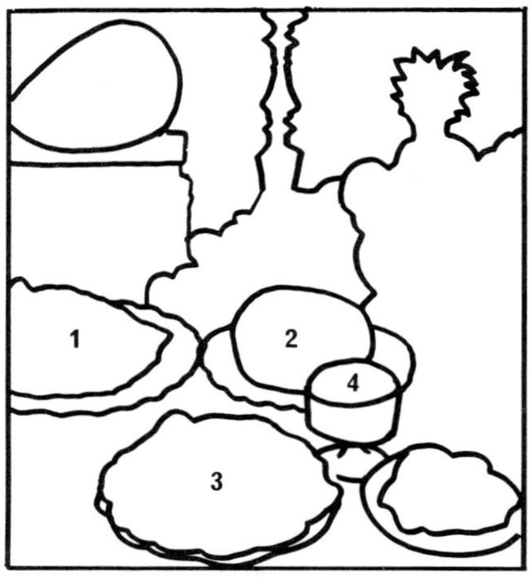

All these dishes are adaptations of seventeenth-century recipes : **1** *Chicken stuffed with grapes (page 98)* **2** *Collared roll of lamb (page 88)* **3** *Butter'd crab (page 33)* **4** *Chocolate Cream (This particular dish was made with seventeenth-century-style chocolate, but a less complicated version of chocolate mousse is on page 124).*

Pâté de canard en croûte

Duck pâté in pastry

A rich forcemeat baked in a boned duck, then covered with a crisp butter pastry. (The duck may be boned, stuffed and cooked at one session, then cooled and frozen ready to be wrapped in pastry when required.)

1 duckling, 4-4½ lb
2 tablespoons brandy
2 tablespoons port
Generous pinch of salt
Pepper

FORCEMEAT
¾ lb lean veal
¾ lb lean pork
½ lb pork fat
1 small onion, finely chopped
1 tablespoon butter
¼ pint port
2 eggs
Salt and pepper
Pinch of thyme

To make the forcemeat, mince the meats together. Sauté the onion in the butter and add to the meats. Mix thoroughly with remaining ingredients.

Next, bone the duck. For this, be sure to use a sharp flexible knife; always cut towards the bone to avoid piercing the flesh and skin. Cut off the wings at the second joint and cut off the legs at the first joint. Lay the bird on its breast and snip the skin and flesh along the underside, cutting from neck to tail. Cut the flesh away from the rib cage with one hand, and pull the skin and attached flesh away with the other. Continue around the ribs on either side of the bird to meet at the breast bone. Lift the loosened carcass and very carefully free by trimming closely along the bone, taking care not to cut the skin.

Cut through the sinews at the wing joints and scrape the flesh along the wing bone, turning the wing inside out as you work. Cut through the leg joint and sinews, then scrape away the flesh in a similar way. When the bones have all been removed, turn the wings and legs right side out and lay the casing, flesh side up, on a board. Sprinkle with the port, brandy, and the seasonings. Roll up and refrigerate for half an hour.

To stuff, open out the boned duck, skin side down, and heap the stuffing in the centre to form a loaf shape. Bring the duck skin up over the loaf to enclose it completely, folding in the end flaps to form a neat parcel shape. Sew the skin in place with a strong large needle and string. Also wrap string around the whole of the bird and tie firmly in three or four places. Place into a cookbag, seal, slash the bag in a few places and cook in the oven at 400°F (gas 6) for about 1½ hours until the skin of the duck is a good golden brown and the flesh tender when pierced with a knife tip. Remove duck from bag and cool.

FOR THE PASTRY: Make a rich short pastry with 1¼ lb plain flour and 10 oz butter. Roll to a rectangle approximately 14 by 10 inches, then carefully lay on a baking sheet. Place the duck, breast side up, in the centre of the pastry. Cut diagonal slashes from each corner in towards the duck, then fold up the pastry to completely cover, mitring at the corners. To hold the pastry in position, brush the under sides at the overlapping points with beaten egg. Glaze the whole of the outside of the pastry and decorate with pastry trimmings. Bake at 400°F (gas 6) for approximately 45 minutes or until a golden brown. Serve cold with salad and green vegetables such as asparagus.

SERVES 6-8. L.B./D.M.

Barbecued duckling

2 4-lb duckling, cut in quarters
Cooking oil

If duckling is frozen, thaw completely, and wash and dry thoroughly. Brush with cooking oil. Put on to grill, cut-side down, and cook over medium heat, about 3 inches from fire, turning frequently for 45 minutes. Serve with a salad of thin orange slices and onion rings.

SERVES 6-8. M.N.

Duck in cider

5 lb duck
2 oz sage and onion stuffing
1 pint cider
1 cooking apple, peeled and chopped
Salt and pepper
14 oz can stoned cherries
Watercress

Remove the giblets, wash and dry the duck. Stand on a rack in a meat tin. Make up the stuffing using ¼ pint of the cider. Fry and chop the duck liver and add to the stuffing with a chopped apple. Stuff the duck with this mixture and season the bird with salt and pepper. Allow 25 minutes per lb and cook at 350°F (gas 4), removing from the oven 30 minutes before the end of the cooking time. Discard the rack and drain off the fat. Drain the cherries from the juice and heat them in the remaining cider and pour over the duck. Return to the oven for the last 30 minutes, basting occasionally. Garnish with watercress.
SERVES 4.   S.W. (1)

Salmis of duck

2 large Spanish onions
4-5 lb duck with giblets
1 pint water
Bay leaf, thyme and parsley
1½ oz butter
1 oz flour
4 oz sliced mushrooms
5 fl oz red wine
4 oz diced fried bacon
10 sliced stuffed green olives
Salt and pepper
Juice and rind of 1 orange

Slice one of the onions and chop the other one. Put the duck into a roasting tin, prick well all over with a very fine skewer or hat pin. Cook at 400°F (gas 6) for 1½ hours until the skin is crisp. Meanwhile, put the giblets, chopped onion, water and herbs into a pan, bring to the boil and simmer for 45 minutes. Strain the liquid. Cool the duck slightly and cut it into joints. Skim fat from the juices in the roasting tin. Heat the butter in a frying-pan and fry the sliced onion and mushrooms. Stir in flour and brown for 2 minutes. Gradually add ¾-pint giblet stock, wine, and juices from the roasting tin stirring all the time. Bring to the boil and add the bacon, olives, orange juice and rind. Season, add duck and bring to the boil again. Serve with croûtons and a watercress and lettuce dressed salad.
SERVES 4.   M.N.

Partridge and quince casserole

2 rashers unsmoked bacon
2 plump partridges
1 onion, chopped
4 oz quinces peeled, cored and finely
    sliced
Butter
Salt and pepper
½ pint stock
Caster sugar
Chopped parsley
4 tablespoons cream

Remove the rind from the bacon and put the rashers on the bottom of the casserole, then put the prepared partridges on top. Add the chopped onion and one quince. Dot with about half the butter. Season with salt and pepper and cook at 350°F (gas 4) for ½ hour. Then lift out the birds, split them right through and put back in the casserole and pour the warm stock over them. Put back in the oven, uncovered, and cook at the same temperature for 30-40 minutes until the birds are tender. Meanwhile, peel, slice and core the rest of the quinces and sauté them in a little butter until golden, then dust with caster sugar. Dish the partridges and strain the gravy into a saucepan, reduce it a little, then stir in some chopped parsley and the cream, mix and then pour over the birds. Garnish with the sautéed quince.
SERVES 4.   W.G.

Partridge casserole, piquante

½ lb smoked bacon
2 partridges
6 oz pickling onions
2 oz chopped mushrooms
¼ pint Madeira
¼ pint stock
Salt and pepper
Flour and water paste
Juice ½ lemon

Spread the bacon on the bottom of the casserole, put the prepared partridges on top, add the onions and mushrooms. Mix the Madeira and stock and pour over the birds, season with salt and pepper. Cover and seal with flour and water paste. Cook at 400°F (gas 6) for about 45 minutes. Remove the lid and add the lemon juice. Serve without delay.
SERVES 4.   W.G.

Partridge in vine leaves

1 partridge
A few vine leaves
4 oz butter
Brandy
Salt and pepper

Wipe the vine leaves and sprinkle a little brandy on them, then stuff the bird with them, season with salt and pepper. Put the butter in a baking dish and add the partridge. Cook at 400°F (gas 6) for 25-30 minutes. To add a final touch, serve with sauerkraut cooked in white wine.
SERVES 2.   W.G.

Braised partridge à la catalone

2 partridges with their livers
4 pork chipolata sausages
¼ lb lean veal
2 oz mushrooms
4 rashers streaky bacon
Parsley, thyme, chives
Salt and pepper
4 silver skin onions
2 tablespoons white wine vinegar
½ bottle red wine
Olive oil
Dried peel of half an orange
1 clove garlic
1 tablespoon melted plain chocolate

Chop the sausages and mince the veal and partridge livers, chop the mushrooms and mix all together and season with salt and pepper. Heat the olive oil and fry these ingredients for a few seconds, until they are soft enough to be mashed. Then stuff the birds with it. Line an ovenware dish with the bacon and put the birds on top. Mince the onions and add a little oil to them, then mix with the chopped garlic and chopped herbs. Put into a saucepan with the dried orange peel and cook for 10 minutes, then stir in the melted chocolate, wine, vinegar, and salt and pepper. Put this mixture on top of the birds, cover the dish and cook at 350°F (gas 4) for 1 hour or until the birds are tender. Serve small croûtons of fried bread with this partridge dish.

SERVES 4.   W.G.

Partridge en papillotes

2 partridges
Fresh mixed herbs, chopped
Shredded peel of half an orange
  and ¼ small lemon
Salt and pepper
¼ lb butter
4 rashers fat bacon

Split the birds along the back. Put 3 oz of the butter in a pan and fry the pieces for about 8-10 minutes, season with salt and pepper and lift out of the pan on to a plate. Mix the herbs, orange and lemon peel and spread on the birds and leave to get cool.

Then take two pieces of cooking foil each large enough to cover half a partridge. Spread with butter and put a piece of bacon on each piece of foil with half a bird on each one. Then fold the foil over, bringing the edges together, then make a perfect seal all round. Put into a fireproof dish and into the oven pre-heated to 350°F (gas 4) and cook for 20 minutes. Open the foil after 10 minutes to allow the partridges to colour a little. Serve in the foil.

SERVES 4.   W.G.

Partridges with red cabbage and chestnuts

4 partridges
1 lemon
4 rashers bacon
Salt and pepper
Medium-sized red cabbage
12 shelled chestnuts
½ pint dry cider
2 oz beef dripping

Put a dusting of flour, salt and pepper and a sprinkle of lemon juice inside each bird. Melt the dripping and slowly brown the birds in it. Remove from the heat and leave to stand until they may be handled, then wrap each bird in a rasher of bacon. Discard any tough leaves of the cabbage, wash the vegetable and shred it, then put into a saucepan with the cider and a little salt. Put the partridges on top and cover tightly, then simmer for 1 hour. Toss the peeled chestnuts in hot butter, cut in half and add to the pan. Simmer for a further 10 minutes.

SERVES 8.   W.G.

Pheasant and partridge pie

1½ lb raw game (pheasant, partridge and
  pigeon are a good combination)
2 tablespoons olive oil
1 tablespoon parsley and thyme
12 oz rump steak
4 oz ham
4 oz button mushrooms
1 onion
1 oz butter
Salt and pepper
½ pint stock
¼ pint red wine
1 tablespoon brandy
Flaky pastry, made with 8 oz flour
Beaten egg yolks

Cut the game flesh into pieces and leave in the wine and brandy for 3 hours. Make stock with the bones and trimmings of the game. Cut the steak and ham into strips and put into a deep pie dish. Sprinkle with finely chopped onion and herbs, and a few chopped mushrooms and season with salt and pepper. Drain the game and brown the pieces lightly in oil and butter. Put them into the pie dish and add the remaining mushrooms, some more chopped herbs and seasoning. Mix the wine, brandy, stock and pan juices from the frying-pan and pour over the meat. Cover with pastry and make a hole in the centre. Brush with beaten egg yolk. Bake at 425°F (gas 7) for 10 minutes, then reduce heat to 350°F (gas 4) and cook for 1½ hours.

SERVES 6.   M.N.

Raised game pie

12 oz plain flour
2 level teaspoons salt
6 tablespoons milk
4 oz lard
2 egg yolks
12 oz sausage meat
4 oz raw lean ham
6 oz lean chuck steak
1 pheasant
Salt and pepper
Good ¼ pint jellied stock
Gelatine

Use a 7½-inch raised game pie mould with a hinged side for this; if not available, use a cake tin. Grease the tin and put it on a baking sheet. Sieve the flour and salt and make a well in the centre. Warm the milk and lard until the lard has melted, and pour into the flour with the beaten egg yolks. Work the mixture together to a smooth pliable dough and knead lightly until smooth. Cool slightly and line the mould with three-quarters of the pastry rolled about ¼ inch thick. Press the pastry to the sides of the tin so there are no cracks. Line the inside of the pastry with the sausagemeat. Cut the ham and steak into small pieces. Cut the flesh from the pheasant and cut it in small pieces. Mix with ham and steak

and put into the pie. Add a little of the stock to moisten and cover with the remaining pastry. Make a hole in the centre for the steam to escape. Bake at 425°F (gas 7) for 30 minutes. Reduce heat to 375°F (gas 5) for 30 minutes. Finally reduce to 350°F (gas 4) for 30 minutes. Cover the pastry with grease-proof paper if it seems to be browning too fast. Remove from oven and fill up with the remaining stock, stiffened with a little gelatine if necessary, when the pie has cooled for about 30 minutes. Leave the tin mould on the pie until it is cold, and the jelly has set.

SERVES 6.   M.N.

Pigeon pie

6 pigeons
8 oz chuck steak
Salt and pepper
Mace
Small mushrooms and/or hard-boiled
  eggs
Shortcrust pastry, made with 8 oz flour
Beaten egg

Use only the breasts of the pigeons, and simmer the remains of the birds in a little water to produce a rich gravy. Put the pigeon breasts into a pie dish with the steak cut into small pieces. Add mushrooms and quartered eggs and pour over pigeon stock. Season well with salt, pepper and mace, and cover with a lid. Cook at 350°F (gas 4) for 1 hour. Cover with pastry, brush with beaten egg and bake at 425°F (gas 7) until golden.

SERVES 6.   M.N.

Spiced turkey pie

Flaky pastry, made with 12 oz flour
2 oz butter
1 oz flour
1 tablespoon mild curry powder
½ pint turkey stock
¼ pint milk
12 oz cooked turkey
Pieces of left-over stuffing (optional)
2 tablespoons sweet chutney
1 tablespoon lemon juice
2 tablespoons double cream
Salt and pepper
Beaten egg to glaze

Melt the butter, add flour and curry powder and cook for 2 minutes, stirring all the time. Take from heat and gradually stir in stock and milk. Return to the heat and bring to the boil, stirring all the time, until thickened. Remove pan from the heat, add chopped turkey, stuffing, finely-chopped chutney, lemon juice and cream, and season to taste. Put into 1½-pint pie dish and leave to cool. Cover with pastry and brush with beaten egg. Bake at 425°F (gas 7) for 30 minutes. This is a good way of coping with cold poultry which can be rather dull.

SERVES 4-6.   M.N.

Turkey croquettes

12 oz turkey, finely chopped
1 medium onion, minced
2 tablespoons celery, finely chopped
2 oz mushrooms, chopped
½ green pepper, minced
Pinch sage
Salt and pepper
2 oz butter
1½-2 oz flour
½ pint chicken stock
4 tablespoons single cream
Dry breadcrumbs
2 eggs, beaten
Fat for frying

Mix together turkey, onion, celery, green pepper, sage, salt and pepper. Make velouté sauce with butter, flour and stock and cook for about 10-15 minutes, stirring until thick and smooth. Add cream. Season as necessary. Remove from heat and add turkey mixture. Chill on flattish dish before forming into croquettes. Coat with breadcrumbs, beaten egg and more breadcrumbs. Chill again. Then leave at room temperature for an hour before deep-frying.
SERVES 6-8.   L.H. (2)

Teal with oranges

Allow one bird per person
1 small orange per bird
1 tablespoon butter
Juice of ½ lemon
2 fl oz sherry

Peel the orange. Stuff the bird with the orange. Soften the butter and mix with the lemon juice. Smear the bird with this all over. Roast for 20 minutes in a moderately hot oven, 375°F (gas 5), basting frequently. Stir the sherry into the juices in the baking tin at the last minute.   J.E. (1)

Guinea fowl with olives

2 tablespoons oil
1 oz butter
1 guinea fowl, jointed into 4 portions
2 medium-sized onions, chopped
½ pint chicken stock
¼ pint dry white wine
3 tablespoons tomato purée
Salt and pepper
1 bay leaf
6 oz button mushrooms
10 stuffed green olives
2 teaspoons cornflour
2 tablespoons cold water

If guinea fowl is not obtainable, this recipe can be used for chicken or pheasant. Heat the oil and butter in a frying-pan, and brown the pieces of guinea fowl quickly over brisk heat. Put them into an ovenware casserole. Fry the onion slowly in the fat left in the pan until soft but not coloured, and add to the casserole. Pour over the stock and white wine, add the tomato purée, seasoning and bay leaf. Cover and cook at 350°F (gas 4) for 30 minutes. Remove from the oven and add the mushrooms and olives, and return to cook for 20 minutes. Mix the cornflour with the water and a little hot sauce from the casserole. Stir into the casserole and return to the oven until the sauce boils. Check seasoning and remove bay leaf before serving.
SERVES 4.   M.N.

Goose en croûte

2½ lb chicken
7 lb goose
1 pigeon
1 oz butter
Livers of the birds
1 onion
4 oz button mushrooms
1 lb sausagemeat
4 oz fresh white breadcrumbs
4 level tablespoons cranberry sauce
1 level tablespoon chopped fresh parsley
Salt and pepper
1 egg
Shortcrust pastry, made with 1½ lb flour
Beaten egg to glaze

Start by boning the chicken. Remove the trussing string and giblets, and cut off the wing tips, parson's nose and ankle bones. Put the bird breast downwards, and using a sharp knife, slit the skin down the centre. Work the skin and flesh from the carcass until leg joint is reached. Cut sinew between ball and socket joint joining thigh bone and carcass. Hold end of joint and scrape away flesh, working from inside of leg. Scrape thigh bone clean. Remove leg bone from carcass. Repeat with other leg. Sever wing joint from carcass. Work down the wing bone, scraping flesh from it, and turning wing inside out. Continue until the bone can be removed, and repeat with other wing. Continue cutting flesh away from the carcass until only attached to breast bone. Gently ease flesh away from the bone to remove carcass. Bone the goose and pigeon in the same way. Remove the outer skin from the chicken and pigeon. To make the stuffing, melt the butter and fry finely chopped livers, onions and mushrooms. Add liver, onion and mushrooms to the sausage-meat with the breadcrumbs, cranberry sauce, parsley, seasoning and beaten egg. Mix well. Lay goose out flat, with skin side down. Then spread three-quarters stuffing over flesh of goose. Lay chicken and pigeon pieces on top of stuffing and spread remaining stuffing over the top. Roll up the goose tightly and shape into a roly-poly and tie with string. Put in a large roasting-tin and bake at 375°F (gas 5) for 1½ hours. Take from the oven and leave until cold. Remove the string.

Roll out the pastry to about 22 by 16 inches. Put the goose in the centre of the pastry with join uppermost. Bring pastry up and over goose to enclose it completely. Moisten the edges with water and seal well. Turn the goose over and place on a baking tray with joins underneath. Decorate with pastry leaves cut from trimmings. Brush with beaten egg and bake at 400°F (gas 6) for 10 minutes. Reduce heat to 350°F (gas 4) for 35 minutes. This can be served hot or cold.
SERVES 8-10.   M.N.

Oiseaux en gelée
Quail in claret jelly

4 small birds (such as quail, pigeon or poussin)
1 bottle red wine
¼ pint olive oil
2 cloves garlic, crushed
1 tablespoon dried rosemary (or a sprig of fresh)
2 tablespoons chopped fresh parsley
Juice of 1 lemon
1 envelope powdered gelatine

Put the birds in an ovenproof casserole. Combine all the remaining ingredients, except the gelatine, and pour over birds. Cover the casserole and leave to marinade overnight. Transfer the casserole to the oven and cook at 300°F (gas 2) for 1½ hours, basting occasionally during cooking. Carefully remove the birds and set aside to cool, then strain the liquor through a muslin lined sieve.

To clarify the stock (which makes a brighter clearer jelly) add an egg white

and an egg shell to the stock in a saucepan over a moderate heat, whisking until a thick foam is formed. Allow the foam to rise up the sides of the pan, then draw the pan from the heat just before the foam boils back into the centre. Repeat twice more, then strain. (If liked a little red colouring may be added to the stock.) Sprinkle the gelatine over the surface and heat gently to allow the gelatine to dissolve, then set aside to cool until the mixture begins to thicken. Arrange the birds on a serving dish or plate, spoon a little jelly over the top and put into the refrigerator for a few minutes. Continue adding jelly gradually to coat lightly the birds and cover the plate.
SERVES 4.   L.B./D.L. (1)

Grouse pie

2 grouse
Hot-water crust pastry,
*   made with ½ lb flour*
Game forcemeat
Salt and pepper
Herbs
Hard-boiled egg yolks
Slices of raw ham
Beaten egg

Cut up a brace of grouse, each of them in five parts, and season with pepper and salt. Mask the bottom of a pie dish with a layer of game forcemeat, in which place the pieces of grouse and sprinkle over a little cooked fine herbs. Fill the cavities between the pieces with a few egg yolks and place a few slices of raw ham on top of the grouse. Pour in good gravy, to

half the height, cover the pie with pastry, brush with beaten egg, and put it in a moderate oven, 350°F (gas 4) for 1½ hours.
SERVES 4.   M.N.

Hare pie

Puff pastry, made with 6 oz flour
½ hare (about 2 lb on the bone)
½ lb beef skirt, trimmed
½ lb lamb kidney, trimmed
4 oz streaky bacon
1 small onion
2 oz mushrooms
½ pint marinade : red wine, bay leaves,
*   onion, seasoning*

First, make the pastry in the usual way. Then put the hare on the bone into a large casserole and add the trimmed skirt and kidney, cut into bite-sized pieces. Remove the rind from the bacon and roughly chop the rashers into the casserole. Slice the onions and mushrooms and add.

Put the ingredients for the marinade into a small saucepan, bring to the boil, cool and pour over the meat. Cover the casserole and leave overnight, turning the meats occasionally. Cook in the oven at 375°F (gas 5) for about 2 hours, then cool. Remove and discard the bones from the hare. Transfer hare filling to a 2-pint pie dish. Cover with the pastry, decorate as liked and brush with beaten egg, then bake about 25 minutes at 425°F (gas 7) or until a good golden brown.
SERVES 4-6.   L.B./C.L.

Zajac ze smietana
Hare in cream sauce

1 hare
2 shallots
1 carrot
Thyme, bay leaves, parsley
¾ pint wine vinegar
1½ pints water
Margarine
¼ pint soured cream
1 oz flour
4 small beetroots

Leave the prepared hare to marinate for 2 days in the chopped shallots, chopped carrots, thyme, parsley, bay leaves, vinegar and water. Then roast for 1½ hours in margarine. Ten minutes before completion of cooking time, stir in the flour, blended with the cream and continue to baste frequently. Serve accompanied by hot beetroot, finely chopped.
SERVES 4-6.   M.D.

Rabbit pudding

Meat from 1 small rabbit
Pinch of nutmeg
Pepper and salt
Slivers of lemon peel
2 sliced onions
A good pinch of sage
Chopped mushrooms
Stock
Suet pastry

Line a buttered basin with the crust. Season the meat well, then add the other ingredients. Fill basin, pour on the stock and close the pudding. Steam for 3½ hours.
SERVES 4.   J.E. (1)

Rehrücken Garniert
Cold saddle of venison

2 lb saddle of venison
Salt and pepper
Crushed juniper berries
2 oz lard
4 rashers of fat bacon
German liver pâté
Black grapes to garnish
Prepared aspic

Carefully skin and wash the saddle of venison. Rub the meat with salt, pepper and crushed juniper berries. Heat the lard in a roasting-pan large enough to hold the venison. Cover the venison with the bacon and then place in an oven pre-heated to 450°F (gas 8) and cook for 30-35 minutes.

Carve the meat off the bone while it is still warm in thin, attractive slices and allow to cool. Cover the bone with liver pâté and place the slices of meat decoratively over the bone. Glaze the saddle with aspic and decorate with black grapes.

Serve with glazed fruit or cranberry sauce.
SERVES 4.   W.S.

VEGETABLES

Vegetables provençale

2 oz shallots
8 oz mushrooms
3 oz butter
2 cloves garlic
Fresh thyme, basil, sage and rosemary
2 tablespoons tomato purée
Salt and pepper
2 medium-sized green peppers
2 large tomatoes
1 tin anchovy fillets

Finely chop the shallots and the mushrooms. Crush the garlic and the herbs together. Sauté the shallots with some of the butter until they become translucent, then add the mushrooms and cook gently for about 5 minutes, stirring frequently. Stir in the garlic and herbs, the tomato purée and seasoning.

Wash the peppers, blanch for 2-3 minutes in boiling water, then cut in half lengthways. Remove the seeds, and fill the pepper halves with the stuffing mixture. Put in a well-buttered oven dish, alternating peppers and tomatoes (which should be cut in half, decorated with a twist of anchovy and seasoned with salt and pepper). Dot butter over the surface, cover and bake at 400°F (gas 6) for 25-30 minutes or until tender.

Serve hot with more butter and chopped herbs and anchovy.
SERVES 4.   L.B./G.R.

Gratin Dauphinoise
Dauphin potatoes

1 lb potatoes
1 egg, well beaten
1 pint milk
3 oz grated cheese
2 oz butter
Clove garlic
Pinch of grated nutmeg
Salt and pepper

Rub round an ovenproof dish with the butter and the garlic clove. Slice the potatoes very finely and put in the dish. Mix together the egg with the milk, nutmeg and seasoning and pour over the potatoes. Cover with the grated cheese and small pieces of the butter. Bake 40 minutes in a moderate oven.
SERVES 4.   M.D.

Les pommes à l'ail
Potatoes with garlic

Peel by hand a few cold, boiled new potatoes. Season them, roll in flour, then in beaten egg yolk, then in bread crumbs. (Do not use breadcrumbs which are already oven-cooked; allow bread to harden 'like a brick', then grate.) Deep-fry potatoes. In a pan crush some garlic and cook a little in butter. Either pour the whole lot over the potatoes or strain through muslin, then pour the garlic-flavoured butter over the potatoes.
N.L.

Pickled mushrooms

These are fine additions to salads accompanying cold meats. Button mushrooms are easy to clean and look neat, but their flavour is negligible compared with the flat, open ones.

3½ lb trimmed mushrooms
1 tablespoon salt
2 small thinly sliced onions
1½ pints white wine vinegar
1 tablespoon cayenne pepper

Wash the mushrooms and dry well, cutting the large ones into quarters. Sprinkle with salt and leave for about 30 minutes, then heat gently until they begin to lose their liquid. Add the onions, vinegar and pepper and simmer for 10 minutes. Separate the onions and mushrooms into hot jars. Boil the liquid, fill the jars, release any trapped air bubbles and seal.   R.L.

Cabbage with green pepper

2 tablespoons bacon dripping
2 tablespoons butter
1½ pint measure of finely shredded
  Chinese cabbage
3 tablespoons finely chopped mild onion
1 large green pepper, seeded and chopped
4 oz cooked rice
1 lb tomatoes cooked to a pulp
Salt and pepper
Grilled bacon rashers

Melt the dripping and the butter, stir in the onion and green pepper and cook gently until just soft, then add the cabbage and cook and stir for 4 minutes. Then stir in the rice and tomatoes and cook to heat through. Season with salt and pepper or paprika. Serve with crisply fried rashers of bacon.
SERVES 4.   W.G.

Red bean salad

¾ lb dried red kidney beans
Large handful of parsley
Good olive oil
Wine or tarragon vinegar
1 clove garlic
Salt and freshly-ground pepper
Very finely chopped onion or shallot

Soak the beans for a few hours (not longer than overnight or they will begin to ferment) and put them in a pan with a bouquet of parsley stalks, bay leaf, celery stalk and thyme and enough water to cover them. Simmer until they are soft, adding salt just before they are cooked; drain and cool. Mix plenty of chopped parsley, some chopped onion, the olive oil, vinegar, crushed garlic, salt and pepper in a salad bowl and mix in the warm beans very gently. Leave for at least an hour for the beans to absorb the flavour of the dressing.
SERVES 6-8.   V.D./V.W.

Danish hot potato salad

1 lb firm potatoes, boiled in their jackets,
  peeled and sliced when cool
1 medium onion, finely sliced in rings
2 oz butter
2 tablespoons water
2 tablespoons white vinegar
2 teaspoons sugar
1 tablespoon cream
Salt and pepper

Melt the butter in a saucepan but take care not to brown. Add onion rings and simmer gently, add water and vinegar and season with sugar, salt and pepper when onions are cooked. Add sliced potatoes and stir carefully into sauce. Finish off with a dash of cream. Serve with meat balls.
SERVES 4.   I.M.

VEGETABLES

Chinese cabbage with olives

Chinese cabbage, finely shredded, enough
to fill a 2-pint measure
4 sticks celery, minced
1 small onion, minced
1 green pepper, de-seeded and chopped
1 pimento, chopped
Mayonnaise
4 tablespoons chili sauce
12 stuffed olives, sliced

Mix the first five ingredients, cover and put in the refrigerator. Just before serving, moisten with mayonnaise mixed with the chili sauce and olives.
SERVES 4-6.   W.G.

Salad with water chestnuts

Chinese cabbage thinly sliced to fill a
3-pint measure
½ lb cold boiled rice
10 oz cooked frozen peas, cooled
5 oz-tin water chestnuts, sliced
¼ pint mayonnaise
¼ pint soured cream
¼ teaspoon salt
½ teaspoon celery salt

Chill all the ingredients (apart from the mayonnaise, sour cream and salts) and then mix together with a light hand. Then mix the mayonnaise, sour cream, celery seed and salt and then combine the two mixtures. Cover and chill until wanted.
SERVES 6.   W.G.

Cabbage-leaf rolls

1 cabbage
¼ lb rice, preferably brown
2 oz mushrooms
6 oz onion
1 oz chopped nuts
1 tablespoon tomato purée
Mixed herbs
Vegetable stock

Break off large cabbage leaves, suitable to roll into cylinders of about 2½ inches long by ¾ inch thick. Wash leaves and place in boiling salted water for a minute or so until pliable, drain and rinse in cold water. Cook rice in twice its quantity of salted water, with a lid on, until water has been absorbed. Sauté chopped onions and mushrooms; carrots, peas or any other convenient vegetable can be added. Add purée, nuts and seasonings.

Roll up mixture in cabbage leaves, place in greased baking dish. Cover with vegetable stock. Cook in oven for 45 minutes to 1 hour at 300°F (gas 2). If desired, the stock can be thickened. Alternatively, the rolls can be cooked in tomato sauce as used for Aubergine Parmesan (see page 115) or cooked in the stock, drained and glazed with a cheese sauce.
SERVES 4.   J.V.Z.

Chinese cabbage and potato salad

4 large waxy potatoes
1 pint measure filled with finely shredded
Chinese cabbage
DRESSING
1 tablespoon cornflour
½ pint thin cream
3 tablespoons white wine vinegar
3 teaspoons brown sugar
1 teaspoon mild mustard
Salt and pepper

Boil the potatoes in their jackets, but do not overcook. To make the dressing, slake the cornflour with the cream, then add the rest of the ingredients given for the dressing. Put in a pan over low heat and cook and stir until it thickens.

Skin the potatoes as soon as they may be handled, then cut them in cubes. When the potatoes and dressing are lukewarm, combine them and leave to get quite cold. Half an hour before the salad is to be served, mix the shredded Chinese cabbage in very lightly and chill it. If liked, a light dash of onion salt can be added to this salad.
SERVES 4-6.   W.G.

Danish red cabbage

3 lb red cabbage
2 oz slightly salted butter
2 oz demerara sugar
3 fl oz water
3 fl oz white vinegar
Salt and pepper

Cut cabbage in quarters. Remove outer leaves and core. Shred finely. Melt the butter in a large flameproof casserole. Add the sugar and cabbage and stir. Add water, vinegar and seasoning. Cover and cook slowly for about two hours. If you have it, add a little cheap red wine or beetroot vinegar to give the cabbage a fine red colour. (This keeps well and improves when reheated.)
SERVES 4-6.   I.M.

Stuffed cabbage

1½ lb cabbage
6 tablespoons butter
1 medium onion, minced
1 tablespoon parsley, chopped
3 tablespoons breadcrumbs
2 eggs, lightly beaten
Pinch nutmeg
Salt and pepper

Discard outside leaves of the cabbage, then peel 5 perfect leaves and reserve them. Core the cabbage, slice and chop the rest finely. Put butter in a heavy casserole and melt, add the cabbage and cook, uncovered, stirring often, over a low heat for about 30 minutes, until it is soft and golden. Add minced onion and chopped parsley and simmer together for 10 minutes. Allow the cabbage to cool and add breadcrumbs, lightly-beaten eggs, nutmeg, salt and pepper, and mix well. Put a clean cloth in a bowl, leaving the edges hanging over the side. Now arrange the reserved cabbage leaves in the bowl, overlapping with stems up to form a large cup, closed at the bottom. Spoon the cabbage mixture into this cup and tie the cloth tightly around it. Drop this into boiling salted water to cover generously and cook at lowest possible temperature for 1 hour, turning once. Unwrap and drain it and put in a serving bowl, stem ends down. Pour a little melted butter over it. Quarter the cabbage with a sharp knife to serve.
SERVES 4.   A.V.

Chinese cabbage Chinese fashion

1 large Chinese cabbage
1 clove garlic, crushed
4 tablespoons soy or peanut oil
Salt
1 tablespoon minced ginger root
1 tablespoon cornflour
1 tablespoon sherry
1 teaspoon soy sauce

GARNISH
Julienne strips cooked ham
Shredded blanched almonds or
*   minced spring onion tops or chives*

Slice the solid part of the cabbage and keep the loose leaf ends. Put the solid part in a large frying pan with the oil and garlic. Cook and stir over gentle heat for 3 minutes, then add the loose leaves, salt and ginger root. Cover the pan and steam until tender. Blend the cornflour with 3 tablespoons of water, add the sherry and soy sauce. Stir into the cabbage and continue to do so until it is thickened and well mixed. Do not cook for more than 3-4 minutes after it is blended. It should be crisp and fresh.
SERVES 4-6.   W.G.

Herbed carrots

1 lb carrots
Large onion
1 teaspoon of rosemary
1 teaspoon of parsley
Salt and pepper
Garlic clove, crushed
Knob of butter
1 tablespoon of water
1 tablespoon cream

Cut the carrots into ½-inch-thick sticks. Place in heavy saucepan with chopped onion. Add the rosemary, parsley, salt, pepper and garlic. Add the butter and water, stir and cover. Cook slowly until the carrots are tender and moisture is absorbed. Stir in the cream just before serving.
SERVES 4.   U.S.

French beans with egg sauce

1 lb French beans
2 eggs
1 lemon
Olive oil
1 tablespoon of grated parmesan cheese

Cook the beans in boiling salted water. Drain them, and keep a cupful of the water in which they have been cooked. Keep the beans hot. Whisk the eggs to a froth with the lemon juice, a tablespoon of olive oil, and the cheese. Add a little water from the vegetables and keep this sauce over a gentle heat, whisking all the time, until the mixture has thickened. It will only take two minutes. Pour over the beans and serve at once.
SERVES 4.   J.E. (1)

Peas with lettuce heart

Put 12 oz shelled peas in a pan with a quartered lettuce heart, a dozen very small onions, a good knob of butter, 2 tablespoons of water and a good seasoning of salt and sugar. Bring to the boil, cover closely and cook for about 40 minutes over a low heat till tender. Stir in another knob of butter before serving.
SERVES 4.   J.E. (1)

Carrots stewed with rice

1 lb carrots
2 tablespoons rice, uncooked
Salt
Parsley
Mint

Clean carrots and cut them in half, lengthways. Cover the bottom of a thick pan with oil. When it has warmed, put in the carrots and let them get impregnated with the oil. Add rice and stir it round with the carrots. Cover the carrots and rice with water. Add salt to taste. Simmer for 25 minutes or until the carrots and rice are cooked and most of the liquid has evaporated. Stir in a little chopped parsley and mint. Serve cold with a squeeze of lemon.
SERVES 4.   J.E. (1)

Carrot, apple and almond salad

¾ lb carrots
½ lb eating apples
Juice of half a lemon
3 oz flaked almonds
½ pint thick home-made mayonnaise
1 medium-sized onion

Carefully shred carrots, apples and onion, combine with mayonnaise, mix in lemon juice and add almonds. Chill and cover to store or it will discolour.
SERVES 6.   V.D./V.W.

Carrots and celery in cider

1 pint medium-dry cider
1 lb carrots
½ head of celery
Salt and pepper
Chopped parsley

Bring the cider to boiling point. Prepare the vegetables and cut into 2-inch strips. The outside stalks of the celery should be used. Add the carrots to the cider and boil gently for 15 minutes. Add the celery with the seasonings and cook for a further 30 minutes. Retaining the liquid, drain the vegetables and keep hot. Boil the cider quickly until reduced to about 4 tablespoons. Pour over the vegetables, sprinkle with parsley and serve.
SERVES 4.   P.M. (1)

Vegetable stew

About 2 lb mixed fresh vegetables
*   (potatoes, swede, carrots, onions,*
*   mushrooms, etc.)*
¼ lb tomatoes
1 tablespoon flour
Vegetable stock
Bay leaf
2 cloves garlic
2 dried pimentos

Dice vegetables, sauté in butter for about 20 minutes until tender. (The best way to cook vegetables but an acquired art. It's essential to use a saucepan with a close-fitting lid. Turn the heat to high for 1-2 minutes to allow steam to develop inside, then turn very low and simmer. Try not to remove the lid—shake the pan if you suspect sticking.) Then add the flour mixed with a little vegetable water, the rest of the stock, tomatoes and and seasoning. Simmer for another 15 minutes.
SERVES 4.   V.G.

VEGETABLES

Danish cucumber salad

1 cucumber
3 tablespoons white vinegar
3 tablespoons water
3 tablespoons sugar
Salt and black pepper

Wash and peel cucumber. Slice thinly, place in bowl and sprinkle liberally with salt. Cover with a place, on which is placed a weight, and leave for 15 minutes. Meanwhile, make dressing of vinegar, water, sugar, black pepper to taste. (As English vinegar is stronger than the Danish variety, you can add a teaspoon of olive oil at the last minute). Stir all ingredients well. Squeeze the cucumber to remove all water, preferably using a cheese-cloth. Cover cucumber with dressing and leave for about ½ hour before serving.
SERVES 4-6. I.M.

Stuffed peppers

4 green peppers
8 oz cottage or curd cheese
3 eggs
Seasoning

Cut lid off peppers and remove seeds. Blanch in boiling salted water for a few minutes. Mix beaten eggs, cheese and seasoning. Stuff peppers, replace lids and bake in moderate oven for 20-25 minutes.
SERVES 4. V.G.

Cole-slaw salad

1 medium-sized cabbage, shredded
1 Spanish onion, shredded
2 large carrots, grated
2-4 apples, grated
Raisins or sultanas to taste

Mix all ingredients and add oil and vinegar dressing or mayonnaise thinned with milk.
SERVES 6. V.G.

Mangetout peas with mushrooms

8 oz mangetout
4 oz button mushrooms
4 oz butter
Salt and black pepper

Wash and dry the mangetout peas and mushrooms. Melt the butter in a saucepan or frying-pan and gently fry the peas for 4-5 minutes, turning occasionally, until they are tender when tested with the tip of a sharp knife. Turn into a serving dish and keep hot, then fry the mushrooms until they are soft but still hold their shape—again about 5 minutes. Season with salt and pepper. Stir the mushrooms into the peas and serve hot.
SERVES 4. L.B./S.H.

Greek salad
Salata

3 tomatoes, cut into wedges
1 cucumber, sliced
1 onion, sliced
2 green peppers, cut in rings
6 tablespoons olive oil
2 tablespoons wine vinegar
Salt and pepper
⅓ lb feta or cottage cheese
24 black olives
Chopped parsley, crumbled dried
*   oregano or dried or fresh mint*

Rub a wooden salad-bowl or open dish with garlic and pile in all the vegetables. Shake in a bottle the olive oil, vinegar, salt and pepper. Pour over the salad. Top with cubed feta cheese, or small knobs of cottage cheese, and the olives. Sprinkle with a fine dusting of the parsley, oregano or mint.
SERVES 6. D.V.

Aubergines bressanes

4 aubergines
3 tablespoons olive oil
4 shallots
1 clove garlic
2 oz mushrooms
1 egg
½ pint tomato sauce

Cut the aubergines into halves and remove the pulp. Fry the shallots, garlic and mushrooms, all chopped small, in 2 tablespoons of the oil. In a bowl mix the pulp with the fried vegetables and stir in the well-beaten egg. Lightly fry the aubergine skins, then stuff with the vegetable mixture and place in an ovenproof dish, having covered the bottom with the remaining tablespoonfuls of olive oil. Bake in a moderate oven for ½ hour. Serve with tomato sauce.
SERVES 6-8. M.D.

Glazed carrots

This is an excellent way to enliven carrots at the end of the season, but it is equally good with small new carrots.

1 lb carrots
2 oz butter
2 oz soft brown sugar

Thinly peel the carrots, cut in fingers and parboil in salted water. Drain and glaze straight away, or set aside to finish later if more convenient. Heat the sugar and butter in a shallow pan until just beginning to become thick. Add the carrots and toss with a fork in the syrup only long enough to coat all the fingers of carrot and they begin to turn crisp and brown. Watch the heat as the sugar can over-brown very quickly. Turn into a hot serving-dish and serve immediately.
SERVES 4. L.B.

Rice salad

8 oz brown rice
1 green pepper
1 medium onion
4 tomatoes
1 small tin sweet corn
Raisins and nuts to taste

Cook rice until tender (about 20 minutes). Don't overcook it; it should still be chewy. Drain, then add mixture of diced pepper, tomatoes, sweet corn, raisins and nuts. Add a little French dressing and seasoning.
SERVES 4. V.G.

Normandy potatoes

In many French provinces, potatoes cooked in this manner are often served as a main-course dish during Lent. Leeks have been included to give extra flavour.

1 medium onion, sliced thinly
2 leeks, washed and thinly sliced
4 oz lean streaky bacon cut into
*   thin strips*
3 oz butter
1½ lb potatoes
Salt and pepper
3 fl oz stock

Lightly fry the onion, leeks and bacon in a little of the butter until tender and translucent but not brown. Peel and slice the potatoes very thinly, then arrange layers of potatoes and the fried vegetables and bacon in a buttered oven dish. Season well and pour over the stock. Dot with small knobs of the remaining butter and bake at 400°F (gas 6) for 1½ hours until the potatoes are tender and well browned.
SERVES 4. L.B./P.M. (2)

New potatoes with cream

Drop cooked, boiled potatoes in a little cream and boil very gently for another 10 minutes. Season with salt, pepper, nutmeg and a little lemon juice and scatter with chopped parsley. J.E. (1)

New potatoes with mustard

Boil potatoes until cooked, then brown in a little melted butter, pour over 4 tablespoons of cream into which 2 teaspoons French mustard have been stirred. Cook for 5 minutes longer.
J.E. (1)

New potatoes, with lots of butter and chopped parsley, are an essential part of summer meals.

VEGETABLES

Lentil cottage pie

12 oz green lentils
4 oz onion
2 oz mushrooms
4 oz carrots
2 lb potatoes
4 oz butter
Salt and pepper
Mixed herbs

Wash lentils and then boil them in three times their quantity of water for about an hour, until tender. (A point to note for the cooking of dried beans and pulses: salt should be added after cooking, as it tends to harden them if it is present during the boiling stage.) When cooked, drain lentils. Meanwhile, boil the potatoes and mash them with butter in the usual way, keeping them fairly dry as they are going to be a topping. Fry the onion, carrot and mushrooms, all of which have been chopped, add herbs and the drained lentils, stir and season. Place lentil mixture in pie dish or suitable casserole. Top with mashed potato. Dot with butter, place in hot oven until browned.
SERVES 4.   J.V.Z.

Favas a Algarvia
Broad beans from the Algarve

1 lb broad beans
4 oz salami
4 oz smoked ham
1 onion
4 oz carrots
½ tablespoon tomato purée
1 pint chicken stock
1 tablespoon olive oil
Salt and pepper

Gently sauté finely chopped onion, chopped salami and sliced ham (parma is suitable) in the olive oil for about 5 minutes. Add stock, beans, sliced carrots, tomato purée and seasoning. Cover and cook in a casserole in a slow oven for about 1 hour until beans and carrots are tender.
SERVES 4.   C.W.

Potatoes vinaigrette

1½ lb small new potatoes
6 tablespoons olive oil
2 tablespoons vinegar
Salt and pepper
1 tablespoon chopped parsley,
*   mint and thyme*

Cook potatoes in their skins, until tender. Peel and, while still warm, moisten with a little French dressing made with oil, vinegar, salt and pepper. Add the herbs to the remainder of the dressing, add to the potatoes and mix together well.
SERVES 4.   V.J.

Norwegian baked mushrooms

Allow 6-8 button mushrooms per person. Blanch the mushrooms. Sprinkle them with nutmeg. Pack them in a fireproof dish, together with some finely chopped onion which has been lightly fried in butter (1 tablespoon per person). Fill available space in the dish with double cream, sprinkle with grated cheese. Bake in a hot oven for 15-20 minutes.   G.B.

Onion pudding

6 small Spanish onions
Butter for frying
4 oz breadcrumbs
1 egg
A little milk
1 tablespoon melted butter
A little grated lemon rind
Pinch of nutmeg
Salt and pepper
Brown gravy

Slice the onions and fry them to a golden brown, then line a small pudding basin with them. Mix the breadcrumbs, well-beaten egg, melted butter, nutmeg and lemon rind together. Add salt and pepper, and mix all well together with a little milk. Pour this mixture over the onions and steam for 1½ hours. Heat the gravy and serve with pudding.
SERVES 4.   J.E. (1)

Ragout of onions

4 large onions
1 oz butter
Flour
Salt and pepper
¼ pint good gravy
1 teaspoon mustard

Peel and cut the onions very small. Melt the butter in pan, fry onions until brown; dust in flour and shake onions until thick. Season with salt, pepper and add gravy and mustard. Stir all together until thick, pour into a dish, garnish with fried crumbs of bread and serve hot.
SERVES 4.   J.E. (1)

Baked stuffed onions

6 large onions
7 oz tuna fish
6 tablespoons soft white breadcrumbs
2 tablespoons chopped parsley
1 egg
Squeeze of lemon juice
Salt and pepper
½ pint stock or water
Grated cheese
Butter

Peel the onions and cook them in boiling water for 20 minutes. Strain. With a sharp knife, scoop out the centres, leaving a 'shell' on each onion a good ¼-inch thick. Chop up the insides of three of the onions fairly finely. Mix with the flaked and mashed tuna fish, breadcrumbs, parsley, lemon juice and seasonings. Bind the mixture with the beaten egg and pile it into the hollow onions. Place them in a fireproof dish and pour around them the stock or water. Dot the top of each onion with butter and sprinkle with grated cheese. Bake in a fairly hot oven, at 400°F (gas 6), for about 40 minutes, according to size. Serve with home-made tomato sauce or cheese sauce.
SERVES 6.   J.E. (1)

Les bouchées aux épinards
Spinach mounds

Make 4 croûtons (about the diameter of a ramekin dish) lightly flavoured with garlic butter. Cut 4 small rounds of ham the same size as the croûtons. Fry ham in butter very gently and flavour with Madeira. Place ham on croûtons. Fill 4 small buttered ramekins with cooked spinach (flavoured with nutmeg, salt and a little sugar). Overturn shaped spinach on ham. Place a good spoonful of thick Hollandaise sauce on spinach. Put the lot in the oven for 5 minutes to warm through.
SERVES 4.   N.L.

Broad beans and bacon

Broad beans are rarely skinned in Britain, but it makes an enormous difference to their flavour.
2 oz diced bacon
Butter
2 lb cooked broad beans
2 tablespoons béchamel sauce
Cream
Chopped parsley

Fry bacon in a little butter. Add cooked, skinned broad beans, thin béchamel sauce, a little cream and a very little chopped parsley. Simmer together for 5 minutes.
SERVES 6-8.   J.E. (1)

Chicory salad

Chicory
Sliced almonds
Sliced apple
French dressing
Mix all the above and serve with chicken and pork dishes.

M.I.

Ratatouille
Vegetable stew from Provence

6 large onions
1 courgette or small vegetable marrow
2 peppers
2 aubergines
4 tomatoes
2 tablespoons olive oil

Prepare all the vegetables, carefully removing seeds from the courgette and peppers. Slice and fry gently in the oil until tender. This can be served either alone or with the addition of previously boiled rice or topped with poached eggs.
SERVES 4-6. M.D.

Southern mashed potatoes

1 lb cooked, floury potatoes
¼ pint milk
½ oz butter
Salt and pepper
Nutmeg
Grated rind of one orange
1 teaspoon grated lemon rind

Mash the potatoes and put through a ricer. Add the milk, which must be boiling hot, a little at a time, and beat very hard with a fork. Add the butter, grated rind and seasonings and go on beating until the potato is really white and as soft as whipped cream. If necessary reheat it by turning it into a fireproof dish standing in a baking tin of hot water in a moderate oven.
SERVES 4. J.E. (1)

Hot lentil salad

½ lb lentils
1 small onion
¼ pint soured cream or yogurt
1-2 tablespoons vinegar

Cook lentils until tender. Mix with chopped onion; add sour cream or yogurt and vinegar to taste. Serve warm.
SERVES 4. V.G.

Stuffed tomatoes

12 large tomatoes
8 oz cheddar cheese
¼ pint soured cream or yogurt
3 eggs
breadcrumbs
Basil

Cut a 'lid' off each tomato and scoop out pulp, leaving shells intact. Mix pulp with grated cheese, beaten eggs, yogurt or cream, breadcrumbs and seasoning. Stuff tomatoes, replace lids and bake for 20 minutes at 350°F (gas 4).
SERVES 6. V.G.

Cucumber salad

1 cucumber
1 small onion
½ pint natural yogurt
2 hard-boiled eggs, chopped
Sultanas and nuts to taste

Dice cucumber and onion, then mix in all other ingredients. (This is also delicious as an accompaniment to cold or hot dishes, particularly curry.)
SERVES 4. V.G.

Caramel potatoes

Melt 1 oz granulated sugar in frying pan. As soon as it turns brown add 1 oz butter. Sauté small cooked new potatoes in this caramel until they are browned.

Aubergine parmesan

1½ lb aubergines
2-3 lb fresh tomatoes or 16 oz tin
2 tablespoons tomato purée
Oil
Onion
Garlic
Vinegar
Sugar
Basil
Oregano
Bay leaf
Flour and milk
3 oz grated parmesan cheese

Slice aubergine fairly thinly, dip in milk and then flour, fry in oil, then drain on kitchen paper. Make tomato sauce by cooking onion in oil, add tomato purée then chopped fresh tomato or tinned, seasonings, garlic, herbs, etc, plus a little vinegar and sugar. Cook for an hour—the longer the better—adding a little water if too thick. Strain, adjust seasoning and consistency. It should be fairly thick.

Alternate layers of aubergine, tomato sauce and parmesan in a flat-bottomed dish, finishing with parmesan. Bake in oven for 45 minutes at 350°F (gas 4) until nicely browned.
SERVES 6. J.V.Z.

Cèpes à la Bordelaise

Whilst mushrooms can never be substituted for cèpes, large dark-brown field mushrooms do make an acceptable alternative. Try to obtain dried or tinned cèpes, if fresh ones are not available. Tinned ones in brine are particularly good.

2 lb cèpes
4 shallots (or pickling-size onions), finely chopped
8 fl oz (scant half-pint) good flavoured olive oil
2 heaped tablespoons fresh parsley, finely chopped
2 large cloves garlic, finely chopped
Salt and pepper
Good squeeze lemon juice

Wipe the cèpes or mushrooms clean with a damp cloth. Remove stems and slice together with the tops into ½-inch-thick pieces. Heat half the oil until smoking in a heavy-bottomed frying-pan. Fry the cèpes until brown and crisp over a high heat. Remove with a draining spoon to a warm serving-dish. Add remaining oil to pan and fry shallots until lightly browned and cooked, adding the garlic towards the end of this process. Return cooked cèpes to pan, mix well in, season carefully with salt and pepper and a good squeeze of lemon juice. Sprinkle with parsley and mix in. Serve very hot.
SERVES 8. M.S.

Old English apple sauce

1 lb Cox's pippins
2 oz butter
1 teaspoon cinnamon
2 good-sized pieces orange rind
1 oz ground almonds
Brown sugar to taste

Rinse out a pan with cold water, leaving the bottom wet. Peel, core and slice the apples into even-size pieces. Put, together with all the ingredients, into the pan. Cover and put on the lowest heat possible, wait for the juices to draw. Toss the pan at regular intervals to prevent sticking. When the juices draw, simmer the apples until completely softened. Remove the rind, whisk the sauce. Serve either hot or cold. The sauce can be puréed in a blender if you wish but this will change the tweedy texture as too much air will be incorporated.   M.S.

Bread sauce

½ pint milk
2 oz butter
1 small onion
1 garlic clove, crushed
Bay leaf or clove or nutmeg
2 oz white breadcrumbs
¼ pint single cream
Salt and pepper

Put all the ingredients, except the cream, into a small saucepan and simmer over a minimum heat for 20 minutes. Remove the onion and bay leaf. Blend until you have the finest purée. Stir in the cream. Season with salt and freshly milled *white* pepper.
NOTE: The quantity of bread required will depend entirely on the type of bread you use. Commercially-made sliced bread does not taste well and produces a slimy sauce. Black pepper, whilst flavoursome, leaves specks in an otherwise smooth creamy sauce.   M.S.

Cumberland sauce

1 lb redcurrant jelly
¼ pint ruby port or red wine
1 small onion, finely shredded
3 oranges
3 lemons
1 teaspoon dry mustard
Pinch powdered mace
3 fl oz cider vinegar

Using a potato peeler, remove the rind from the citrus fruits. Collect the strips together into manageable piles and with a sharp knife shred these as finely as you possibly can—trying to get them as thin as thread. This will ensure a good-looking sauce. Put the shredded peel into a pan and cover with water. Bring to the boil and simmer for a minute. Strain and

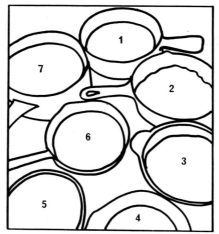

Traditional English sauces:
1 *Cumberland (this page)* **2** *Old English Apple (this page)* **3** *Parsley (see Rich White sauce recipe on page 121, to which is added finely-chopped parsley or parsley juice)* **4** *Rich White sauce in the making (page 121)* **5** *Egg sauce (page 121)* **6** *Bread sauce (this page)* **7** *Tomato*

put on one side. Squeeze the juice from two of each of the fruits. Bring this to the boil together with the jelly and the other ingredients. Boil over a low heat. As soon as the sauce starts to thicken somewhat add the shredded rind and continue boiling, removing any scum which may come to the surface. Cool the sauce, then refrigerate. Serve chilled and unstrained. (The consistency should be that of a hot pouring sauce. If you have problems arriving at the right consistency, re-heat the sauce and add a teaspoon of gelatine, softened in a little hot water, cool and chill again.)   M.S.

Tomato sauce

2 lb tomatoes
1 tablespoon tomato purée
1 small onion
1 garlic clove, crushed
2 oz green bacon
½ pint chicken stock
½ oz white flour
1 oz butter
¼ teaspoon grated lemon rind
¼ teaspoon rosemary
1 teaspoon lemon juice
2 fl oz dry sherry
Little caster sugar (see method)
Salt and freshly milled pepper

Chop onion and soften in the butter. Let this get golden coloured. Cut bacon into striplets and add to pan, frying until cooked. Add purée, stir well in. Add flour and stir in. Skin and de-seed the tomatoes, add half of these to the pan together with all remaining ingredients.
Simmer the sauce for 20 minutes,

press through a hair sieve seasoning again, adding a little sugar if necessary. Chop remaining de-seeded tomatoes and add to strained sauce. Re-heat and serve.
If a creamy sauce is required, add ¼ pint double cream after sieving, check seasoning again, re-heat, serve. Keep hot in bowl over simmering water; cover surface of sauce with buttered paper.
M.S.

Breton sauce

½ pint mayonnaise
1 tomato
Tomato purée
A few tarragon leaves
Pinch of cayenne pepper

Cut the tomato and the tarragon leaves into small pieces and stir into the mayonnaise with remaining ingredients.
S.W. (3)

Home-made salad cream

1 oz butter
1 oz plain flour
2 teaspoons mustard
Pinch of sugar
¼ pint milk
1 egg
2 tablespoons wine vinegar
Salt and pepper

Put butter, flour, mustard, sugar and milk into a saucepan. Bring to the boil, whisking all the time and continue for 2-3 minutes until smooth and well thickened. Remove from the heat and immediately beat in the egg very thoroughly, wine vinegar and salt and pepper to taste. Cool.
Serve with a mixture of chopped celery, cubed dessert apples, and chopped walnuts.   L.B./J.G.

Hollandaise sauce

2 egg yolks
6 oz butter
Lemon juice
Salt and pepper
A pinch of cayenne pepper
2 tablespoons vinegar or white wine
2-3 shallots, finely chopped

Simmer shallots with a little pepper in the vinegar or wine. Add 1 teaspoon of water and the egg yolks. Stir over a slow heat until creamy. Remove from heat and stir in the melted butter. Strain and season to taste adding a pinch of cayenne and a few drops of lemon juice.   S.W.

Chantilly sauce

Make a Hollandaise base with the addition of 4 teaspoons of whipped cream.   S.W. (3)

Sauce Bearnaise

2 tablespoons dry white wine
1 tablespoon tarragon vinegar
1 shallot, finely chopped
Black pepper
2½ oz butter
2 egg yolks
Lemon juice
1 teaspoon tarragon, chervil, parsley

Put white wine and tarragon vinegar in a small pan with the shallot and a grinding of black pepper. Reduce to half by fast boiling. Cool and strain into top of a double boiler, adding a few drops of cold water. The water in bottom of pan should be warm but not boil. Add 1 oz butter cut into small pieces. Stir, and when melted, add another 1½ oz butter and beaten egg yolks. Stir all the time until sauce thickens, then add a few drops of lemon juice, a few drops of cold water and seasoning to taste. Remove from heat and stir in chopped tarragon, chervil and parsley.   J.E. (1)

Bordelaise sauce

5 tablespoons Bordeaux wine
3 shallots
1 stock cube
¼ pint water
1 lemon
1 bay leaf
Thyme
2 to 3 peppercorns
1 teaspoon tomato purée
4 oz cooked beef marrow

Reduce by boiling the wine with the chopped shallots, the peppercorns, a little thyme and the bay leaf. Add the stock cube blended with a cup of water and boil for 5 minutes. Add the tomato purée and remove from the heat. Strain. Before serving, add the diced or sliced beef marrow and a little lemon juice.   S.W. (3)

Aioli
Garlic mayonnaise

Known as 'the butter of Provence', and often served smeared copiously over mixed vegetables. It is particularly good with hard-boiled eggs, potatoes in their jackets (hot or cold) and boiled fish. A big blob with cold lobster is excellent too. Pound finely 4 or 5 cloves of garlic, stir in an egg-yolk and seasonings and start adding olive oil, drop by drop, proceeding exactly as for mayonnaise. If necessary, thin with a teaspoon of water. Add the juice of half a lemon instead of vinegar. Chopped parsley or breadcrumbs can be added if desired.   L.H.

To make a good French dressing, it is essential to use good-quality oil and wine vinegar, rather than malt.

Lobster sauce

Delicious with spinach soufflé (see page 29) but may also be served with a cheese soufflé.

2 6-oz tins lobster
3 tablespoons butter
1½ tablespoons flour
Dash of paprika
½ pint thin cream
2 egg yolks
3 tablespoons sherry

Drain the juice from the lobster and cut up the flesh. Make a roux from the butter, flour, paprika, a little salt; add the cream. Bring slowly to boiling point. Beat the egg yolks, just to blend them, add a little of the hot sauce to the eggs and then return all to the pan. Add the sherry and lobster and reheat but do not boil. This makes about a pint of sauce.   W.G.

Basic barbecue sauce

¼ pint cooking oil
6 fl oz wine vinegar
2 fl oz water
1 teaspoon salt
2 tablespoons sugar
1 teaspoon Tabasco sauce
¼ teaspoon Worcestershire sauce
1 bay leaf

Put all ingredients into a small saucepan and bring to the boil over medium heat. Keep warm by the side of the fire while using, and brush over steaks, chops or poultry.   M.N.

1812 Chicken sauce

1 lemon
1 chicken liver
3 oz butter
Salt and pepper

Peel the lemon and remove all pith. Cut the lemon into thin slices, take out the pips, and cut the lemon flesh into tiny pieces. Melt 1 oz butter and cook the chicken liver until just cooked through but still juicy. Cut the liver into tiny pieces. Melt the remaining butter, stir in the lemon and liver, and season well with salt and pepper. Serve hot with chicken. This family recipe was originally devised for 'boiled fowls' but is just as good today with our often-tasteless roasting birds.   M.N.

Lemon dressing

Juice of 2 lemons
1 tablespoon clear honey
Chopped fresh herbs

Mix all the ingredients and dress a lettuce salad just before serving. With fresh mint or basil, this is a good dressing for tomato salads.   M.N.

Barbecue marinades

The following are all suitable for barbecue cooking. Combine the ingredients and marinate fish or meat, turning occasionally, before cooking.

FOR MEDITERRANEAN PRAWNS

3 tablespoons wine vinegar
2 tablespoons sherry,
3 tablespoons oil
1 teaspoon soy sauce
Pepper

FOR KEBABS

1 clove garlic, crushed
1 small onion, finely chopped
1 teaspoon Worcestershire sauce
3 tablespoons wine vinegar
1 teaspoon soy sauce
Pinch of mustard
2 tablespoons red wine
3 tablespoons oil

SWEET AND SOUR: FOR SPARE RIBS

3 tablespoons pineapple juice
1 oz brown sugar,
3 tablespoons wine vinegar
1 teaspoon soy sauce
2 tablespoons oil
Salt and pepper
1 small onion, finely chopped
¼ green pepper, blanched and finely chopped   M.N.

Salsa Mexicana
Mexican tomato sauce

1 lb tomatoes
2 medium onions
3 chillis
Salt and pepper

Chop up the tomatoes and onions and place in large bowl. Clean and chop the chillis and add 1 teaspoon. Add seasoning and gently mix together. Do not leave for more than six hours before serving. Serve with *tacos*.   J.D. (2)

Sauce tartare

To home-made mayonnaise add 2 tablespoons of finely chopped fresh herbs, parsley, chives, chervil, tarragon and a tablespoon of very finely minced shallot. Gherkins and capers can also be added.   J.E. (1)

Spicy tomato sauce

½ pint water
1 × 15-oz tin tomatoes, chopped
2 tablespoons chopped parsley
1 teaspoon sugar
1 teaspoon oregano
1 teaspoon salt

Mix the ingredients in the order given and simmer in a saucepan for 30 minutes. Stir often.   W.G.

SAUCES

Mayonnaise variée

An electric whisk or liquidizer will make mayonnaise in under five minutes, and with a good-quality olive oil it may be stored in the refrigerator for some time without deteriorating in quality. The new lighter, vegetable oils serve very well for making mayonnaise and they will take on olive flavour if used to store olives.

2 egg yolks
Pinch of dry mustard
Salt and pepper
1 tablespoon wine vinegar
½ pint olive oil

Beat together all the ingredients, except the oil, in a narrow basin, or measuring jug. Then, if you are making the mayonnaise by hand, add the oil drop by drop until it has 'taken'. Then you can add more oil at a time—but still proceeding slowly. If you are using an electric whisk, turn the beaters to high speed, then slowly and gradually pour the oil straight into the revolving beaters. Continue beating until a very thick creamy mass is formed and all the oil is used. Adjust the flavouring to taste, using more vinegar and pepper and salt, or leave until required, then flavour as liked:

TOMATO MAYONNAISE
Mix with tomato purée to taste and serve with sea food or hard-boiled eggs.

GARLIC MAYONNAISE
Store a clove of crushed garlic in some of the mayonnaise and remove before serving. Good with cooked green beans.

LEMON MAYONNAISE
Add a little finely-grated lemon rind and some lemon juice to taste, then serve with whole sardines.

ORANGE MAYONNAISE
Add grated orange rind and orange juice. Good with asparagus spears.

SAUCE VERTE
Make a purée of watercress and parsley and stir into the plain mayonnaise. An excellent sauce for sliced new potatoes or hard-boiled eggs.

CURRY MAYONNAISE
A very little curry paste mixed with the basic mayonnaise makes a really first-class *hors d'hoeuvre* with fresh grapefruit segments and smoked, tinned oysters.

L.B.

Horseradish sauce

If fresh roots are not obtainable, there is some excellent preserved grated horseradish available in jars.

With fresh horseradish, wash and scrape off the surface skin and finely grate the root; with the preserved variety, it is ready to mix straight from the jar. To 2 tablespoons of the grated horseradish mix in 2 tablespoons lemon juice, 1 teaspoon dry mustard, 2 teaspoons sugar, 1 teaspoon salt, a little freshly-ground pepper, and ¼ pint double cream whipped to a floppy consistenty. It is equally delicious with hot or cold beef.

L.B. E.S.

Cucumber mayonnaise

Make the mayonnaise, omitting the cucumber, anything up to four weeks in advance; store it in a polythene container in the refrigerator. On no account freeze mayonnaise—it will curdle when thawed.

2 egg yolks
½ teaspoon made mustard
⅛ teaspoon pepper
½ teaspoon caster sugar
¼ pint olive oil, vegetable or corn oil
1 tablespoon lemon juice
1 tablespoon white wine vinegar or
  distilled malt vinegar
½ cucumber

Stand the bowl on a damp cloth to prevent it slipping on the table. Put the egg yolks, mustard, salt, pepper and sugar into a bowl and mix well. Add the oil drop by drop, beating well after each addition with a whisk until the sauce is thick and smooth. In order that the oil may be added a drop at a time, put into the bottle neck a cork from which a small wedge has been cut. Add the lemon juice and vinegar. Remove the peel and pips from the cucumber and cut into small cubes. Stir into the mayonnaise just before serving.   M.B. (1)

Rich white sauce

1 oz flour
2 oz butter
¾ pint (plus) milk
¼ pint single cream
1 tablespoon roughly-chopped onion
Half clove garlic
6 peppercorns
Half a bay leaf
Salt

Melt the butter in a heavy-bottomed saucepan, swirling the pan around as you do this to avoid any discolouration. Don't let the butter get too hot.

Stir in the flour. Gradually incorporate the cold milk, stirring and beating or whisking as you go. Allow the sauce to come to the boil, reduce the heat to an *absolute minimum*, add the rest of the ingredients except the cream. Cover with a lid and simmer for 15 minutes, when the sauce will be bright and slightly reduced. Check seasoning. Strain into a clean pan or bowl, stir in the cream, re-heat and serve either plain or with one of the garnishes given below. (Makes 1 pint.)

NOTE: To keep the sauce hot, stand the saucepan in another containing simmering water, or arrange a basin over a pan of simmering water, cover the surface of the sauce with a circle of buttered paper to prevent a skin forming.

The following garnishes are for ½ pint of basic sauce:

MUSHROOM
2 oz very finely sliced white button mushrooms which have been quickly fried in a scant 1 oz of butter. Swirl the pan out with 3 tablespoons medium sherry, reducing it to 1 tablespoon before adding to sauce.

PARSLEY
2 heaped tablespoons freshly chopped very green parsley. Gathering the chopped parsley into the corner of a tea-towel and squeezing the green juice into the sauce after rinsing it under cold water. Season with lemon juice only.

MUSTARD
Add two heaped teaspoons of Dijon mustard, 1 tablespoon medium-dry sherry and ¼-inch of stock cube. Strain before serving.

CHEESE
1½ to 2 oz grated Cheddar (mild or strong or a mixture, develop your own 'blend'), ½ teaspoon made English mustard and 1 teaspoon lemon juice.

CELERY
3 oz celery washed and shredded as fine as thread! Soften this carefully in an ounce of butter in a small lidded pan over a very low heat. This will take about 15 minutes. Stir in the sauce, season with a drop of lemon juice and a turn or two of the mill. Do not strain.

ONION
Very finely slice a 3-oz onion. Soften this completely in butter as above; taking care not to permit the onion to colour. Season with the merest touch of curry powder *or* grated nutmeg, lemon or powdered mace.

EGG
Hard-boil 2 eggs (8 minutes should do). Shell and chop. Stir into the sauce—it is better when the yolk is just soft in the centre. Season well with grated nutmeg and a scant tablespoon dry sherry.   M.S.

Sour cream dressing

Flavour sour cream with grated lemon rind, lemon juice and salt.

Serve with sliced avocado and shrimps on a bed of chopped lettuce.   L.B./J.G.

French dressing

Wine vinegar, olive oil and seasoning to taste shaken up in a screw top jar.

Serve with watercress, chicory and sliced oranges.   L.B./J.G.

Meurette sauce

1 tablespoon flour
¼ pint red wine
½ oz butter

Melt the butter, stir in the flour and add, gradually, the wine. Stir until it thickens. (This is a popular accompaniment in France for eggs, fish or meat.)   M.D.

Aioli, a pungent garlic-flavoured mayonnaise from Provence, is served with cold seafood and raw summer vegetables (page 119).

Hot orange soufflé surprise

8 egg whites
Butter and sugar for the dish
4 sponge fingers, split
½ pint orange juice
6 egg yolks
4 oz caster sugar
3 oz plain flour
Scant ½ pint milk
1½ tablespoons grated orange rind
6 tablespoons Grand Marnier

Prepare a soufflé dish as above. Put the split sponge fingers in a single layer in a shallow dish and sprinkle with the Grand Marnier. Beat the egg yolks at high speed until thick and pale (it takes about 3 minutes), then beat in the orange juice; add the flour and beat to incorporate. Put the milk in a large pan with ¼ of the caster sugar and heat until bubbles appear at the edge of the pan. Stir this hot milk into the egg yolk mixture and return to the pan, cook carefully over low heat until it thickens. This will take about 10 minutes (you may find it better to use a double saucepan). Turn into a large bowl, add the orange rind and leave to cool. Beat the egg whites at high speed until foamy, then slowly beat in the remaining caster sugar and beat until very stiff. Now fold into the orange mixture. Turn half of this into the prepared dish and arrange the soaked sponge fingers on it, then pour the rest of the soufflé mixture on top. It is possible to refrigerate this as below, but it is better to bake it at once at 350 F (gas 4) for 45-50 minutes. Serve at once with chantilly cream.
SERVES 8.   W.G.

Hot lemon soufflé

6 egg whites
4 egg yolks
Butter and sugar to line dish
1 oz flour
2 oz sugar
Pinch salt
¼ pint milk
3 tablespoons lemon juice
1½ tablespoons grated lemon rind
1½ tablespoons butter
1 teaspoon cream of tartar
1 tablespoon icing sugar

Grease and prepare a soufflé dish as usual and sprinkle with sugar. Put a paper band round the dish. Separate the eggs. In a saucepan put the flour, sugar, salt, ¼ pint of cold water and the milk. Cook and stir until smooth. When thickened, remove from the heat. Beat

A lot of confidence and a little skill is all you need to produce the most breathtakingly delicious of all finales to a meal: a soufflé. This one is orange-flavoured. (Recipe above.)

the egg yolks with a wooden spoon or whisk, add a little bit of the sauce to the eggs, then put all back into the pan, reheat but do not let it boil. Take off the heat, add the lemon juice, rind and the butter and beat until blended. Add the cream of tartar to the egg whites and beat at high speed in an electric mixer until stiff, then fold in a third of the lemon mixture and blend well. Fold in the rest very gently. Turn into the prepared dish. The mixture may be refrigerated for not more than four hours. Bake at 350°F (gas 4) for 35 minutes. Sprinkle with icing sugar and serve. (If wished, chantilly cream may be served with this soufflé. To make this, whip 2 tablespoons of icing sugar into ¼ pint of whipping cream.)
SERVES 6-8.   W.G.

Hungarian rice soufflé

2½ oz rice
1 pint milk
5 oz sugar
2 eggs
Strawberry jam
Tin chestnut purée
Brandy

Cook the rice and milk in the top of a double saucepan until soft and creamy; cool slightly. Mix 1 oz of the sugar with the egg yolks and add to the rice, then put ⅓ of this into a greased fireproof dish and spread with jam. Continue with layers of rice and jam and then spread the chestnut purée on top. Make a meringue from the egg whites and the rest of the sugar and put on the pudding, bake at 350°F (gas 4) for 20 minutes. Heat the brandy, pour it over the pudding, set fire to it and send blazing to table.
SERVES 4.   W.G.

Surprise soufflé

2 oz black grapes, cut in halves
1 orange
1 small crisp dessert apple
Juice of ½ lemon
1 oz butter
1 oz plain flour
1 oz caster sugar
9 fl oz milk
3 oz Sbrinz cheese, grated
3 eggs

Carefully remove seeds from grapes and halve; peel and segment the orange; quarter the apple, remove the core, then cut in thin slices; place all the prepared fruits in a basin with the lemon juice and leave while the soufflé is being made.
Put the butter, flour, sugar and milk into a saucepan and bring to the boil whisking vigorously, then continue to cook for 2-3 minutes over a low heat. Thoroughly beat in the cheese then the egg yolks. Whisk the egg whites until

stiff and peaks are formed which turn over, and fold lightly into the cooked mixture.
Place alternate layers of soufflé mixture and drained fruit in a buttered 2-pint soufflé dish, beginning and ending with the soufflé mixture. Bake approximately 35 minutes or until well risen, golden brown and just set at 350°F (gas 4). Sprinkle with sugar; serve at once.
NOTE: Sbrinz cheese is the best for this recipe, but if it is not available, gruyère may be used. Care chould be taken in measuring the milk.
SERVES 6.   L.B./J.G. (2)

Liqueur soufflé

2½ oz butter
2 tablespoons plain flour
Pinch of salt
2 tablespoons sugar
¼ pint boiling milk
2 egg yolks
3 egg whites
5 tablespoons Cointreau or Grand
    Marnier

Melt together the butter and flour. Stir in the salt, sugar and milk, and cook until smooth and thick. Cool. Add the egg yolks, one at a time, and beat well. Stir in the liqueur and fold in the stiffly-whipped egg whites. Put into a buttered 1-pint soufflé dish and bake at 350°F (gas 4) for 20 minutes, then at 400°F (gas 6) for 10 minutes. Eat at once with more liqueur and cream if liked.
SERVES 4.   M.N.

Orange mousse with lychees

3 eggs
2 egg yolks
3 oz caster sugar
½ oz gelatine
5 tablespoons water
¼ pint double cream
1 can frozen orange juice
1 large can lychees
TO FINISH
¼ pint double cream
Angelica or pistachio nuts

You will need an angel cake tin, lightly oiled.
Place the whole eggs and yolks in a basin, add the sugar and whisk over a pan of hot water until thick. Remove from heat and continue whisking until cold. Put the gelatine in the water and dissolve it over the heat. Partially whip first ¼ pint cream and quickly stir this, the orange juice and gelatine into the egg mousse. As mixture begins to set, pour it into tin. Cover the mousse with foil and leave to set in fridge. (A minimum of 2 hours.) Turn it out onto a serving-dish and fill centre with drained lychees. Decorate with rosettes of whipped cream and angelica or pistachio nuts.
SERVES 4.   M.L.

PUDDINGS AND BAKING

Wengen lemon mousse

4 eggs
4 oz caster sugar
2 large lemons
½ oz gelatine
3 tablespoons water

Separate the eggs and place the yolks in a bowl with the sugar and beat until creamy.

Grate the rind and squeeze the juice from the lemons and add to the egg yolk mixture. Put the gelatine in a small bowl or cup with cold water, leave to stand for 3 minutes to become a sponge. Stand the bowl in a pan of simmering water and allow the gelatine to dissolve. Cool slightly and stir into the lemon mixture. Leave for a few minutes until the mixture starts to set.

Whisk the egg whites until stiff and fold into the lemon mixture. Put into a 2 pint straight-sided dish and chill for at least 2 hours.

Just before serving decorate with swirls of whipped cream and lemon slices.

SERVES 6.   M.B. (1)

Chocolate mousse

8 oz sweetened dark chocolate
¼ pint water
1½ oz butter
1 tablespoon rum
4 small eggs

Break up the chocolate and put in a saucepan. Add the water. Boil, stirring until it is smooth and has the consistency of very thick cream. Cool slightly and stir in the rum and the butter. Separate the eggs. Beat the yolks into the chocolate. Whisk the whites until stiff but not dry-looking, and fold into the mixture. Pour into individual pots, glasses or coffee cups. Refrigerate overnight. The mousses can be decorated with whipped cream or chopped nuts, but classically they are served as they are. For a lighter less rich mousse, leave out the egg yolks, and use an extra egg white.

SERVES 4-6.   P.L.

Chocolate mousse (2)

4 oz of bitter chocolate
4 egg yolks
4 egg whites
1 teaspoon vanilla
6 tablespoons sugar
⅛ lb butter
Pinch of salt

To melt chocolate, put in a saucepan; cover it with a little very hot water, and then place lid on saucepan. Let it stand — not over heat. The water will melt the chocolate after about 5 minutes, but if it is not quite melted, drain water and add more hot water. Drain off water when soft. Add yolks and stirring with a

whisk cook over a very low heat until thick. Remove saucepan from heat and add the butter, vanilla and dash of salt. Mix well and cool a little. Do not let it become solid. Then beat egg whites, adding sugar gradually. Beat until stiff. Add one large tablespoon of the white to the chocolate, mix well, then gently fold in the remainder. Pour into individual serving dishes and refrigerate until needed. Decorate with whipped cream, chopped nuts. (This pudding can be served immediately or kept in the refrigerator for a day.)

SERVES 4.   K.K.

Chocolate and orange mousse

12 oz plain cooking chocolate
⅓ pint whipping cream
2 oranges
½ oz agar-agar (obtainable at most health food shops)
2 oz sugar

Melt chocolate in a bowl over hot water, add sugar and stir until smooth. Grate the zest off the oranges, and add juice to the zest in a small pan, add a tablespoon of water, add agar-agar and stir over low heat until dissolved. Whip cream until stiff. Add orange and agar to chocolate and stir until cool. Fold in whipped cream, keeping some back for decoration. Pour in desired mould and refrigerate until set. (Agar-agar sets quicker than gelatine.) Immerse mould in hot water to turn out on to plate, then decorate.

SERVES 4.   J.V.Z.

Chocolate praliné pudding

This is very rich, so it is best served with simple boudoir biscuits.

12 oz dark chocolate
¼ pint black coffee
3 oz unsalted butter
3 oz caster sugar (optional)
1 tablespoon brandy
½ pint double cream
FOR THE PRALINE
5 oz blanched almonds
5 oz caster sugar

Praline may be made at anytime, and kept in an airtight container. Cook slowly the almonds and sugar together until both turn a deep golden brown.

Turn the mixture out on to a flat greased surface. When hard, break up into small pieces.

Break the chocolate into small pieces and put into a double saucepan with the coffee, stir until melted and quite smooth, and put aside to cool. Cream butter and sugar, if included, with a mixer if possible, then beat in the chocolate until all is well blended. Add the praline and the brandy, mixing well. Whip half the cream separately and fold into the chocolate, once again being careful that all the ingredients are well blended. Spoon into a well-oiled round-sided two-pint basin. Put in the fridge to set, overnight if necessary.

To turn out the pudding on a dish, either dip very quickly in hot water or cover with a hot wet cloth and shake. Decorate with piped cream round the base and medallions of chocolate.

SERVES 6-8.   A.R. (1)

Apricot flummery

4 oz dried apricots
½ pint water
1 oz plain flour
6 oz caster sugar
¼ pint orange juice
1 tablespoon lemon juice
½ tablespoon gelatine
3 tablespoons hot water
¼ pint double cream

Put the apricots and water into a saucepan. Bring to the boil and simmer over low heat for 1 hour. Purée the apricots in an electric blender or push them through a sieve into a bowl. Put the flour and sugar into a saucepan. Blend in the orange juice, lemon juice and purée of apricots. Bring to the boil, stirring continuously, and cook for 3 minutes until the mixture has thickened.

Dissolve the gelatine in the hot water in a small bowl over a pan of hot water. Stir the dissolved gelatine into the apricot mixture and leave to one side until the mixture is thick and syrupy for about 30 minutes. Whisk with a balloon or rotary whisk until it is frothy and doubled in bulk. Pour into a serving dish and chill in the refrigerator. Whip the cream until stiff and spoon on to the flummery.

SERVES 4.   M.N.

Lemon flummery

½ pint water
¾ oz butter
1 lemon
1 oz plain flour
4 oz caster sugar
1 large egg
Macaroons or digestive biscuits

Put the water, butter and grated lemon rind into a pan and bring to the boil. Mix the flour and sugar in a bowl and make a well in the centre. Pour in the hot liquid, whisking to avoid lumps. Put the egg yolk into a small bowl and stir in a little of the hot mixture. Put the remaining mixture into a saucepan and whisk in the egg mixture. Bring slowly to the boil, and then cook gently for 10 minutes. Whisk the egg white until stiff. Add the juice of the lemon to the mixture in the saucepan. Pour the lemon mixture into a bowl and fold in the egg white. Cool and then scatter the top with crushed macaroons or digestive biscuits. Serve cold with cream. This is a very cheap pudding, and more refreshing than the usual mousse.
SERVES 4.   M.N.

Syllabub

Double cream is a must for this rich dessert. Make it in small pots, ramekins, glasses or demi-tasse coffee cups. Make the day before and keep in refrigerator.

1 large lemon
2 tablespoons medium sherry
2 tablespoons brandy
2 oz caster sugar
½ pint double cream
Lemon slices

Finely grate the rind from the lemon and squeeze the juice out. Put in a bowl with the sherry, brandy and sugar. Stir until the sugar has dissolved. Pour in the cream and whisk until the mixture will form soft peaks when the whisk is lifted out. Spoon into individual glasses and leave in a cool place until required. Top each glass with a slice of fresh lemon just before serving.
SERVES 4.   M.B. (1)

Crème brulée

This recipe is an interesting variation of a classic dish.

½ pint double cream
2 large eggs
1 oz soft brown sugar
1 tablespoon sherry
TO FINISH
Soft brown sugar

Heat the cream in a basin over hot water until steaming. Beat together the remaining ingredients, then stir in the hot cream. Return to the heat and cook over hot water, stirring frequently, until the custard forms a coating on the back of a metal spoon and falls from the spoon in large thick drops. Remove from the heat immediately and pour straight into 4 individual heat-proof dishes. Chill well, then sprinkle generously with more soft brown sugar and put under a hot grill until the sugar melts. Serve well chilled, but do not prepare the caramel topping until a short time before serving as it may melt and lose its crunchy character.
SERVES 4.   L.B.

Norwegian cream

1 pint milk
5 eggs
1 teaspoon caster sugar
1 vanilla pod
4 tablespoons apricot jam
¼ pint double cream, whipped with 1 egg white

Heat milk with vanilla pod and sugar. Mix three whole eggs and two yolks together, keeping a white separate for the cream. Cream eggs until pale yellow, then pour in the hot milk and mix all well together. Cover the bottom of a 7½-inch soufflé dish with apricot jam, and pour in the eggs and milk mixture. Cover with tin-foil, stand in a baking dish of cold water in the oven and bake at 350 F (gas 4) until set, about an hour. When cold, sprinkle with chocolate vermicelli, covering the surface well. Decorate with cream whipped with egg white.
SERVES 6.   A.R.

Grand Marnier creams

¾ pint milk
4 oz caster sugar
4 egg yolks
2½ tablespoons Grand Marnier

Heat the milk and sugar gently together until the sugar has melted. Beat the egg yolks and continue beating while the warm milk is added. Cook gently over a low heat (or in a double saucepan) until the custard thickens but does not boil. Remove from the heat and stir in the Grand Marnier. Pour into four individual dishes and chill before serving. If liked, a little caster sugar can be sprinkled on each dish just before serving, and the top glazed under the grill.
SERVES 4.   M.N.

Caribbean cream

A delicious concoction of eggs and cream with Tia Maria to flavour. The caramel web on top gives a crunchy contrast to the velvet smooth custard.

¾ pint double cream
Few drops vanilla essence
4 eggs
4 tablespoons Tia Maria
Soft brown sugar to taste
2 oz caster sugar for the caramel

Scald the cream in a basin over hot water then whisk into the eggs, vanilla, and Tia Maria. Return to the basin and cook over a gentle heat, stirring frequently to clear the mixture away from the sides of the basin. The custard will take approximately half an hour to thicken and will be cooked when it coats a spoon thickly and falls from the spoon in thick drops like jelly. Add sugar to taste and turn into a serving dish.

Heat the caster sugar in a heavy small saucepan over a gentle heat without stirring until it turns a rich caramel colour. Carefully dribble over the surface of the custard and chill well.
SERVES 4.   L.B./H.C.

Polly's strawberry cream

1 lb strawberries
½ pint milk
2 eggs
5 tablespoons caster sugar
½ pint double cream
1 miniature bottle kirsch
3 drops rosewater

Make a custard with the milk, the egg yolks and 1 tablespoon sugar. Cool and stir in half the kirsch. Chill this custard. Whip the cream and the rosewater. Cut the strawberries in half and soak them in remaining kirsch. Whip the egg whites and fold in the remaining sugar. Carefully fold the custard into the cream. Add the strawberries, and finally the whipped egg white and sugar mixture. Serve chilled.
SERVES 4-6.   A.S. (2)

Apple and blackberry whip

1 lb cooking apples
½ lb very ripe blackberries
¼ lb granulated sugar
2 oz caster sugar
Whites of 2 eggs

Press the blackberries on a hair sieve to extract the juice. Put this juice into a pan. Peel, core and cut the apples, and add them to the blackberry juice. Then add the granulated sugar. Stew until tender, rub through a sieve and leave until cold. Whisk the whites of eggs to a froth, and stir the caster sugar into them. Beat the apples and the blackberry pulp for a few minutes, add the whisked egg and continue beating until thick.
SERVES 4.   J.E. (1)

Lemon sauce pudding

8 oz caster sugar
1½ oz plain flour
½ teaspoon baking powder
Pinch of salt
2 eggs
1 tablespoon melted butter
⅓ pint milk
1½ teaspoons grated lemon rind
4 tablespoons lemon juice

Sift 6 oz sugar with the flour, baking powder and salt. Separate the eggs and beat the yolks until light and creamy. Fold in the butter, milk, lemon rind and juice, and stir into the sugar mixture. Beat the egg whites until stiff, fold in the remaining sugar and beat well, and then fold into lemon mixture. Put into a buttered pie dish and bake at 350°F (gas 4) for 1 hour. Serve warm with cream. The result is a light sponge with its own lemon sauce underneath.
SERVES 4.   M.N.

Gâteau de crêpes à la Normande
Apple-pancake gateau

12 thin pancakes (using 3-egg batter)
2 lb cooking apples
8 oz caster sugar
¼ pint sweet cider
9 tablespoons calvados
3-4 tablespoons double cream
2 oz ground almonds
1 oz melted butter

Peel, core and chop the apples then cook with 6 oz sugar, cider, and 3 tablespoons calvados until the mixture becomes

A pyramid of profiteroles is deliciously decorative (recipe on page 152). At right, a variation of Black Forest cherry torte (page 149).

thick enough to hold its shape. Stir in the double cream.

Stack the pancakes and apple mixture in alternate layers on a suitable serving dish, sprinkling between the layers with the ground almonds. Pour the melted butter over the top, sprinkle with the remaining 2 oz sugar, then heat the remaining 6 tablespoons calvados, set alight and pour over the top of the gateau. Serve cut in wedges, with thick pouring cream.
SERVES 8.   L.B. D.G.

Crêpes au confiture
Crêpes with black cherry preserve

4 oz plain flour
Pinch of salt
1 egg
½ pint milk
1 tablespoon vegetable oil
4 tablespoons clarified butter
Strawberry or black cherry preserve
Kirsch or lemon juice

Sift the flour and salt together into a mixing-bowl. Using a wooden spoon, make a hollow in the centre and add the egg. Mix the egg with some of the flour from around the hollow, then gradually add half the milk, beating in the flour all the time. Stir in the remaining milk and the oil.

Heat ½ tablespoon clarified butter in a 7-inch-diameter heavy crêpe pan, until very hot. Pour off excess butter, then add enough batter to cover the base of the pan thinly. When the crêpe is golden brown underneath and all the bubbles on top have burst, flip it over with a palette knife and cook the other side. Place the cooked crêpe on a clean tea-towel. Continue cooking the remaining batter in the same way.

Place 1 tablespoon of preserve for each crêpe, in a small bowl, stir in kirsch

or lemon juice to taste.

Place 1 tablespoon of prepared preserve in the centre of each crêpe and fold in quarters. Place the crêpes in an ovenproof serving-dish, cover with foil and, just before serving, reheat gently at 350°F (gas 4) for about 15 minutes, immediately before serving.
NOTE: The addition of oil to the batter will help prevent the crêpes from becoming tough.
SERVES 4-6.   A.B.

Liqueur pancakes

½ pint milk
Pinch of salt
1 oz sugar
2 eggs
4 oz plain flour
1 oz melted butter
SAUCE
Juice of 2 oranges
2 oz sugar
2 oz butter
5 tablespoons Grand Marnier

Put two-thirds of the milk into a bowl and beat in the salt, sugar, eggs and flour until the batter is smooth. Gradually add enough of the remaining milk to make a thin creamy consistency. Stir in luke-warm melted butter. Fry thin pancakes (this quantity should make 12 pancakes). Fold each pancake in quarters and put on a serving dish. While the pancakes are cooking, melt the sugar and butter in the orange juice and simmer until syrupy. Stir in the Grand Marnier and pour over the pancakes just before serving.
SERVES 4.   M.N.

French orange pancakes

3 eggs
½ lb flour
1 pint milk
Salt
2 tablespoons brandy
2 tablespoons rum
Juice of 1 orange
2 tablespoons caster sugar
Butter for greasing

Separate yolks and whites of the eggs. Put the flour into a bowl and stir in, very slowly, the milk and then the yolks of eggs. Add the salt, orange juice, brandy and rum, stir again and set aside for several hours—6 is not too much.

Just before cooking the pancakes, whip egg whites very stiff and fold lightly into pancake mixture.

Grease the pan and, when it is very hot, pour in just enough of the mixture to cover the base thinly. Let the pancake cook only a few seconds, then turn it and cook the other side. Keep hot.

When all the pancakes are done, roll them, sprinkle with the sugar and serve piping hot.
SERVES 3-4.   J.E. (1)

PUDDINGS AND BAKING

Rote Grütze mit Sahne
German fruit jelly

As the season for fresh strawberries and raspberries is so short, best-quality German tinned varieties can be substituted during the winter and spring seasons.

1 small tin raspberries
1 small tin strawberries
2 cloves
1 small piece cinnamon
Small piece of lemon peel
¼ pint red wine
3 tablespoons cornflour
Sugar to taste—if necessary

Place the tinned fruit together with their juices, cloves, cinnamon and lemon peel in a saucepan and slowly bring to the boil. Add sugar if necessary. Then blend in the red wine and cornflour, stirring until the mixture thickens.

To test whether the jelly is ready, dip a large spoon in the mixture and see if the jelly remains on the back of the spoon. Pour while still hot into attractive tall wine or champagne glasses. Chill and serve with single cream.
SERVES 4. W.S.

Wine jelly with fruit

8 fl oz sherry or marsala
2 oz sugar
½ oz gelatine
Juice of ½ orange
Juice of ½ lemon
Pinch of ground coriander
Fruit and cream to taste

Boil ½ pint water and stir in the sugar and fruit juices until the sugar as dissolved. Melt the gelatine in a little water and then stand the bowl of gelatine over hot water, stirring until the gelatine is syrupy. Mix with the water and fruit juice mixture and add the coriander and sherry or marsala. Leave until almost set in a cool place. Arrange some fruit in individual glasses and pour in some of the jelly. When set, cover with more fruit and remaining jelly. When completely set, top with whipped cream and decorate to taste. This jelly is best with a bland fruit such as bananas.
SERVES 4. A.S. (2)

Fruit Romanoff

Either melon or pineapple is suitable. Cut in half across (lengthways for pineapple), scoop out the flesh with a sharp knife and cut into pieces. Mix with any other fruit in season such as grapes, strawberries, blackberries, etc, and sprinkle with kirsch, maraschino, or curacao. Leave overnight in a covered container in the refrigerator to marinate and serve piled in the fruit shells. Excellent with fresh cream or water ice.
L.B./S.J.R.

Summer pudding

6 to 8 large fairly thin slices of white
  bread, crusts removed
½ lb rhubarb
½ lb blackcurrants
½ lb sugar
6 tablespoons water
½ lb strawberries
½ lb raspberries

Put one slice of bread on one side for the top, use remainder to line base and sides of a 2 pint round fairly shallow dish. Put rhubarb cut in ½-inch slices with the blackcurrants in a saucepan. Add sugar and water, bring to the boil, simmer until barely tender, stirring; this will take only a few minutes. Add strawberries and raspberries; cook for a further minute.

Turn the mixture into the prepared dish, place a slice of bread on top and bend over top of sliced bread at the sides towards centre. Put a sauce on top, pressing down a little until the juice rises to the top of the dish.

Leave to soak until cold or overnight in the refrigerator. Turn out just before serving and serve with lots of cream.
SERVES 4-6. M.B. (1)

Summer pudding (2)

2-3 tablespoons water
4 oz sugar (or to taste)
1½ lb mixed fresh fruit, such as
  raspberries and redcurrants
8 large slices of white bread

Gently simmer together the water, sugar, and fruit for 2-3 minutes just until it becomes juicy. Cut the crusts from the bread and dip each slice into the juice then press the slices around the sides and bottom of a 1½ pint basin or mould, overlapping to ensure a complete coverage. Into the centre of the lined basin, spoon some of the fruit and its syrup, then cover with a slice of bread. Continue this layering until the basin is full, finishing with a bread layer. (We used a fluted aluminium mould.)

Set the filled basin onto a plate to catch the overflowing juices, set a small plate on top of the pudding then weight it down with some heavy tins or other weights. Set in a cool place and leave for at least 8 hours. Turn out and serve with cream.
SERVES 6-8. L.B. .G.W. (1)

Red fruit salad

Use the same fruits as for Summer Pudding (see this page) with the same amount of sugar syrup. Place in a dish and leave to become quite cold. Stir in a little brandy or cherry brandy and serve with plenty of cream.
SERVES 4-6. M.B. (1)

Fruit vol-au-vents

Although vol-au-vents are often thought of as cases for savoury fillings, they make an excellent sweet course, particularly for stand-up informal meals. The cases may be made in advance, frozen, then just recrisped in the oven after thawing.

Puff pastry made with 2 lb flour
1 egg, for glazing
½ pint double cream, whipped
Assorted fresh fruits : orange segments,
  slices of pineapple, peach etc.

Roll the pastry to ½-inch thickness between two sheets of greaseproof paper. This prevents rolling extra flour into the pastry, and helps reduce distortion. With a sharp 5-inch pastry cutter, stamp out twelve rounds with a firm downward pressing action (for good even rising it is important to use sharp cutters so the edges are not pulled unevenly). With a smaller cutter, cut out the centres from six of the circles and carefully lift out. This leaves six plain circles and six rings with borders of about ¾-inch width.

Brush the edges of the complete circles with egg glaze, then very carefully lift one ring on to each with a fish slice—this provides a wall around a centre well when the cases are baked.

With a sharp knife flake the edges of the six completed cases by slashing with short sharp cuts parallel to the counter to assist in a good rise. Cut the paper around each of the cases then transfer paper and pastry to baking-sheets. Glaze the tops of the cases around the rims with egg wash and bake at 425°F (gas 7) for about 20 minutes until the cases have risen well and are crisp and golden brown.

Transfer to a cooling rack and scoop out the centres with a spoon or the tip of a sharp knife. Remove the paper and allow to cool. Fill the vols-au-vent with fruit, flavoured with kirsch, and dredge with sugar. Serve with whipped cream.
SERVES 6. L.B./D.L. (2)

Mixed summer fruits, piled together and flavoured with kirsch, make a colourful and refreshing dessert.

Vacherin with raspberries

This sweet can be made with a variety of soft fruits such as strawberries or peaches and can be made up an hour before serving.

3 egg whites
6 oz caster sugar
8 oz fresh or frozen raspberries
8 oz double cream
Icing sugar

Whisk the egg whites until stiff. Add 1 tablespoon of sugar and continue whisking for a few minutes. Fold in the remaining sugar and spoon into a piping bag fitted with a $\frac{5}{8}$-inch éclair pipe. Have ready two baking trays greased and covered with greaseproof paper. Pipe two rounds of meringue 7 inches in diameter. Sprinkle lightly with caster sugar and bake in a cool oven 250°F (gas $\frac{1}{2}$) for about 2 hours until lightly coloured and crisp. Gently peel off paper and cool. When cold, sandwich the two rounds with half the cream and the raspberries, reserving some for decoration. Dust the top with sifted icing sugar and decorate with 6 rosettes of cream using a 6-cut vegetable rose pipe. Decorate each with a raspberry.
SERVES 4.   V.J.

Entremet surprise
Baked alaska surprise

This variation of Baked Alaska, with alternate piping of plain and chocolate cream, can be prepared well in advance.
Layer of sponge, approx 6 inches diameter
Round tub of rum and raisin ice-cream to fit the cake
FOR CHOCOLATE CREAM
6 oz plain chocolate
2 oz unsalted butter
3 fl oz double cream
FOR WHITE CREAM
$\frac{1}{4}$ pint double cream
2 tablespoons rum

A few hours before required, make the chocolate cream. Break the chocolate into pieces and melt in a basin over hot water, then gradually beat in the butter. Stir in the cream and leave for about 2 hours or until very thick, stirring occasionally to keep smooth. When stiff enough to hold its shape, put into a piping bag fitted with a star nozzle.

To make the white cream, whip the cream and the rum to piping consistency and put it into a second piping bag fitted with a star nozzle.

Just before dinner begins, place the cake on a serving plate and turn the tub of ice-cream out onto it. Pipe all over the ice-cream with alternate lines of chocolate and plain cream, or in any pattern to suit. Keep in the refrigerator until required to serve. The ice-cream

must be soft enough to cut easily but not so soft that it collapses. If need be, the dish may be put into the freezer for a few minutes to maintain a suitable consistency.
SERVES 8.   L.B./A.P.

Pineapple granito

1 medium-sized pineapple
$\frac{1}{4}$ pint water
3 oz caster sugar
Rind and juice of 1 lemon
2 tablespoons Maraschino liqueur
10 Maraschino cherries

Cut the pineapple in half lengthways and carefully scoop out the flesh and juice over a bowl, taking care not to break the shells. Dredge the inside of the two shells with sugar, wrap closely in aluminium foil and freeze.

Purée the flesh and juice from the pineapple in an electric liquidizer (or chop the flesh very finely with a sharp knife and mix with the juice which collects). Put the purée, water, sugar, lemon juice and thinly-pared lemon rind into a saucepan and boil gently for 5 minutes. Remove the lemon rind, turn into the freezer tray and leave until quite cool (about 1 hour), then freeze for about $\frac{3}{4}$ hour until mushy. Spoon this mushy mixture out into a bowl, beat well and add the liqueur and the cherries. Return to the freezer tray, cover tightly with the lid and freeze until firm—a further $2\frac{1}{2}$-3 hours.

Leave the pineapple shells for about 30 minutes at room temperature and the ice for about 15 minutes then scoop it into the shells with a tablespoon or ice-cream scoop and place on a bed of crushed ice on a serving dish.
SERVES 4-6.   L.B. V.A.

Grapefruit water-ice

This ice is excellent to serve in summer after salmon or other rich fish dishes. It is best prepared several days in advance to allow the flavour to develop.
1 pint water
10 oz caster sugar
Juice and finely-pared rind of 2 grapefruit
Juice of 1 lemon
2 egg whites

Put the water and sugar into a medium-sized saucepan with the grapefruit rind and stir over a low heat until the sugar is dissolved. Bring to the boil and boil fairly rapidly for 5 minutes. Remove from the heat and add the fruit juices. Leave to get quite cold.

Strain the cooled syrup into a basin, add the egg whites and mix well. Pour into the freezer tray and freeze until beginning to set ($1\frac{1}{2}$-2 hours) then spoon into a chilled bowl and whisk until creamy in texture and white in colour. Return to the freezer tray, cover tightly and re-freeze until quite firm, $1\frac{1}{2}$ hours.

Spoon into individual serving glasses just before serving.
SERVES 4.   L.B./C.P. (2)

Fresh pineapple ice-cream

You can make endless variations of this basic ice-cream, but pineapple and coffee are particularly good. And as it is made with real cream, not custard, there are no trips to the freezer for whisking every hour or so.
1 small pineapple
Juice of $\frac{1}{2}$ a lemon
1 oz icing sugar
4 eggs, separated
4 oz caster sugar
$\frac{1}{4}$ pint double cream

Cut the pineapple in half lengthways and cut out the hard core down the centre of each side. With a grapefruit knife or sharply pointed spoon scoop out all the flesh and keep the pineapple shells intact. Place the pineapple flesh with the lemon juice and icing sugar in a liquidizer and purée, turn into a container, cover and freeze until just set.

Meanwhile, mix the egg yolks until well blended. Whisk the egg whites until they are stiff, then whisk in the sugar a spoonful at a time. Whisk the cream until it holds a soft peak, then fold it into the egg white mixture with the yolks and frozen pineapple purée. Turn into a rigid container, cover, label and freeze.

Leave the ice-cream to thaw at room temperature for about 5 minutes, then scoop out the ice-cream and pile into the pineapple shells.
SERVES 6-8.   M.B. (1)

Brown bread ice-cream

6 oz fresh wholemeal bread
1 pint double cream
8 oz sugar
4 tablespoons water
Crystallized violets

Cut the bread into slices and put into a low oven 250°F (gas ½) until dry. Break into coarse crumbs. Whip the cream to soft peaks and mix in 6 oz sugar. Freeze this cream for 1 hour. Melt the remaining sugar in the water and cool. Pour on to the breadcrumbs and then mix the breadcrumbs and syrup into the cream mixture. Put into freezer tray and freeze about 2 hours until firm. Sprinkle thickly with crystalized violets before serving.
SERVES 4. M.N.

Coffee nut ice

6 oz mixed nut kernels
6 oz caster sugar
Pinch of salt
1 pint cream
2 eggs
2 teaspoons coffee essence

Use a mixture of walnuts, almonds, hazelnuts and brazils if possible. Blanch and chop the nuts finely. Mix the sugar salt and nuts and stir in the cream carefully until well mixed. Put into a bowl over hot water and cook for 10 minutes. Take off the stove and stir in the beaten eggs very gently. Freeze for 1 hour to a mush. Beat well and add the coffee essence. Continue freezing for 2 hours.
SERVES 4. M.N.

Peppermint whirl

A cool-green ice-cream with a subtle mint flavour, layered with rich chocolate sauce; this is expensive but delicious.
ICE-CREAM
2 large eggs, separated
2 oz icing sugar
¼ pint double cream
5 tablespoons creme de menthe
SAUCE
1 oz plain chocolate
¼ pint water
2 teaspoons cornflour
1 oz caster sugar
Few drops vanilla essence
Knob of butter

For the ice-cream, whisk together the egg yolks and sugar until very pale and the consistency of lightly whipped cream. Whip the cream until it just holds its shape then fold it and the crème de menthe into the cream. Whisk the egg whites to form soft peaks and gently fold into the mixture. Turn into a freezer tray, cover firmly and freeze for about 2 hours or until firm.

For the sauce break the chocolate into

small pieces and melt with most of the water in a small saucepan. Mix the cornflour and sugar smoothly with the rest of the water, then add to the saucepan. Boil gently for 3 minutes stirring constantly. Remove from the heat and beat in the butter and essence. Chill thoroughly. (The sauce is not suitable for freezing.)

Remove from the freezer only when required and spoon in alternate layers in tall glasses with the chocolate sauce. This ice-cream softens quickly at room temperature.
SERVES 4. L.B./S.P. (2)

Biscuit tortoni

2 oz blanched almonds or macaroons
2 tablespoons water
2½ oz caster sugar
3 egg yolks
½ pint double cream

Toast the almonds and then blend them until well ground. If macaroons are being used instead, crush them into fine crumbs. Put the water and sugar into a thick pan and bring to the boil. Boil for 3 minutes. Put the sherry and egg yolks into a bowl, mix well and gradually pour on the hot syrup, blending well. Whip the cream to soft peaks and fold in the syrup mixture and nuts or crumbs. Freeze for 2 hours without beating.
SERVES 4. M.N.

Orange sorbet

A refreshing water ice served in the orange shells.

2 teaspoons gelatine
½ pint water
6 oz caster sugar
7 oranges
Grated rind and juice of 1 lemon
4 egg whites

Soak the gelatine in a little of the water and put the rest on to heat with the sugar.

When the sugar is completely dissolved, bring to the boil and boil for 10 minutes to form a syrup.

Meanwhile, slice the tops from six of the oranges and remove the pulp with a teaspoon, leaving the skins intact, then squeeze the pulp to make ½ pint juice (use the seventh orange if necessary). Add the lemon juice and rind and grated rind of one orange.

Stir the gelatine into the syrup and leave to cool, then add the grated fruit rinds and fruit juices. Put into the freezer trays and freeze to a mush (about ½ hour). Beat the egg whites until they form soft peaks and fold into the mush. Return to the freezer trays, cover tightly and freeze for 2-2½ hours (this ice does not freeze hard). The orange skins and their lids should be wrapped in foil and frozen separately.

Remove from the freezer and spoon into the unthawed shells, then return to the freezer until ready to serve. If preferred, the ice may be served in glasses.
SERVES 4. K.W.

Gooseberry sorbet

2 lb green gooseberries
6 oz caster sugar
1½ pints water
Juice of 1 lemon
Green vegetable colouring
2 fl oz Maraschino
2 fl oz white rum

Cook gooseberries with sugar and water, add lemon juice and a little green colouring, and put through a sieve. Cool and freeze to a thick batter. Add Maraschino and rum, and continue freezing. This ice will not become solid.
SERVES 4-6. M.N.

Summer fruit bowl

Any melon in season is suitable for this dish. We used a mixture of watermelon and honeydew.

1 melon (approx 3 lb weight)
6 oz strawberries
4 oz cherries, stoned, or fresh raspberries
Caster sugar to taste
2-3 tablespoons kirsch

Slice off the stem end of the melon (or a long melon, cut in half). Remove the seeds from the flesh and scoop out the flesh with a tablespoon. Pile back into the shell along with other fresh fruits of your choice—our picture on page 99 shows mango, strawberries and raspberries. Sprinkle with sugar and spoon over the liqueur.

Wrap melon in food film or foil and chill well before serving with fresh cream if liked.
SERVES 6. L.B./F.B.

Canadian tea ice

2 oz tea
1 pint water
3 eggs
½ teaspoon vanilla essence
3 oz caster sugar
¼ pint double cream, thickly whipped

Warm a teapot, put in the tea and pour
on boiling water. Leave to infuse for 5
minutes, strain and cool. Beat eggs with
the sugar and vanilla for about 5
minutes, until white and thick. Add
the cold tea by degrees, whipping all the
time. Fold in cream and freeze for two
hours, stirring once during freezing.

SERVES 4.   M.N.

Coupe glacée créole

2 tablespoons double cream
2 scoops vanilla ice-cream
2 heaped tablespoons chestnut cream
6 tablespoons hot melted chocolate
Chantilly cream
2 tablespoons almonds, flaked and grilled
2 marron glacé

Mix the fresh cream with the chestnut
cream without blending completely. Put
this mixture into a champagne glass.
Place a scoop of ice-cream on top, and
cover with the hot chocolate. Decorate
with chantilly cream, grilled almonds
and marron glacé.

SERVES 2.   A.V.

Banana ice-cream

3 small, very ripe bananas
Small tin sweetened condensed milk
¼ pint double cream
5 drops vanilla essence
Squeeze of lemon juice

Mash the bananas to a froth with the
lemon juice. Beat the condensed milk
for a couple of minutes until light and
frothy, add the banana and vanilla
essence, beat well then pour in the
cream. Keep beating for at least two
more minutes. Turn into an ice-cream
tray and freeze. You do not have to re-
beat this during freezing.

SERVES 4-6.   G.C.

Tosca orange cream ice

3 oranges
½ pint creamy milk
2½ oz caster sugar
5 egg yolks
¼ pint double cream

Peel the oranges very thinly and put peel in a pan with the milk and sugar. Boil gently for 10 minutes. Pour on to egg yolks, and stir gently until mixture thickens without boiling (this is best done in a double saucepan or in a bowl over hot water). Put through a sieve and cool. Add the strained juice of the oranges, and freeze this custard to the consistency of batter. Add whipped cream and continue freezing for 1½ hours. This ice is attractively served in orange skins which have been hollowed out and frosted lightly in the freezer.
SERVES 4.   M.N.

Caribbean ice-cream

A rich, smooth ice-cream with raisins soaked in coffee, served with Tia Maria liqueur.
4 oz seedless raisins
2 tablespoons strong black coffee
4 eggs
4 oz icing sugar
½ pint double cream
4 tablespoons Tia Maria

Soak the raisins in the coffee for 2 hours to plump them well.

Beat the egg yolks and icing sugar together until light in colour, thick and fluffy. Beat the cream until it just holds its shape, then fold into the egg yolk mixture. Whisk the egg whites until they form soft peaks and lightly fold in.

Pour into the freezer tray and freeze for 45 minutes to an hour, or until the mixture begins to thicken, then stir in the raisins and coffee. Cover the tray firmly and freeze completely, for 2½ hours.

Place the container in the refrigerator 20 minutes before required, then spoon or scoop into individual dishes and serve with the liqueur poured over.
SERVES 4.   L.B./E.P.

Raspberry honey ice

1 lb raspberries
¼ pint double cream
¼ pint natural yogurt
10 tablespoons clear honey
2 tablespoons lemon juice
Pinch of salt
4 egg whites

Sieve the raspberries and mix the purée with the cream, yogurt, honey, lemon juice and salt. Put into a freezing tray and freeze for about 1 hour until mushy. Whip the egg whites to stiff peaks, and

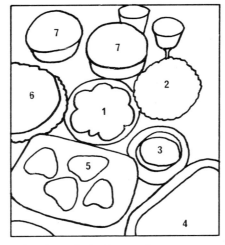

A handsome fruit gâteau enhances a picnic for a special occasion—perhaps at Glyndebourne. **1** *Hors d'oeuvre roll (page 32)* **2** *Hare Pie (page 107)* **3** *Avocado Soup (page 22)* **4** *Oiseaux en gelée (page 106)* **5** *Coeurs à la creme (page 137)* **6** *Strawberry Gâteau (page 137)* **7** *Green salad and orange chicory salad.*

stir in the frozen ice until soft and smooth. Continue freezing until firm.
SERVES 4.   M.N.

Liqueur ice

7 oz sugar
¾ pint water
Juice of 1 lemon
⅛ pint liqueur
¼ pint whipped cream

This is particularly good with Benedictine, but is worth trying with any available liqueur. Make a syrup with the sugar, water and lemon juice. Put into a freezing tray at lowest refrigerator setting until 'mushy' which will take about 1 hour. Whip in a cold basin and fold in the cream and liqueur. Freeze again until just firm. Scoop out into tall glasses and pour a little extra liqueur on top. For a very special ice, chop a few pieces of glacé fruit and soak them in the liqueur before folding into the syrup.
SERVES 4.   M.N.

Vienna redcurrant ice

1 lb redcurrants
¼ lb redcurrant jelly
1 pint water
1 large ripe tomato
¼ lb raspberries
Juice and rind of ½ lemon
3 oz caster sugar
Red vegetable colouring
4 egg yolks
2 fl oz white rum or brandy
½ pint double cream

Remove currants from stalks and simmer with redcurrant jelly, hot water, tomato, raspberries, juice and rind of lemon,

sugar and colouring until the fruit is a pulp. Cool and add well-beaten egg yolks and rum or brandy. Rub through a sieve, and freeze to a batter. Add whipped cream and continue freezing for 2 hours.
SERVES 6.   M.N.

Coffee ice in cups

4 tablespoons freshly-ground coffee
1 pint water
3 oz caster sugar
½ pint single cream

Put coffee into a hot dry pot, pour on boiling water, and leave to stand for 10 minutes. Strain and mix with sugar. Cool and mix with cream. Freeze for 45 minutes, stir and continue freezing for 1½ hours. Pile into small cups to serve.
SERVES 4.   M.N.

Apple sultan sorbet

ICE
1½ lb cooking apples
6 oz caster sugar
Peel of 1 lemon
1-in cinnamon stick
1 pint water
Juice of 2 lemons
Green vegetable colouring
2 fl oz brandy
¼ pint double cream
COMPOTE
8 oz sultanas
½ pint water
1 oz white rum
3 oz caster sugar
1 bay leaf
Strip of lemon peel

Peel and slice apples, and put into pan with sugar, lemon peel, cinnamon and water. Cook until apples are tender, add lemon juice, and colour lightly green. Put through a sieve, cool and add brandy. Freeze to a thick batter, add whipped cream and continue freezing for 1½ hours. Serve topped with sultana compote, made by simmering all ingredients together until like thick cream, removing bay leaf and lemon peel, and chilling compote before using with the apple ice.
SERVES 4.   M.N.

Ice-cream chocolate sauce

3 oz cocoa
6 oz soft brown sugar
½ pint milk
A few drops of vanilla essence

Put all the ingredients into a saucepan. Stir until the sugar has dissolved and boil for about 2 minutes or longer if a thicker sauce is required. Serve hot or cold. Delicious with ice-cream, sponge puddings, etc.
K.K.

Passionfruit Babylon

24 passionfruit
1 pint milk
4 eggs
¾ oz gelatine

Scoop out the passionfruit pulp and sweeten very slightly—sugar easily hides the flavour. Make a thin custard with the milk and yolks, being specially watchful against boiling. Soak the gelatine in warm water, then add to the custard, stirring well. When cold, fold in the fruit pulp, whip the egg whites until stiff but not dry. Fold in gradually, then either leave to set in the bowl or pour gently into moulds or one large mould. Using large eggs, this can easily fill a 3-pint mould.
SERVES 6-8.   G.C.

Baked orange Suzanne

4 large oranges
3 oz sugar
1 teaspoon cornflour
¼ pint water
1 tablespoon grated orange rind
1 tablespoon sherry
4 Maraschino cherries

Peel the oranges and cut off any white pith. Trim the bottom of each one evenly so that it will stand straight. Slice each orange crosswise into five slices but keep them in order so that the oranges look complete. Secure the slices with a cocktail stick and stand the oranges in a shallow baking dish. Blend the sugar and cornflour together in a small pan and stir in the water and grated orange rind. Cook over a medium heat, stirring constantly until the syrup is thick and clear.

Remove from the heat. Spoon a third of the syrup over the oranges and bake at 350°F (gas 4) for half an hour, basting the oranges with the remainder of the orange syrup once during the baking time. Remove from oven, stir in the sherry and baste the oranges frequently with the syrup while they are cooling so that they are well glazed with it. Just before serving remove the cocktail sticks and garnish with a cherry.
SERVES 4.   J.E. (1)

Flan con platanos
Banana caramel custard

CARAMEL
3 oz caster sugar
3 tablespoons water
CUSTARD
4 eggs
1½ oz caster sugar
2 ripe bananas
1 pint milk
A strip of lemon rind

Heat the oven to 300°F (gas 2). Put the sugar for the caramel with the water in a heavy pan over a very low heat, allow the sugar to dissolve slowly, without

French country dishes adapted to a summer buffet in Britain, with Cherry Tarts providing a colourful finale :
1 *Cassoulet (page 85)* **2** *Vegetables provençale (page 109)* **3** *Artichokes à la greque (page 39)* **4** *Whipped cream for the Cherry Tarts* **5** *Cherry Tarts (page 145)* **6** *Pears in coffee (page 136)* **7** *Rillettes (page 40)* **8** *Anchovy cream (page 36)*.

boiling. Then bring the syrup to the boil and keep boiling until a pale golden brown. Quickly pour into the base of a 1¾ to 2 pint charlotte mould or cake tin.

Now prepare the custard: blend together the eggs and sugar in a bowl. Peel the bananas and sieve into the egg mixture. Warm the milk and lemon rind in a pan until hand hot, then strain on to the egg mixture.

Butter the sides of the mould or tin above the caramel with a butter wrapper. Pour the custard into the mould and place in a meat tin half filled with hot water.

Bake in the centre of the oven for about 1½ hours or until a knife inserted in the centre comes out clean. Remove from the oven and leave to become completely cold, at least 12 hours or overnight.

Turn out carefully on to a serving dish and decorate with slices of fresh bananas.
SERVES 4.   M.B. (2)

Tangerines in caramel sauce

12 satsumas, tangerine, or mandarin
2 large juicy oranges
8 oz caster sugar
1 pint water

Peel the tangerines and remove as much pith as possible, while keeping the fruit whole. Put them into a glass bowl. In a heavy saucepan melt 4 oz of the sugar slowly. When it is bubbly and brown, pour on the water. It will fizz dangerously, so take care. Add the rest of the

sugar. Re-boil stirring, and then boil the sauce until it is of a syrupy consistency. When cool pour over the tangerines, and chill before serving. A tablespoon of liqueur such as Cointreau, Van de Hum or Grand Marnier is a magical addition.
SERVES 4-6.   P.L.

Butter'd orange

2 large juicy oranges
2 oz caster sugar
5 egg yolks
2 teaspoons rose or orange-flower water
4 oz unsalted butter
¼ pint double cream
1 tablespoon grated candied orange peel
Crystallized rose petals or whipped cream
for decorating (see method)

Decide whether you will serve this confection in emptied orange shells, or custard cups and prepare whichever accordingly.

Grate the zest from the two oranges, which should yield a level tablespoonful when pressed down. Avoid getting any of the pith into this.

Squeeze the oranges. Separate the eggs—using the whites for meringues later. Select a round-bottomed basin that will fit nicely and firmly into the top of a pan of boiling water. In this basin mix the juice, grated rind, yolks, sugar and flower water. Make sure the boiling water *is* in contact with the bottom of the basin as you sit it into the pan. Whisk until thick. Remove from the heat, allow to cool a little, then stir in bits of the unsalted butter which should be soft but not melted. As the mixture begins to cool further, half whip the cream and fold it into the mixture. Finally, as the mixture starts to set, fold in the grated *peel* so that it stays suspended in the mixture and doesn't sink to the bottom. Fill the orange shells or custard cups and put to chill.

To empty orange shells for filling with Butter'd Orange, reverse the orange so that the 'stalk' is at the base. Holding a small pointed cook's knife at a diagonal angle, insert the tip into the orange an inch down from the apex, cut round and remove the 'lid'.

Take an old teaspoon—for these are usually somewhat sharp due to use—and using the palm of the hand as a protective 'wall', scoop out the flesh. Take care not to pierce the skin. Should you do so, seal this with a little unsalted butter. Afix any decoration to the lid at this stage. Any flesh and juice from this method has to be used in another recipe, or for breakfast.

(Note: cut the butter into ½-inch cubes whilst it is firm, and leave on a piece of greaseproof paper to soften; this way you may find things easier as the pieces can be dropped into the orange mixture with a teaspoon.)
SERVES 4.   M.S.

PUDDINGS AND BAKING

Chestnut compote

6 oz caster sugar
1 pint water
½ teaspoon vanilla essence
1 lb chestnuts, peeled

Dissolve the sugar in the water over a medium heat, then bring to the boil and boil for 5 minutes. Add the vanilla essence and chestnuts, cover and simmer for 45 minutes-1 hour until the chestnuts are tender and the syrup thick. Allow to cool before pouring into a glass serving dish. Chill well before serving. If liked, stir in 2 tablespoons kirsch, or to taste, before serving.

SERVES 4.   H.W.

Christmas ginger meringues

Add half-a-teaspoon ground ginger to your usual meringue mixture. Sandwich with whipped cream to which you have added ½ oz caster sugar, 1 oz grated stem ginger, 1 tablespoon brandy per ½ pint of whipping cream.

Decorate with slivers of stem ginger after piping cream into meringues.

M S.

Caramel oranges

4 oranges
6 oz sugar
¼ pint water

Peel oranges carefully, leaving no pith. Take the peel of two oranges, and cut into very fine 1½-in-long strips. Stir the sugar into the water, and cook until the syrup is thick. Dip in and turn the oranges for a couple of minutes until well coated with syrup. Arrange them in a dish. Put the strips of peel into boiling water and cook for 7 minutes. Drain them thoroughly and then cook them in the sugar syrup until they become transparent and begin to caramelise. Spoon the peel over the oranges. Serve very cold.

SERVES 4.   A.S. (2)

Marrons dessert de Tours

5 oz dark chocolate, broken into pieces
3 oz butter, softened
3 oz caster sugar
1 lb unsweetened chestnut purée
1½ fl oz brandy
DECORATION
¼ pint double cream, whipped
3 oz strawberries

Lightly oil a 2 lb tin or mould. Melt the chocolate in a bowl placed over a saucepan of warm water. Leave to cool slightly. Cream the butter, then beat in the sugar, followed by the chestnut purée, chocolate and brandy. Spoon into the mould and chill for at least 6 hours. Turn out onto a chilled serving plate and decorate with the cream and strawberries, cut into halves or quarters as appropriate.

SERVES 4-5.   H.W.

Oeufs à la neige
Snow eggs

1¾ pints milk
9½ oz caster sugar
14 yolks
2 vanilla pods
8 egg whites

For the custard, bring the milk to the boil with the vanilla. Cream the yolks and sugar and stir with a wooden spatula until they turn white. Add the boiling milk to the mixture. Heat, stirring continually. Remove from heat. Pass through sieve then cool.

Add a little sugar to egg whites and whip them until stiff. Poach tablespoonfuls of mixture in milk and water. Lift out and neaten shapes with a spoon. Drain on a cloth.

Pour custard into the serving dish. Arrange the egg-white ovals on custard. Top with caramel.

SERVES 6.   M.R.

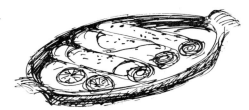

Ginger syllabub

1 pint thick cream
¼ pint advocaat liqueur
4 tablespoons ginger marmalade
2 or 3 pieces preserved ginger

Whip the cream stiffly and stir in the advocaat and the ginger marmalade. Spoon into small glasses or little china pots or coffee cups. Put two or three thin slivers of preserved ginger on top of each syllabub.

SERVES 4-6.   P.L.

Ratafia cream

This rich crème patissier, with the extra texture of crisp ratafia biscuits, is delicious served with peaches, redcurrants or other similar summer fruits but raspberries and strawberries might tend to overpower the delicate cream.

1 oz cornflour
1 oz caster sugar
2 egg yolks
1 pint milk
2 oz ratafia biscuits, crushed coarsely
½ pint double cream
3 tablespoons kirsch
2 egg whites
Peaches, redcurrants, etc

In a saucepan, mix together the cornflour, sugar and egg yolks, then stir in the milk and cook over a low heat, stirring constantly, until thick and smooth. Remove from the heat and

lightly stir in the crushed biscuits. Whip the cream until it holds its shape, then fold into the cooked mixture along with the kirsch.

Whisk the egg whites into soft peaks and fold gently into the creamy mixture to give a light fluffy pudding. Turn into a suitable serving dish and chill well before serving with fresh fruit.

SERVES 6.   L.B./S.P. (1)

Pears in coffee

4 large firm pears
2 oz demerara sugar
½ pint made-up coffee
1 miniature or 3 tablespoons Tia Maria
Double cream

Peel, halve and core the pears, then place in an ovenproof dish. Sprinkle the sugar over and pour on the coffee and the liqueur. Cook covered at 325°F (gas 3) for about 35 minutes, or until just tender (the time will vary with different pears). Take care not to overcook, as pears quickly lose their shape. Cool, cover and store in the refrigerator until required— up to one week. Serve cold with lots of thick cream.

SERVES 4.   L.B. H.S.

Bananas with B & B

6 bananas
1 oz granulated sugar
4 oz butter
4 tablespoons B & B

This liqueur is a mixture of brandy and Bénédictine in which the brandy 'cuts' the sweetness of the basic liqueur. Peel the bananas and roll them in the sugar. Melt the butter in a frying pan and brown the bananas all over. Add the liqueur. Have ready a heated serving dish and arrange the bananas on it. Pour over the liquid from the pan and light with a match.

SERVES 4.   M.N.

Lemon fluff

1 oz gelatine
1 pint water
Finely grated rind and juice of 2 lemons
Whites of 2 eggs
½ lb sugar

Soak the gelatine in the water. Put in a pan with the lemon rind and juice. Add the sugar. Simmer gently for half an hour. Then strain the mixture into a basin and leave in a cold place until it begins to thicken. Beat the whites of eggs until frothy. Stir them into the mixture and continue beating until it is a white snow. Pile into glasses and serve with sponge fingers.

SERVES 4.   J.E.

Coeur à la crème
Hearts of cream

These delicate cottage-cheese hearts, with their fresh taste of lemon, are delicious with fresh redcurrants and a light sprinkling of sugar.

8 oz sieved cottage cheese
½ pint double cream, whipped until thick
Juice of ½ lemon (or to taste)
2 teaspoons grated lemon rind
1 tablespoon sugar (optional)
2 egg whites, stiffly beaten
Fresh redcurrants or raspberries

Place the sieved cheese in a bowl and mix with the whipped cream. Add the lemon juice, grated rind and sugar if liked. Finally fold in lightly the beaten egg whites.

Line six traditional heart-shaped moulds with single thickness cheesecloth (this is essential in order to unmould the hearts). Divide the mixture among the moulds, pressing it well down into the corners. Set the dishes on a baking sheet and place in the refrigerator until firm— 1½-2 hours. Unmould on to a serving dish, remove the cheesecloth, sprinkle with sugar and serve with the redcurrants immediately.

NOTE This recipe freezes well if you prefer to make it to have ready when you wish. When the moulds are set, unmould each on to a piece of freezer film, remove the cheesecloth and wrap carefully. Label and freeze until required. To thaw, unwrap and place the little moulds in serving dish.
SERVES 6.   L.B./L.H. (1)

Almond trifle

1 packet boudoir biscuits
1 pint double cream
4 oz crushed almond macaroons
8 oz blanched whole almonds
3 fl oz Amaretto liqueur, kirsch or
* brandy*
1 teaspoon lemon juice
1 oz caster sugar
Extra ½ pint cream for decorating

To make the case: Select a suitable tin or mould about 6 inches in diameter. Stand this on the plate, on which you will eventually serve the trifle, bottom side up. Glue two tabs of tape onto the bottom to aid lifting out the tin mould.

Fix the boudoir biscuits around the *outside* of the tin. You will have to stick the first one to the plate with a tiny knob of butter. Dip the narrow *edges* of each biscuit in beaten egg-white and stand them vertically around the mould. Tie with a piece of broad tape or bandage and stand the finished case in an airing cupboard to dry out the egg white.

When ready for use, carefully remove the tin by lifting with the tape loops.

To make the filling: Mix cream, sugar and liqueur. Whip until it ribbons well, but is not stiff enough to stand in firm peaks. Chop half the almonds and fold in with the crushed macaroons. Now stir until it just holds its shape without 'sinking'. Fill into case. Pipe unsweetened whipped cream over the top. Spike with remaining whole blanched almonds. Leave to chill for an hour. Remove tape and serve.

The case must not be filled more than an hour before serving, and if you 'split' the cream, this will be too wet to fill the case and will have to be served in a glass bowl.
SERVES 6.   M.S.

Chocolate trifle

This trifle has alternating layers of rich chocolate and vanilla custard. The flavours are improved if the different parts are made a day in advance and stored separately in the refrigerator until needed.

7-inch (or equivalent) sponge
1 lb 3 oz can raspberries
2 tablespoons kirsch
CUSTARD
4 oz butter
3 oz flour
1 pint milk
1 oz sugar
4 egg yolks
1 tablespoon kirsch
4 oz plain chocolate, melted
Few drops vanilla essence
TO FINISH
½ pint double cream
Chocolate squares to decorate if liked

Break the sponge into pieces and use to cover the base of a dish 6-8 inches in diameter. Add the 2 tablespoons kirsch to the tin of raspberries and pour over the sponge. Cover the dish with foil or film and store in the refrigerator for 1-2 days.

Place the butter, flour and milk in a saucepan and bring slowly to the boil, stirring all the time, then continue to cook and stir for 2-3 minutes until thickened and smooth. Remove from the heat and thoroughly mix in the sugar, egg yolks, and the remaining 1 tablespoon of kirsch. Divide the mixture evenly between 2 basins.

To one half, stir in the melted chocolate, and to the other a few drops of vanilla essence. When the custards are cool, cover tightly and store in the refrigerator with the sponge base.

Shortly before serving, spoon first the vanilla custard, then the chocolate, over the soaked sponge. Whip the cream and spread over the surface, then decorate with chocolate squares if liked.
SERVES 8-10.   L.B./G.G.

Strawberry gâteau

Crushed caramel is a delicious texture combination with the soft sponge and the cream and is very easy to make.

3 8-inch genoese sponges
8 oz sugar
1-1½ lb strawberries
¾ pint double cream

Make the caramel for coating the sides of the sponges by melting the sugar in a heavy saucepan over a low heat, then bringing to the boil and cooking gently until it turns a rich brown colour. Take off the heat and pour immediately on to greased greaseproof paper. When cold, break up coarsely by pounding with a rolling-pin, then put into a plastic bag and roll with the pin to form small pieces of crystal. Store in a closely-covered jar until required.

Sandwich the cakes together with whipped cream and sliced strawberries. Coat the sides of the cake with more whipped cream and roll in the crushed caramel until well coated. Decorate the top as liked with whole berries and cream.
SERVES 8-10.   L.B./G.L.

Pear and chestnut flan

1 16-oz tin pears
1 sponge flan
3 tablespoons sherry
¼ pint whipped cream
6 tablespoons chestnut purée

Put the flan on a serving plate and pour the sherry over it. Put half the purée on the flan and arrange the drained pears on it. Whip the cream and fold the rest of the purée into it and pile on top of the pears. Serve cold. May be kept in the refrigerator for 1 hour but no longer.
SERVES 4.   W.G.

Fruit flan

4 oz plain flour
2 oz cornflour
¼ oz caster sugar
3 oz butter
1 egg yolk
1 large can sliced peaches
4 tablespoons apricot jam

Sift the flour and cornflour together and stir in the sugar. Rub in the butter and mix to a stiff dough with the beaten egg yolk. A little cold water may be necessary to bind the mixture, but it should remain stiff. The pastry is rather difficult to handle. Roll it out and line a 7-inch flan ring or dish. Prick the bottom of the pastry and bake at 425°F (gas 7) for 20 minutes. Cool. Drain the peaches completely and arrange in circles in the flan case. Sieve the apricot jam and heat gently with a little water. Cool slightly and pour over peaches. (Canned or poached fresh apricots can be used in the flan, with apricot glaze, or fresh strawberries or raspberries, with raspberry glaze made in the same way from raspberry jam.)
SERVES 4.   A.S. (2)

Spicy plum flan

This delicious and handsome flan is very simple to make. The base is a cinnamon-flavoured French pastry, the filling simply whipped cream and stewed plums —the whole glazed with plum jam.

PASTRY
10 oz plain flour
Pinch of salt
1 tablespoon ground cinnamon
5 oz caster sugar
5 oz butter, cut in small pieces
5 egg yolks
FILLING
2 lb red plums
4 oz caster sugar
¼ pint water
1-2 tablespoons plum jam
TO FINISH
½ pint double cream

Sieve the dry ingredients for the pastry on to a work surface, then make a well in the centre and drop in the butter and egg

The plum flan in the middle of the photograph has an unusual cinnamon-flavoured pastry. **1** *Spicy plum flan (recipe on this page)* **2** *Exotic apple crumble (page 141)* **3** *Kipper pâté (page 33)* **4** *Chocolate trifle (page 137)* **5** *Savoury fondue (recipe for Swiss fondue on page 48, to which is added chopped garlic and fresh sage, plus finely-chopped continental sausage).*

yolks. Using the fingers of one hand, draw the dry ingredients into the butter and egg yolks and continue working until a smooth dough is formed. Wrap closely in film or foil and chill in the refrigerator for at least one hour before using, but this pastry may be stored for a day or two before baking if preferred.

Roll the pastry thinly on a lightly-floured table and use to line a flan dish or ring 12 inches in diameter and bake blind at 350°F (gas 4) for 20-25 minutes or until quite dry. Do not over brown. Cool and use as required: either immediately, or wrap closely and store in a cool place for 2-3 days.

The plums also may be prepared in advance and stored in a covered container in the refrigerator. Cut in half lengthways and remove the stones. Place the water and sugar in a saucepan and bring to the boil, then add the plums, reduce the heat, cover the pan and simmer gently until tender. This will take approximately 5 minutes and care should be taken not to overcook the fruit as the skins should remain whole. Drain off the plums and use the juice to make a glaze.

Boil the juice until syrupy, add the jam and stir until melted. Cool and store in a covered jar in the refrigerator. If preferred, the syrup may be thickened with arrowroot instead of with jam but the colour will be less bright and the eating quality less luscious.

To assemble: whip the cream and spread over the base of the baked flan case, then carefully arrange the plums, cut side down, on top of the cream. Spoon the glaze over the whole and chill for about 1 hour before serving.
SERVES 10.   L.B. H.C. (2)

Cranberry flan

Puff pastry made with 8 oz flour
1 lb cranberries
8 oz sugar
½ pint water
Egg-milk for glaze

Simmer the berries and sugar in the water for about 10 minutes or until the skins all burst. Strain and allow the cranberries to cool; reserve the syrup.

Roll out the pastry on a lightly-floured board to about 12 inches square. Turn the rolled pastry over the rolling pin then unroll on to a 9-inch foil pie plate. Support the pastry with one hand, and gently shape it into the dish with the other. Trim the edges with scissors, then fill with the cooled cranberries.

Gather together the remaining pieces of pastry and roll out again and cut into strips ¼-½ inch wide by about 10 inches. For an attractive edge, cut the strips with a pastry wheel. Dampen the edges of the flan and weave the strips of pastry across the top to form a lattice. Trim the ends of the strips and gently press down on to the edge.

Flake the pastry edges with a slashing action with a small sharp knife, cutting into the pastry parallel to the edge of the plate. Pour a little of the reserved syrup into the flan, taking care not to run on to the lattice. Glaze the top of the flan with egg and bake at 425°F (gas 7) for about 30 minutes or until the pastry is golden brown and moves easily on the plate. For serving, slide on to a large plate.

Serve hot or cold with thick cream, egg custard, or the syrup from the berries.
SERVES 6-8.   L.B./H.L.

Pumpkin pie

Shortcrust pastry made with 8 oz flour
14 oz can pumpkin
2 large eggs
4 oz soft brown sugar
½ pint single cream
Pinch of salt
½ level teaspoon each of grated nutmeg, ginger and cinnamon

Use the pastry to line a deep ovenproof dish of approximately 2-pint capacity. Prick the base of the pastry, line with foil and bake as for the Apple Custard Pie on page 140. When baked, remove from oven and turn heat down to 350°F (gas 4).

Beat all the filling ingredients together to mix thoroughly, then pour as much as possible into the baked pastry. Bake for approximately one hour until the custard is firm. If the pie is served hot, serve additional whipped cream separately, or leave the pie to get quite cold and cover the top with a layer of whipped cream.
SERVES 6.   L.B.

PUDDINGS AND BAKING

Raisin pie

A double-crust, plate tart is good to eat hot or cold, and it carries well for picnics. Stoned raisins may be used, but the smaller, dark, seedless ones are even better. The filling is simple to make and may be kept in the fridge for several days ready for use.

Canadian pastry (made with 10 oz flour, see page 157)
10 oz seedless raising
½ pint water
2 oz soft brown sugar
1 tablespoon cornflour
2 tablespoons cold water
Grated nutmeg to taste
3 tablespoons rum

Simmer the raisins in the water for 7-10 minutes until they are well plumped. Mix the sugar and cornflour smoothly with the 2 tablespoons cold water and stir into the raisins. Cook for a further 2-3 minutes, stirring until thickened. Add grated nutmeg and rum to taste. Leave to cool.

Thinly roll half the pastry on a lightly-floured board and use to line an oven-proof plate approximately 9 inches in diameter. Spread the filling over, and dampen the edges of the pastry with water. Roll out the rest of the pastry and carefully place over top of the filling. Press the edges together firmly, then trim and decorate as liked. Pierce the top of the pie with a sharp knife or skewer to allow steam to escape, then brush over the surface with milk. Bake for about 45 minutes, or until the pastry is well browned and moves on the plate, at 400°F (gas 6). Serve hot or cold with ice-cream or cream.
SERVES 6.   L.B.

Lemon chiffon pie

A baked pastry case with a hot lemon soufflé filling, which, if possible, should be taken to the table at the peak of its glory, but even after it has settled down into itself, it is still delicious.

Canadian pastry (using ½ quantities given on page 157)
3 large eggs
6 oz sugar
Grated rind and juice of 1 large lemon
3 tablespoons water

Roll the pastry thinly and use to line a deep ovenproof plate approximately 9 inches in diameter. Prick the base, line with foil and bake as for Canadian Apple Custard Pie. Remove from the oven, and turn the heat down to 325°F (gas 3).

Put the yolks of the eggs and 4 oz of the sugar into a basin with the lemon juice, lemon rind, and water. Set over a saucepan of water on a low heat and whisk until the mixture is very thick and pale and forms a trail after the whisk. Whisk the egg whites with a pinch of

salt until they form soft peaks, then gradually whisk in the remaining 2 oz sugar. Continue whisking until the mixture forms into stiff peaks, then lightly fold in the cooked lemon mixture.

Pile the filling into the baked case, return to the oven and bake for about 20 minutes or until the filling has puffed up well and turned a light golden brown. Serve as soon as possible—within about 15 minutes of baking.
SERVES 5-6.   L.B.

Tarte Normande
Plum flan

Plums stuffed with tiny ratafia biscuits are baked in a sweet pastry. Very good cold, but even better hot with thick cream.

PASTRY
10 oz plain flour
3 oz caster sugar
8 oz butter
1 egg
Approx 1 tablespoon milk
FILLING
1 lb plums
2 oz ratafia biscuits
1 oz caster sugar
GLAZE
3 tablespoons glacé icing

Rub the butter finely into the flour and sugar, then mix to a smooth dough with the egg and milk. Work with the hand until quite even, then wrap and chill in the refrigerator for an hour before using so that the pastry is easier to handle.

Cut the plums in half and remove the stones, then press a ratafia biscuit into the cavity in each half plum. Roll about two-thirds of the pastry out thinly and fit into a swiss-roll 12 × 8 × ½ inch. Arrange the filled plums over the surface of the pastry, cut-side down, and sprinkle with the caster sugar. Dampen the edges of the pastry, roll out the rest of the pastry and fit on over top. Pinch together around the edges to seal, and drizzle over the surface the glacé icing. (Yes, the icing goes on *before* baking. It gives a lovely crispy glazed surface which crackles and blisters during cooking.) Bake for 40-45 minutes at 350°F (gas 4), until the juices begin to bubble through and the top is browned. Cut in squares and serve hot.
SERVES 6.   L.B./A.K.

Canadian apple custard pie

Shortcrust pastry made with 8 oz flour
1 large cooking apple
Ground cinnamon
2 large eggs
½ pint soured cream
2 oz sugar
Demerara sugar to sprinkle on top

Lay lifting 'straps' of aluminium foil across the bottom and up the sides of a deep 7½-inch sandwich tin, then line the tin with the pastry. Prick the bottom, press a piece of foil around the inside of the pastry and bake for 10 minutes at 400°F (gas 6). Remove the lining foil and bake the pastry for a further 10 minutes. Remove the pastry from the oven and turn the heat to 350 F (gas 4).

Peel, core and thinly slice the apple over the bottom of the baked pastry case and return to the oven for 15 minutes. Mix together thoroughly the eggs, soured cream, and sugar. Sprinkle cinnamon generously over the surface of the apples, then carefully spoon the egg mixture on top and return to the oven. Continue to bake at 350°F (gas 4) for about ¾ hour or until the custard is set firmly. When the custard is nearly baked, sprinkle the surface generously with demerara sugar.

To serve, cool slightly then carefully lift from the tin with the foil strips and transfer to a serving plate. Best served while still warm.
SERVES 4.   L.B.

Apple pie with cheddar crust

5 oz flour
Pinch of salt
5 oz butter
5 oz cheddar cheese
¼ egg yolk (approx)
4 Bramley apples
1 oz brown sugar
1 tablespoon cornflour
¼ teaspoon cinnamon
Pinch of nutmeg
Unsalted butter
Lemon juice

Sift flour and salt together, then rub in 5 oz butter. Combine with grated cheese and enough egg yolks to bind the pastry. Wrap in greaseproof paper and chill overnight. Peel, core and slice Bramley apples—tartness is important—and toss with a mixture of brown sugar, cornflour, cinnamon and nutmeg. Place in an 8-inch tart ring lined with two-thirds of the cheddar pastry, alternating layers of apples with small knobs of unsalted butter, and a liberal sprinkling of lemon juice. Cover with a lattice crust, binding edges with a strip of pastry. Pastry breaks easily, but do not worry—just patch as needed. Bake for 10 minutes at 425°F (gas 7), then for 25 minutes at 375°F (gas 5). Best served warm.
SERVES 6.   A.S. (1)

Traditional apple pie

PASTRY
8 oz plain flour
2 oz butter
2 oz lard
FILLING
2 lb cooking apples
4-5 oz sugar

Slice the apples thinly and pack as firmly as possible in alternate layers with sugar into 2-pint pie dish.

Make the shortcrust pastry in the usual way and roll out on a lightly-floured board. Trim with a sharp knife to roughly the size and shape of a dish. Dampen the edges of the dish and use the trimmings to form a rim of pastry around the dish, then dampen this pastry edge. Roll the pastry shape onto a rolling-pin, then unroll over top of the pie. Trim the edges and decorate as liked.

Make a few slashes in the top of the pie to allow the steam to escape and brush over the top with milk or egg and milk mixed. Bake at 400°F (gas 6) for about 45 minutes or until golden brown and crisp. Serve with cream.
SERVES 8.   L.B./E.T.

Upside-down apple tart

The prepared tart can be wrapped in foil or film and stored in the refrigerator ready to be baked just before required.
2 lb cooking apples
3 oz butter
4 oz sugar
Puff pastry made with 8 oz flour
2 oz brown sugar

Using all the butter, thickly cover the inside of a deep oval pie dish of 2-pint capacity. Peel, core and thinly slice the apples, then pack into the pie dish alternately with the sugar. Place on a baking-tray and cook at 400°F (gas 6) for 20-30 minutes until the apple slices are just tender but have not lost their shape. Leave to cool.

On a lightly-floured board, roll out the pastry, wrap around the rolling-pin then unroll over the top of the cooked apples. Trim off any excess pastry and flake the edges with a knife, but no particular care is necessary as the edge does not show very much in the pudding when it is reversed for serving. Wrap and leave in the refrigerator overnight or bake at once at 425°F (gas 7) for 35-40 minutes until the pastry is well risen and golden brown.

To turn the tart out, place a large oval platter over the pastry and invert the dish quickly. Give a good shake to loosen all the apples. Sprinkle the soft brown sugar over the apples and put under a hot grill for a few minutes to caramelize the apples. Serve immediately.
SERVES 6-8.   L.B./M.B. (3)

Tarte aux pommes
French apple flan

PASTRY
4 oz butter
6 oz plain flour
1 oz sugar
1 egg yolk
½ teaspoon water
FILLING
1½ lb cooking apples (approx 4 large)
1 cinnamon stick or ground cinnamon
2 tablespoons caster sugar
TOPPING
1 lb dessert apples
2 oz soft brown sugar
¼ pint sweet cider
1 tablespoon apple jelly
3 tablespoons demerara sugar

To make the pastry, finely rub the butter into the flour and sugar and mix to a firm paste with the egg yolk and water. Wrap and chill for about half an hour before using to line a loose-bottomed flan tin of approximately 8-inch diameter (the loose bottom is necessary to make possible removal from the tin on completion). Prick the base, line with foil, chill again for a few minutes then bake for 20-25 minutes at 375°F (gas 5) or until the pastry is lightly browned and firm to the touch. Cool before filling.

For the filling, peel, core and roughly chop the cooking apples, then put into a saucepan with the cinnamon stick and sugar. Simmer over a low heat for 15-20 minutes, stirring occasionally until tender. Remove the cinnamon stick and beat the apples to a pulp. Cool.

For the topping, put the cider and soft brown sugar into a saucepan and stir over a low heat until the sugar is dissolved. Peel the dessert apples, cover and cut in segments. Bring the syrup to the boil, add the apple slices and gently poach for 3-4 minutes until just tender but still holding shape. Drain off the

apples with a draining spoon, add the apple jelly to the syrup remaining, melt over the heat then bring to a rapid boil until the syrup thickens to coat thickly the back of a metal spoon.

To assemble the flan, leave in the flan ring for support, fill with the apple purée, arrange the cooked apple slices over top, and finally spoon the syrup glaze over. Sprinkle with the demerara sugar and brown under a hot grill until the sugar bubbles and browns. Remove the flan ring just before serving, but leave the flan on its base. Serve with whipped cream fairly soon as the pastry is tender and may break if left too long.
SERVES 6.   L.B./P.M. (2)

Exotic apple crumble

1 lb cooking apples
2 tablespoons of water
1 level teaspoon ground cinnamon
2 oz soft brown sugar
2 oz raisins
9 oz crumble mix (see below)
¼ pint natural yogurt

Peel, core and slice the cooking apples into a pan with the water, cinnamon, brown sugar and raisins. Cook slowly, stirring occasionally, in a covered pan until the apple forms a pulp. Turn into a buttered 1-1¼-pint oven-proof dish.

Spread the yogurt over the top of the fruit pulp, then sprinkle on the crumble mixture. Bake about 20 minutes, or until crisp and brown at 400 F (gas 6).
CRUMBLE MIX: This will keep in a plastic bag, closed tightly with a wire closure, for several weeks in the fridge, so it may be convenient to make a large quantity. For the pudding given here: rub together to form fine crumbs 5 oz plain flour, 2½ oz butter, and 1½ oz caster sugar. Alternatively, the spice may be omitted from the apples and included in the crumble mix.
SERVES 4-5.   L.B./M.T.

Pineapple millefeuilles

Puff pastry made with 1 lb flour
1 egg for glazing
1 pint double cream
2 oz sugar
1 fresh pineapple
Few strawberries or raspberries to
*   decorate*

Roll the puff pastry on a sheet of lightly floured greaseproof paper to a rectangle 15 by 12 inches. Trim the edges using a positive downward stroke with a sharp large knife, being careful not to drag or stretch the pastry as you cut. Cut through the paper also. Divide the pastry into three smaller pieces 12 by 5 inches, again cutting through the paper.

Transfer the pastry slabs on to baking-sheets, using the paper as a slide to prevent stretching or pulling the pastry out of shape. Flake the edges of each piece of pastry with a sharp knife and a short chopping action parallel to the board. Be sure to flake right into the corners so the pastry will rise to a true rectangle.

Leave the pastry pieces in the refrigerator for ½ hour before baking, then glaze over the surface of each with beaten egg. Bake at 425°F (gas 7) for 10-15 minutes or until well risen and golden brown. Slide off on to cooling racks and when cool peel off the paper.

At this stage the pastry slabs may be made up into the gateau or they may be packed carefully into a plastic container and frozen for use at a later date. On thawing, the pastry may be refreshed by placing it in a hot oven for 5-10 minutes and cooling as before.

To make up the finished gateau, whip the cream until stiff and gently fold in the sugar. Remove the rind from the pineapple and cut it into slices; cut out the hard centre core with a small biscuit cutter. Reserve four even-sized rings for the top and cut the rest in half.

Set aside the most attractive piece of pastry for the top. Lay one slab of pastry on a suitable serving dish, cover with whipped cream and pineapple pieces. Repeat with the second layer, more pineapple and the rest of the cream then finally place the last piece of pastry on top and decorate with the whole pineapple slices.
SERVES 8.   L.B./A.B.

Tarte au fromage blanc

Shortcrust pastry made with 6 oz flour
2 oz imported fromage blanc,
*   such as Gervais*
1 oz caster sugar
2 eggs
½ pint double cream

Bake blind an 8 inch pastry shell for about 10 minutes at 400°F (gas 6) until just beginning to colour; cool and fill with a mixture of the *fromage blanc,*

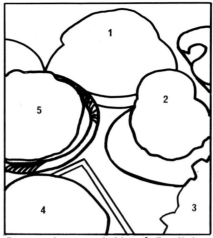

Sweet and savoury baking : 1 Candied Fruit Cake (page 152) 2 Savoury Brioches (page 101) 3 Danish pastries (page 156) 4 Savarin aux framboises (page 154) 5 Ginger Crown (page 151).

creamed with the sugar into which the eggs and cream have been gradually beaten. Bake at 375°F (gas 5) for about 25 minutes, or until the top is risen and browned.
SERVES 4.   A.S. (1)

Suffolk pie

2 egg yolks
1 oz sugar
8 fl oz milk
1 oz breadcrumbs
2 oz ground almonds
1 oz butter
Almond or vanilla essence
1 egg white
1 tablespoon raspberry jam

Make a custard by blending the egg yolks with the sugar and pouring the warm milk over, mixing well. Return to the pan and cook over gentle heat, stirring all the time, until the custard just coats the back of the spoon. Do not allow it to boil. Stir in the crumbs, almonds, butter and flavouring, then fold in the stiffly-whisked egg white. Spread the jam over an 8-inch pastry case, pour in the filling and bake for 35-40 minutes in a fairly hot oven, 350°F (gas 4).
SERVES 4-6.   M.N.

Orange tart

Puff pastry made with 8 oz flour
2 oranges
2 tablespoons sugar
2 oz butter
2 eggs
2 oz finely-crushed biscuits
Caster sugar

Line a tart tin with the pastry. Rub the grated rind of the oranges with the sugar and then cream these with the butter. Add to them the yolks of the eggs, crushed biscuit and the strained juice of

the oranges. Beat the whites of eggs to a stiff froth, stir them in and pour the mixture into the pastry case. Bake the tart in a fairly hot oven until the pastry is lightly brown and the mixture is set. Just before serving, the surface should be sprinkled with caster sugar.
SERVES 4.   J.E. (1)

Banana tart

Shortcrust pastry made with 4 oz flour
½ pint milk
2 oz flour
4 oz caster sugar
Pinch of salt
2 eggs
1 tablespoon lemon juice
2 bananas
10 drops of lemon essence.

Line a sandwich tin with the pastry and bake blind at 425°F (gas 7). Cool and remove from tin. Mix together the flour, salt, and 2 oz of sugar and sift them. Whip the egg yolks and mix them in. Heat the milk, then add it gradually. Turn into a double saucepan and stir well until it thickens, then cook slowly 10 minutes longer. Then add the lemon juice and the bananas, peeled and cut in slices. Leave until cold, and turn into the pastry case. Beat the whites of eggs until quite stiff and stir in gently the remainder of the sugar and the lemon essence. Pile this on the tart and then colour slightly in a cooling oven. Serve cold.
SERVES 3-4.   J.E.

Bakewell tart

PASTRY
8 oz plain flour
6 oz butter
1 tablespoon caster sugar
1 egg yolk
2-3 tablespoons water
FILLING
2 oz ground almonds
2 oz caster sugar
2 oz butter
1 egg
Raspberry jam

First, make the pastry. Sift flour. Work in softened butter. Add sugar. Stir 1 tablespoon of water into the beaten egg yolk. Tip it into the flour, and work the mixture to a dough, adding the rest of the water as you need it. Wrap the pastry in foil and leave to rest in a cool place for 30 minutes.

Line a 7½-inch or 8-inch tart tin or flan mould with two-thirds of the pastry. Cover with a fairly thick layer of jam. Cream butter and sugar, beat in the egg and add the ground almonds. Mix together. Spread this mixture on top of the jam, criss-cross the top with narrow strips of pastry and bake at 400°F (gas 6) for 30 minutes, until risen and brown.
SERVES 4.   F.M.

Peach flan

A pastry sweet course makes a good finish to a summer meal. Many fruits are suitable, and the pastry case may be made well in advance, then frozen ready for use as required. This pastry is simple to make and holds its shape well during baking. It is particularly suitable for fruit fillings.

4 oz plain flour
1 oz caster sugar
2 oz butter, soft enough to spread
1 egg yolk (large egg)
1 tablespoon cold water

Mix together the flour and sugar and make a well in the centre. Drop in the butter, then pour over the egg and water well mixed together. Draw the flour into the centre and work with the fingers until a smooth paste is formed. Knead lightly, wrap in foil or film and chill in the refrigerator for an hour or until firm.

Roll thinly on a lightly-floured board and use to line a shallow, fluted flan-tin approximately 8 inches in diameter. Press the pastry neatly into the tin, trim the edges, then prick all over with a fork. Line with a square of aluminium foil and bake at 375°F (gas 5) until a light golden brown and quite firm. Remove the foil after the first 10 minutes, and cook for 20 minutes in all (the thinner the pastry, the more quickly it bakes).

Leave the pastry to cool in the tin, then carefully lift out. Wrap in foil or freezer film and freeze for use when required, or use straight away. While the pastry is being baked, prepare the filling:

¼ pint double cream
2 tablespoons kirsch
3-4 small peaches
2-3 tablespoons redcurrant jelly
2 tablespoons water

Lightly whip the cream with the kirsch and spread into the cooled pastry. Peel, halve and stone the peaches then lay cut side down onto the cream. Heat the jelly and water until a thick syrup-like consistency and spoon over the fruit.
SERVES 4.   L.B.

Date and orange glazed pie

Flaky pastry made with 14 oz flour
3 satsumas
4 oz dried figs
6 oz grapes
1 tablespoon golden syrup
1 egg white
Caster sugar

Roll out half the pastry and line a shallow 9-inch pie plate. Peel and segment the satsumas, chop the figs, and cut the grapes in half, removing the pips. Pile the fruit into the pastry case and add the syrup. Roll out remaining pastry and

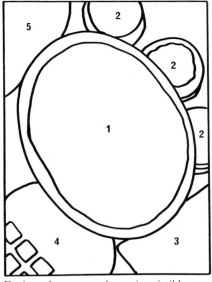

Fruit and pastry make an irresistible combination: 1 Upside-down Apple Tart (page 141) 2 Fruit Vol-au-vents (page 128) 3 Pineapple Millefeuilles (page 142) 4 Cranberry Flan (page 138) 5 Plum Jalousie (page 148).

cover the fruit, sealing the edges with a little water. Bake at 425°F (gas 7) for 10 minutes. Reduce to 350°F (gas 4) for 10 minutes. Take from oven and brush with lightly-beaten egg white. Sprinkle with a little caster sugar and return pie to oven for 10 minutes. Serve hot or cold. (Mrs Beaton liked to glaze her sweet pies in this way in place of the earlier method of covering with a thick cake icing and further baking.)
SERVES 4-6.   M.N.

Orange puff-balls

Crisp, puffy pastry with an orange flavoured soufflé. The irregular shapes are caused by baking the pastry on the outside of deep patty tins (to get better baking).

Puff pastry made with 8 oz strong flour
3 eggs
6 oz caster sugar
3 oz butter
Grated rind of one orange
3 tablespoons brandy

Roll the pastry to the thickness of a coin and with a sharp plain cutter of approximately 3-4 inch diameter cut out as many circles as possible. Refold the pastry trimmings carefully to preserve the flaky layering, wrap and chill before re-rolling. Press each pastry circle firmly onto the outside of an upturned patty tin or small pudding mould. Set the moulds on a baking tray, cover with foil or film and chill for 30 minutes before baking.

Meanwhile, make the fillings by beating together the eggs and sugar in

a basin until they form a smooth creamy mixture. Set over a pan of hot water on a low heat and gradually whisk in the butter, orange rind and brandy. Remove from the heat.

Bake the pastry cases at 425°F (gas 7) for about 10 minutes until brown, well risen and crispy. Prise each case away from its tin and ensure the centres are baked. Set all the cases upright on the baking tray. Divide the filling among the baked cases and return to the oven for approximately 10 minutes or until the filling is set.

Serve the puffs as soon as possible with coffee, or as a rich pudding.
MAKES 14 PUFFS (approx).   L.B./M.P.

Lady Abbess tarts

3 oz ground almonds
2 oz butter
2 oz caster sugar
Jam
Whipped cream

The mixture is very delicate to handle. Work the almonds, butter and sugar together to form a paste. Roll out carefully, using a little icing sugar on the rolling pin if the mixture sticks. Line small tartlet tins and bake at 350°F (gas 4) for 20 minutes. Remove carefully from the tins, cool and fill with jam and whipped cream on top.   M.N.

Cherry tarts

1 lb fresh cherries
Red cherry jam
2 tablespoons kirsch
PASTRY
4 oz plain flour
2 oz butter
2 oz sugar
2 egg yolks

Sieve the flour on to a clean working surface and make a well in the centre. Place the slightly softened butter, the sugar, and the egg yolks into the well, then start to mix together with the hands, gradually drawing in the flour from the outside to the centre. Continue to work with the hand to obtain a smooth even pastry, the consistency of almond paste.

Roll out thinly and use to line six 4-inch fluted tart tins. To prevent the bases rising during baking, prick with a fork and line with small pieces of aluminium foil. Bake until a light golden brown at 375°F (gas 5) for about 15 minutes. The cases will move in the tins when they are fully baked. Cool, then remove carefully from the tins.

Heat together some cherry jam with kirsch, then sieve to form a glaze. Stone the cherries, place into the pastry cases and spoon the glaze over. Serve with whipped cream.
MAKES 6 TARTS.   L.B./R.W.

PUDDINGS AND BAKING

Strawberry pudding

2 oz margarine
3 oz sugar
4 oz flour
½ teaspoon baking powder
½ pint strawberries, thawed if frozen
2 eggs
2 tablespoons milk
Pinch of salt

Sprinkle 1 tablespoon of sugar over thawed strawberries. Beat the margarine and 2 oz of sugar to a soft cream. Mix the flour, baking powder and salt; rub the creamed margarine into them.

Whisk the eggs well and then beat them in. When the mixture has been well beaten, add the strawberries and last of all the milk. Turn into a greased mould and steam for two hours. Turn out, sift remainder of sugar over and serve with cream or custard.

SERVES 4.   J.E. (1)

Ginger fruit pudding

8 oz self-raising flour
½ teaspoon salt
2 teaspoons powdered ginger
4 oz butter
3 oz brown sugar
4 oz mixed dried fruit
2 large eggs
About 6 tablespoons milk to mix

Sift the dry ingredients together. Rub in the butter, add the sugar and fruit. Mix to a soft dropping consistency with the well-beaten eggs and the milk. Turn into a well-greased fluted mould. Cover with buttred greaseproof paper or foil and steam for 1½ hours. Serve with a sauce of hot, melted marmalade.

SERVES 4-6.   J.E. (1)

Le gâteau au chocolat
Chocolate gateau

3 boxes of sponge fingers
1½ tablespoons of brandy
¼ pint milk
12½ oz plain chocolate
4 oz butter
5 oz caster sugar
2 egg yolks
3 egg whites
Chantilly cream (optional)

Melt chocolate with a little water and the butter in a bain-marie. When completely smooth, allow to cool. Mix the 2 egg yolks and the caster sugar to a creamy consistency and pour into cold chocolate mixture. Beat the egg whites until they form peaks and fold carefully into the mixture. Leave to set in the fridge.

On a large piece of foil, lay out 9 sponge fingers which have been dipped in the brandy and milk. Spread an even layer of chocolate over the biscuits and then add another layer of biscuits, following through until you finish with a layer of sponge fingers, each one having been dipped in the brandy and milk. Cover the cake with the foil and leave in

the fridge overnight. To finish off, spread the Chantilly cream all over the cake, dot the sides with a handful of crushed almonds and place 9 strawberries on the top. This cake should be left in the fridge until it is served.

SERVES 6.   N.L.

Royal pudding

3 oz seedless raisins, roughly chopped
2 tablespoons rum
3 oz self raising flour
2 tablespoons cocoa
1 oz fresh white breadcrumbs
3 oz soft margarine or butter
3 oz caster sugar
2 eggs
½ pint pudding basin, ready greased

Soak the raisins in rum for about ½ hour. Sieve the flour and cocoa into a bowl. Add remaining ingredients and the raisins, beat together for about 2 minutes until well blended. If necessary, add a little milk to make a soft dropping consistency. Turn mixture into prepared basin and cover with greased foil or graseproof paper. Steam for 1¼ hours.

Turn out the pudding and pour the cream or custard. (The pudding may be baked in a moderate oven, 350°F gas 4, for 45 minutes.)

SERVES 4.   K.K.

Bread and butter pudding

Thin slices of buttered stale white bread
Home-made marmalade
Sultanas
1 tablespoon brown sugar
2 large eggs
1½ pints milk (approx)

Line a 2-pint soufflé dish with the bread which should be really stale. (Freshly bought bread just doesn't work.) Continue filling dish with slices, layered with home-made marmalade, sultanas and sugar. Beat the eggs. Pour over mixture with the milk (nearly boiling). The pudding should look really flooded. Leave for a while to see if more milk should be added. Sprinkle with addition-

al brown sugar to form a really good crust. Bake at 325°F (gas 3) until the pudding has risen and looks like a soufflé. It should be served straight away.

SERVES 4.   U.S.

Golden pudding

2 eggs
4 oz caster sugar
4 oz self-raising flour
2 oz butter
2 tablespoons marmalade
SAUCE
2 tablespoons marmalade
Juice of 1 orange
1 tablespoon of caster sugar
¼ pint water

Beat the eggs with the sugar; add the melted butter. Then beat in the flour gradually. Stir in the marmalade and, when mixed, turn into a buttered basin, cover with buttered paper and steam for 1½ hours.

For the sauce, put the marmalade, strained orange juice, sugar and water in a saucepan; boil until a thick syrup.

Turn out the pudding and pour the sauce over.

SERVES 4.   J.E. (1)

Toffee apple pudding

6 oz self-raising flour
3 oz shredded wheat
Pinch of salt
4 oz brown sugar
2 large cooking apples

Sift the flour with a pinch of salt and stir in the suet. Add enough water to give a firm paste which should leave the bowl perfectly clean. Roll out about ¼ inch thick. Use about two-thirds to line the pudding basin and roll out the rest to fit the top. Before lining the basin, butter it thickly and press half the sugar against the sides. Line smoothly with the crust and fill with the sliced apples sprinkled with the rest of the sugar. Put on the pastry lid and pinch the edges well together. Cover with greased paper and steam for 2 hours.

SERVES 4.   J.E. (1)

Prune pudding

4 oz self-raising flour
4 oz breadcrumbs
2 oz suet
1 egg
¼ lb sugar
¼ lb prunes
¼ pint milk
Good pinch of salt

Stone the prunes and chop them. Add the salt to the flour, stir in the breadcrumbs, the suet, the prunes, sugar and the prune kernels. Beat the egg, add milk, pour it in. Mix well and steam for three hours in a well greased basin.
SERVES 4.   J.E. (1)

Pear dumplings

PASTRY
4 oz lard
4 oz butter
12 oz plain flour
Approx ¼ pint cold water
FILLING
4-5 large pears
2 oz golden syrup
1 oz butter

Cut the fats into pieces the size of sugar cubes then rub coarsely into the flour. Mix to a smooth paste with the water and knead lightly on a floured board. Wrap and chill before using.

Roll the pastry to the thickness of a coin and cut into strips about ¾ inch wide. Peel and core one pear at a time, then wrap in pastry by winding in a spiral, starting at the bottom. Wet the end of the pastry strips to help them stick at the top. Carefully set onto a low-sided ovenproof dish.

Heat the syrup and butter in a small saucepan until the butter has melted, then brush liberally over the pastry (it won't hurt to have a little more syrup if you like pears to be sweeter). Bake at 400°F (gas 6) for 30-40 minutes until the pastry is a rich golden brown and the pears are tender when pierced with a skewer.
SERVES 4-5.   L.B./S.P. (1)

Fairy butter

The Georgians were very fond of Fairy Butter. It also makes eccles cakes extra special when the cakes are warmed through.

4 oz unsalted butter
3 hard-boiled egg yolks
2 oz caster sugar
1 tablespoon orange flower water, rum, brandy or lemon juice

Cream butter and sugar. Mash egg yolks and beat in with chosen flavouring. Press through a hair sieve and carefully pile into a serving bowl, using two forks for lifting. This way you won't destroy the 'fairy' texture.   M.S.

Russian cherry cheesecake

1½ oz margarine or butter
3 oz digestive biscuits
2 × 15 oz cans pitted black cherries
8 oz full fat soft cheese
3 oz caster sugar
2 eggs
2 oz ground almonds
1 tablespoon kirsch
1 teaspoon arrowroot

Grease the base and sides of a 6-inch round cake tin with removable base. Melt the fat and add the crushed biscuits, mixing well. Press into the tin and bake at 350°F (gas 4) for 10 minutes. Drain the cherries, reserving the juice. Put a layer of cherries on the biscuit base. Soften the cheese with the sugar and gradually add the egg yolks, beating until smooth. Stir in the ground almonds. Beat the egg whites until stiff and fold into the cheese mixture. Pour into the cake tin and bake at 350°F (gas 4) for 1¼ hours. Cool and remove from the tin. When the cake is cold, pour over the kirsch, and arrange the remaining cherries on top of the cake. In a basin, mix the arrowroot with a little of the cherry juice and boil the remaining juice. Add the boiling juice to the arrowroot, then return to the saucepan and boil, stirring until thick and clear. Pour over top and sides of cake, brushing the side to give an even coating. Chill thoroughly.
SERVES 4.   M.N.

Lemon cheesecake

2 oz margarine or butter
2 oz caster or soft brown sugar
4 oz digestive biscuits
8 oz full fat soft cheese
3 oz caster sugar
2 eggs
¼ pint natural yogurt
1 lemon
½ oz gelatine
⅛ pint water
¼ pint double cream

Melt the margarine (or butter) and sugar. Crush the biscuit into fine crumbs with a rolling-pin. Remove the fat from the heat and stir in the biscuit crumbs until well mixed. Press into the base of a greased cake tin measuring 8 inches, with removable base. Leave for 10 minutes in a cool place for the base to harden slightly. Break up the cheese with a fork and cream with the caster sugar until smooth. Separate the eggs, and gradually work in the egg yolks and yogurt, together with the grated lemon rind and lemon juice. Dissolve the gelatine in the water in a basin over a saucepan of hot water until the mixture is syrupy. Cool slightly, then add to the cheese mixture, blending thoroughly. Whip the cream into soft peaks and fold into the mixture. Finally, whip the egg whites until stiff and fold carefully into the mixture.

Pour on to the base and chill in the refrigerator until firm. Remove the base from the tin, and serve the cheesecake on the metal base.

If liked, decorate the top of the cheesecake with whipped cream and mimosa balls.
SERVES 4.   M.N.

Almond cheesecake

2 oz butter
2 oz caster sugar
Grated rind of 1 lemon
3 egg yolks
1 lb cottage cheese
2 oz ground almonds
1 oz sultanas
2 oz soft white breadcrumbs
Pinch of salt

Cream the butter and sugar with the lemon rind, and beat in the egg yolks. Sieve the cottage cheese and stir into the mixture. Add almonds, sultanas, breadcrumbs and salt, and put into a greased 8-inch cake tin. Bake at 400°F (gas 6) for 40 minutes. Leave to cool with the oven turned off. Sprinkle the top of the cheesecake with sugar.
SERVES 4-6.   M.N.

Continental cheesecake

PASTRY
8 oz plain flour
½ teaspoon salt
4 oz butter
2 oz caster sugar
2 tablespoons water
FILLING
1 lb cottage cheese
4 egg yolks
4 oz caster sugar
1 oz ground almonds
Grated rind of 1 lemon
¼ pint soured cream
2 oz sultanas
2 oz chopped candied peel

Make the pastry by rubbing the fat into the flour and salt and working in the sugar, moistening with the water. Roll out to line a Swiss-roll tin and reserve any trimmings. Cover the pastry with foil and baking-beans or rice. Bake at 425°F (gas 7) for 15 minutes. Remove beans and foil, and continue baking for 7 minutes. Remove pastry from the oven, and reduce the temperature to 325°F (gas 3). Sieve the cottage cheese. Cream the egg yolks and sugar. Stir the almonds, eggs and sugar, lemon rind, soured cream, sultanas and peel into the cheese and mix well. Fill the pastry case with the mixture and top with a lattice made of pastry trimmings. Put cheesecake into the oven and bake for 1½ hours. Turn off the oven and leave the cheesecake in for 30 minutes. Cool completely before serving. This cheesecake is better for keeping a couple of days.
SERVES 6.   M.N.

PUDDINGS AND BAKING

Grapefruit cheesecake

This is uncooked, very quick to make, and goes well with the red fruit salad (see page 128). Use a rolling pin to crush the biscuits in a thick polythene bag. If you have a spring mould, put the crumb crust on the base; if you are using a cake tin, put the crust on top and it will be right way up when you turn out the cheesecake.

½ oz gelatine
3 tablespoons cold water
1 lb Philadelphia cream cheese
6¼ oz can concentrated grapefruit juice,
  thawed
3 oz caster sugar
½ pint double cream
2 oz digestive biscuits
2 oz gingernut biscuits
2 oz butter
1 oz demerara sugar
Strawberries

Place the gelatine in a basin with the cold water and leave to stand for 5 minutes, then place in a pan of simmering water and leave until the gelatine has dissolved and become clear, remove and leave to cool. Cream the cheese until soft and gradually beat in the grapefruit juice and sugar. Stir in the cooled gelatine.

Whisk the cream until thick but not stiff and fold into the cheese mixture. Turn into a lightly oiled 8-inch cake tin. Place in the refrigerator. Crush the biscuits finely. Melt the butter in a pan and stir in the crumbs and sugar. Press over the creesecake and leave in the refrigerator for several hours.

Dip into a bowl of very hot water then turn out onto a serving plate and decorate with strawberries.

SERVES 8.   M.B. (1)

Refrigerator log cake

¼ pint double cream
Vanilla essence
Packet of gingernuts
Fresh orange juice

Squeeze the orange juice into a shallow bowl. Whip the cream with 3-4 drops of vanilla essence; it should be a spreading consistency. Dunk each biscuit in the orange juice then stick them together with a smear of cream to form a log shape. Cover this with the rest of the cream, draw a fork over this to make a pattern, then leave the cake in the refrigerator for a couple of hours at least—overnight is better. The variations are infinite: biscuits with chocolate and nut chips, for example, are ideal. By adding cocoa powder to the cream, you can make a very presentable chocolate log cake for Christmas.

G.C.

Plum jalousie

Puff pastry made from 1 lb flour
½ lb fresh plums
1-2 oz sugar
Beaten egg white to glaze
2 oz whole blanched almonds

Roll out the pastry on a piece of grease-proof paper to a rectangle 12 by 11 inches and trim the edges neatly with a clean downwards cut of a sharp knife. Cut the pastry in two lengthways to give one piece 12 by 5 inches and one 12 by 6 inches, cutting through the paper as well as the pastry. Lift the paper containing the narrower piece of pastry on to a baking tray and leave in the refrigerator while the top and the fruit are being prepared. This piece of pastry forms the base of the jalousie.

Halve and stone the plums, then arrange in rows on the pastry base, cut side down, leaving a border of ½ inch around the edge. Sprinkle with the sugar.

To make the slatted top, fold the remaining paper and pastry in half lengthways then peel the paper back to the fold. Make cuts at ½-inch intervals across the pastry from the folded edge inwards to within ½ inch of the cut edges. Dampen the edges of the pastry base, then carefully lift the paper containing the slashed top and invert over the plums with the fold down the centre. Unfold the other half of the pastry and peel off the paper.

Gently press around the edges to seal, then slash the pastry sides all around with a sharp knife, making frequent cuts into the pastry with the knife parallel to the base. This helps it to rise well and evenly. Brush the top with egg white and decorate along the long sides with whole or halved almonds. Rest in the refrigerator for 15 minutes, then bake at 425°F (gas 7) for 15-20 minutes or until well risen and golden brown. Serve hot or cold.

SERVES 6.   L.B./J.B. (2)

Black Forest cherry torte

9 oz plain chocolate
1 jar German sour cherries
3-4 tablespoons kirsch
1 pint double cream
2 tablespoons top-of-the-milk
10-inch chocolate sponge, cut into three
*   layers*
Few fresh cherries

Using a potato-peeler, and with the chocolate at room temperature, 'shave' the block into thin curls; chill. Drain the syrup from the cherries and mix with the kirsch. Whisk cream and milk. Prick cake layers and place one on a serving-dish. Soak it with half the cherry juice, then add a layer of cream and half the cherries, leaving a 1 inch margin. Repeat with second layer. Position the third layer and press together. Mask the cake in cream. Spoon chocolate curls over the cake, leaving a gap in the centre. Decorate with more chocolate and fresh cherries. Chill for 1-2 hours.
SERVES 12.   W.S.

Kugelhopf

Blanched slivered almonds
½ oz fresh yeast
2 oz caster sugar
½ teaspoon salt
3½ fl oz cold milk
1 lb flour
4 eggs
5 tablespoons schnapps or kirsch
7 oz unsalted butter
2 oz raisins
1 egg yolk
Icing sugar

Butter a 1½-litre earthenware *kugelhopf* mould and scatter the bottom with the blanched almonds. Dissolve the yeast in a tablespoon of warm water; dissolve the caster sugar and salt in the cold milk.

Sift the flour on to a pastry-board and make a well in the centre into which you pour the dissolved yeast. With the fingers of one hand work this into the surrounding flour; work in 3 of the eggs, then the salted and sugared milk, the schnapps or kirsch and another egg. Work all together into the flour and knead for 15 minutes—the dough should become shiny and very elastic. Work this dough into the hand-softened unsalted butter. Reflour the board and spread the

dough into a rectangle. Scatter over it a handful of raisins. Roll the dough into a sausage shape and place it in the mould, sealing the join with egg yolk. Cover with a cloth and allow the dough to rise in a warm place for about 2 hours, until the mould is threequarters full. Bake in a pre-heated oven at 400°F (gas 6) for 30 minutes, checking after 20 minutes. If colouring too quickly, cover the *kugelhopf* with a piece of greaseproof paper. It is done when the blade of a knife tests clean. Remove from the oven and unmould after 5 minutes. When cold, sprinkle liberally with icing sugar.
A.S. (1)

Angel's hair gâteau

Choux buns filled with strawberries and cream, dipped in syrup and cloaked in spun sugar. The buns may be made in advance and frozen.
6-egg quantity choux pastry
1 lb fresh or frozen strawberries
Sugar to taste
¼ pint double cream
3 tablespoons kirsch
FOR THE SPUN SUGAR
12 oz caster sugar
2 oz liquid glucose
¼ pint water

Make about forty equal-sized buns of choux pastry and bake until crisp. Slit to allow the steam to escape immediately on removal from the oven and cool on a wire rack.

Roll the strawberries in sugar. Add the liqueur to the cream and whip until thick. Into each bun place about a teaspoon of cream, then a strawberry, and finally top with more cream. Put the lids on to the buns.

To make the syrup for the glaze and the spun sugar, place the sugar, liquid glucose, and water in a saucepan about five inches in diameter (1½ pint size) and slowly dissolve the sugar over a low heat. Wash down the pan sides with a wet brush, turn up the heat and boil to 295°F without stirring (too high a temperature makes the sugar brittle, too low makes it difficult to spin) for approximately ½ hour.

While the syrup is cooking, prepare for the spinning by covering the worktop and floor with paper. Set two saucepans

or other weights about twelve inches apart on the counter and, under each, insert the blade of a palette knife so that the handles protrude from the counter edge. Oil the knife handles.

When the syrup is ready, plunge the pan immediately into cold water to stop the cooking, then, working as quickly as possible, dip the top of each bun into the syrup and pile in a pyramid on a serving plate.

To spin the sugar, enmesh the prongs of two forks and use to pick up a small amount of the syrup. As soon as a thread forms when the forks are raised, flick the forks back and forth from one knife handle to the other lifting as high as possible to obtain long thin strands of spun sugar. If the syrup becomes too thick, warm gently. Continue spinning as long as the syrup will spin. Then carefully lift the whole mass of spun sugar off and set over the top of the pyramid of buns, gently pressing into position. (This will hold for several hours in a cool, dry place.)
SERVES 12.   L.B./E.B. (2)

Ginger ale cake

2 lb mixed dried fruit
2 8-9 oz bottles ginger ale
½ lb butter
½ lb sugar
4 large eggs
Rum, lemon, almond and vanilla essences
1 teaspoon baking powder
1 lb plain flour (or a mixture of
*   wholewheat and white flour)*

Soak the fruit overnight in the ginger ale and essences—about a teaspoon of each, but taste again in the morning. Cream the butter and sugar and add the eggs one at a time. Add the flour sieved with the baking powder and the fruit alternately, using all the liquid.

Bake in a deep, well-lined tin for at least three hours at 325°F (gas 3).   G.C.

Chocolate cream cake

1 oz cocoa
3 oz butter
4 oz apricot jam
2 oz soft brown sugar
6 oz plain sweet biscuits (Marie or Nice)
¼ pint double cream
2 oz plain chocolate

Heat the cocoa, butter and jam and cook gently until smooth. Take off the heat and stir in the sugar and coarse biscuit crumbs (roll the biscuits with a rolling pin, but don't make them too powdery). Press into a tin so mixture is about 1½ inches deep and refrigerate for 4 hours. Turn out, cover with whipped cream and coarsely grated chocolate.
SERVES 4.   M.N.

Lemon curd sponge

2 large eggs
4 oz caster sugar
2 oz butter
2 oz margarine
4 oz self-raising flour
1 tablespoon milk
2 tablespoons lemon curd
2 tablespoons double cream
Icing sugar

Cream the butter and margarine until soft and add the sugar, a little at a time. Beat until light and fluffy and then add the beaten eggs, beating all the time so as not to curdle the mixture. Fold in half the sieved flour along with the milk and then add the remaining flour. Spoon the mixture into two 7 inch sandwich tins which have previously been greased and floured. Bake at 350°F (gas 5) for 20 minutes. Take out and cool on a wire rack and sandwich with the lemon curd and whipped cream. Dust the top with icing sugar.   V.J.

Lemon cake

1½ oz butter
6 oz caster sugar
3 egg yolks
¼ teaspoon lemon essence
6 oz self-raising flour
6 tablespoons milk
Pinch of salt
ICING
1 tablespoon grated orange rind
3 tablespoons soft butter
12 oz icing sugar
2 tablespoons lemon juice
1 tablespoon water
Pinch of salt

To make the cake, cream the butter until light and gradually add the sugar, egg yolks and lemon essence. When the mixture is soft and fluffy, add the flour alternately with the milk. Add the salt and beat well. Grease two 8-inch round tins and line the bottoms with greased

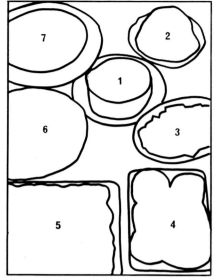

Baking with the flavours of Normandy:
1 *Gâteau de Crêpes à la Normande (page 126)* **2** *Entremet Surprise (page 130)* **3** *Sablés de Caen (page 156)* **4** *Pear Dumplings (page 147)* **5** *Tarte Normande (page 140)* **6** *Orange Puff-Balls (page 145)* **7** *Tarte aux Pommes (page 141).*

paper. Put in the mixture and bake at 350°F (gas 4) for 25 minutes. Meanwhile prepare the icing. Mix the orange rind with the butter and cream well. Cream in one-third of the icing sugar and the salt. Mix the lemon juice and water and add to the mixture alternately with the remaining icing sugar. Beat well until smooth. Cool the cakes, and sandwich together with icing. Cover top and sides with the remaining icing.
                                    M.N.

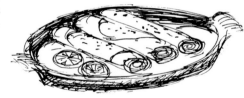

Ginger crown

The spicy taste of ginger and cinnamon gives an interesting variation to ordinary white bread dough.

¾ pint milk
1 teaspoon sugar
½ oz dried yeast
1½ lb strong plain flour
1 teaspoon salt
1 oz butter
2 teaspoons ground ginger
½ teaspoon ground cinnamon
3 oz sultanas
Stem ginger and syrup

Bring the milk to the boil and allow to cool to blood heat (test with a finger), then stir in the sugar and sprinkle the

yeast on top. Set to one side until the yeast dissolves in the liquid and forms a layer of thick froth on top—about 10 minutes.

Rub the butter into the flour and salt sieved together, then stir in the yeast mixture and mix together thoroughly. Turn out onto a clean table and knead well until the dough becomes quite smooth and loses any tackiness—do not use any flour on the board unless the dough is very sticky. Put the kneaded dough back into its bowl and place inside a large plastic bag. Set in a warm place, away from direct heat, to allow the dough to rise to approximately double in bulk—about 1½-2 hours.

Turn out once more onto the board and work well to remove the air from the dough and shape into 20 balls. Arrange a layer of these balls over the surface of a greased 9 inch tin. Sprinkle the spice/sugar mixture and the sultanas over the dough in the tin and cover with the remainder of the dough balls in a smaller ring set back slightly behind the outside lower ring. Replace into the plastic bag and leave to rise until double in bulk—1½-2 hours. Brush well with the ginger syrup and bake at 350°F (gas 4) for about 1 hour until well risen and browned.

Cool on a wire rack and brush again with ginger syrup and decorate with slices of the stem ginger.

                                    L.B./C.P. (2)

Aunt Rene's amazing orange cake

CAKE
3 eggs plus their weight in butter, sugar, self-raising flour
1 teaspoon of finely-grated orange rind
Orange juice
GLAZE
8 oz icing sugar
1 teaspoon orange rind
Orange juice

Set oven to 325°F (gas 3). Line a cake tin with greased paper, allowing it to come well above the rim. Cream butter and sugar, add eggs one by one, and flour, beating well. Mix in enough orange juice to make batter the consistency of thick double cream; add orange rind. Cook for about an hour—possibly more, depending on how wet you made the mixture.

Cool in the tin for 10 minutes.

Meanwhile mix the glaze ingredients to make a thin icing. Turn out the cake, pour the glaze over it and keep spooning it back as it runs off. The cake should then be put into an airtight tin and not cut for at least three days. Decorate with whipped cream and grated orange peel. Some Curaçao or Cointreau in the cream would do no harm.   G.C.

PUDDINGS AND BAKING

Moist banana cake

4 oz butter
6 oz sugar
2 eggs
2 bananas, well-mashed
1 teaspoon bicarbonate soda
2 tablespoons boiling milk
1 teaspoon baking powder
8 oz plain flour
ICING
1 lb icing sugar
Melted butter
1 banana, mashed
Rum
Cocoa powder

Set oven at 350°F (gas 4). Cream butter and sugar, beat in eggs one at a time, then add mashed bananas, followed by the soda dissolved in the milk. Sift together and mix in the flour and baking powder. Bake in two greased sandwich tins for about 20 minutes, or add a touch more baking powder and bake in one deeper tin for about 50 minutes. Fill with whipped cream and sliced bananas soaked in lemon juice.

For the icing, combine all the icing ingredients thoroughly. Spread over the cake. G.C.

Candied fruit cake

Madeira cake soaked with wine and decorated with an exotic mixture of crystalized fruits.

CAKE
12 oz butter
1 lb caster sugar
6 eggs, lightly beaten
1 lb plain flour
2 teaspoons baking powder
Grated rind of 3 large oranges
Juice of 1 orange
TOPPING
¼ pint Madeira
Selection of crystallized fruits
2 oranges, peeled and segmented
2 oz sugar
4 tablespoons water

To make the cake, remove the butter from the refrigerator in advance so it is quite soft for creaming. Thoroughly beat together the butter and sugar until quite light coloured and fluffy. Gradually add the eggs, beating in well after each addition. Stir in the grated orange rind and the flour and baking powder sifted together. Finally, add enough orange juice to give a soft dropping consistency and turn the cake mixture into a greased lined 9-inch tin. Bake in the centre of the oven at 325°F (gas 3) for approximately 2 hours, or until a good golden brown colour and the centre is baked when tested with a skewer. Cool on a wire rack.

When cool, drizzle with the Madeira and decorate the top with the crystallized

Festive dishes for Christmas: **1** *Bauble Cake (traditional Christmas cake, topped with almond paste and soft white icing to which is added a little lemon juice, then decorated with baubles)* **2** *Almond Trifle (page 137)* **3** *Chicken, Cheese and Chive Terrine (page 43)* **4** *Mushroom and Cauliflower Vinaigrette (page 44)* **5** *Fairy Butter (page 147) to serve with mince pies.*

fruits and the segments of the two remaining fresh oranges. Dissolve the sugar in the water, bring to the boil and simmer without stirring for about 1 minute then pour over the fruits (the syrup should be thick but not brown). L.B./H.C. (1)

Spiced cake for Easter

6 oz self-raising flour
5 oz caster sugar
5 oz margarine
3 large eggs
½ teaspoon mixed spice
¼ teaspoon cinnamon
SPICED CREAM
3 oz icing sugar
¼ teaspoon mixed spice
1½ oz butter
1 egg yolk
ICING
12 oz icing sugar
Warm water
Few drops of vanilla essence
EGGS
2 oz ground almonds
1 oz caster sugar
1 oz icing sugar, sieved
Few drops of almond essence
1 egg yolk
Vegetable colouring
Crushed chocolate vermicelli

Cream together margarine and sugar until soft and light. Sieve the dry ingredients. Beat the eggs, add flour mixture and eggs, alternately to the margarine mixture, taking care not to overbeat. Put the mixture into two 7-inch sandwich tins and bake for 20-25

minutes, at 350°F (gas 4).

For the spiced cream, sieve together the icing sugar and mixed spice, add butter and beat until light. Add egg yolk slowly to the mixture and beat briskly to a smooth cream.

When cold, sandwich together, with spiced cream.

For the icing, mix 8 oz icing sugar with enough warm water to make a very flowing icing and add a few drops of vanilla essence. Pour it over the sponge and leave to set. Make a stiffer icing with 4 oz icing sugar and spread it over top of cake.

Finish decorating sponge with marzipan eggs: mix ground almonds, caster sugar, sieved icing sugar with a few drops of almond essence and a little egg yolk, and colour with vegetable colouring. Sprinkle with crushed chocolate vermicelli. J.E. (1)

Profiteroles

CHOUX PASTRY
3¾ oz plain flour
3 oz butter
8 fl oz water
3 eggs

Prepare pastry, pipe out, or put (measured in teaspoons) on lightly-greased baking tin. Bake in moderate oven 15-20 minutes until firm. Put on rack to cool.
CHOCOLATE CREAM FILLING
1 whole egg
1 egg yolk
⅔ oz chocolate, bitter
2 oz caster sugar
¾ oz flour
½ oz cornflour
½ pint milk

Separate egg. Cream yolks and sugar together until light. Add flour and a little cold milk making smooth paste. Melt chocolate in remainder of milk. Pour on egg mixture, blend and return to pan. Stir over gentle heat until mixture boils. Whip egg white until stiff, turn a little of the boiling cream into a bowl and fold in white. Return this to pan and stir carefully 2-3 minutes over heat to set egg white. Fill the profiteroles with chocolate cream. Pile up in serving dish. Pour over chocolate sauce just before serving.
CHOCOLATE SAUCE
¼ pint cream
6 oz dessert chocolate
4 oz sugar
½ pint water

Break up chocolate, put in pan with a little water and melt slowly. Tip on rest of water, add sugar, when dissolved simmer with lid off the pan 10-15 minutes. Pour off and cool. Whip the cream and fold in 2-3 tablespoons of chocolate sauce.
SERVES 8. S.T.

PUDDINGS AND BAKING

Apple strudel

PASTRY
8½ oz plain flour
1 oz butter
1 egg
2 tablespoons water
Pinch of salt
Oil
FILLING
1½ lb apples, peeled, cored and cubed
    finely
2½ oz raisins
1½ oz flaked almonds
1½ oz sugar
½ oz cinnamon
1 oz breadcrumbs
3 tablespoons rum
1 egg yolk
ICING
½ lb icing sugar
3 teaspoons lemon juice

Sieve flour on to a clean board, make a well in the centre, pour in water and melted fat, add salt and egg, at the same time drawing in the flour from well sides to make a thick paste. Starting from the middle, knead well and roll into a ball. Brush with oil and leave in a warm place for 1 hour.

Mix all filling ingredients with the exception of the breadcrumbs. Roll out three-quarters of the dough, brush with oil and pull until very thin and transparent in texture; cut into a rectangle. Place on a greased, floured baking-tray and sprinkle the top evenly with breadcrumbs. Spread the mixture evenly over the breadcrumbed dough leaving a border of ⅛ inch, and roll out the remainder of the dough until transparent. Cut off any thick borders, then cut in half. Place two halves around pastry with filling, seal joins with water, pressing together firmly with wet fingers. Brush the whole strudel with egg yolk and bake in the middle of an oven heated to 350°F (gas 4) for ¾ hour.

Mix icing sugar with lemon juice and pour over hot strudel; cool and serve.

W.S.

Savarin

1 lb flour
¾ lb butter
5 teaspoons sugar
⅔ oz fresh yeast
8 eggs
¼ pint warm milk
SYRUP
1 lb sugar
1 pint water
Pinch of cinnamon
Pinch of coriander
Pinch of mace
2 tablespoons kirsch or rum

Dilute the yeast in the warm milk. Sift flour and a pinch of salt into large bowl, make a well in the middle and add yeast and milk mixture, mix roughly together with wooden spoon and then add eggs, one at a time, beating all the while. Detach any of the mixture that has stuck to the sides, and distribute softened butter in small portions over the paste.

Cover and leave it to rise in a warm place until it has double in size.

Sprinkle the sugar over the risen paste and knead well so that all the butter is absorbed. Put the mixture into two well-buttered 2-pint ring moulds or Savarin moulds, taking care to fill only three-quarters full and let the savarins rise to the top of the mould.

Bake in a hot oven pre-heated to 425°F (gas 7) for three-quarters of an hour. Allow to cool completely before turning out.

Meanwhile, make the syrup. Melt the sugar in the water, then add cinnamon, coriander and mace whilst it is boiling. Add kirsch or rum.

Turn the cooled savarin onto a dish and pour over hot syrup, reserving a small amount to pour over just before serving.

This cake freezes well.

R.J.

Savarin aux framboise
Raspberry babas

Using the same basic dough as small babas, this is made in a ring mould and soaked in a richly-flavoured syrup. The centre is piled with fresh raspberries sprinkled with kirsch. If liked, it may be served with whipped cream.

YEAST BATTER
6 tablespoons lukewarm milk
1 teaspoon sugar
1 tablespoon dried yeast
2 oz strong plain flour
DOUGH
4 eggs
6 oz strong plain flour
½ level teaspoon salt
1 oz caster sugar
4 oz softened butter
SYRUP
4 oz sugar
¼ pint water
Juice and thinly-pared rind of ½ orange
2 tablespoons kirsch
FOR SERVING
¾ lb fresh raspberries
A little icing sugar
2-3 tablespoons kirsch

Beat the yeast batter ingredients together in a bowl until a smooth mixture is formed. Cover and leave in a warm place for about 20 minutes or until frothy.

Beat the eggs and add to the yeast batter with the other dough ingredients. Beat for 4-5 minutes until quite smooth, then pour into a greased 3-pint ring mould. Place in a plastic bag and leave in a warm place, away from direct heat, for about 30 minutes or until the mould is two-thirds full, the dough is glossy, and has the thick bubbled appearance of a thick batter.

Remove from the bag and bake at 400°F (gas 6) for approximately 35 minutes or until well risen and golden brown. Turn out onto a wire cooling rack and while still warm baste with the syrup.

TO MAKE THE SYRUP: Carefully dissolve the sugar in the water, then bring to the boil with the orange rind and juice and simmer for a few minutes to form a syrup. Add the kirsch and spoon over the savarin. When cool, fill with fresh berries and sprinkle with icing sugar and kirsch. Serve with a bowl of whipped cream.

SERVES 6.

L.B. D.M.

Arusha

8 oz unsalted butter
11 oz flour, sifted
Large pinch of salt
¼ pint double cream
6 oz blanched slivered almonds
Caster sugar

Cream together the softened butter, sifted flour, salt, cream and almonds. Wrap in greaseproof paper and chill several hours. Roll dough ⅛-inch thick— it will be very fragile—on floured board, cut rounds with 2½ inch scalloped cutter and then carefully remove centres of half the rounds with a 1-inch cutter.

Sprinkle with caster sugar and bake on buttered baking sheets at 350°F (gas 4) for about 12 minutes, until just browning. Transfer to racks and, when cooled, sandwich pairs with raspberry jam.

MAKES ABOUT 36.

A.S. (1)

Date fingers

4 oz rolled oats
4 oz flour
½ teaspoon baking soda
4 oz margarine
2 oz soft brown sugar
DATE FILLING
½ lb dates
2 oz sugar
Little water

Make the filling first. Chop the dates finely and stew in the water with the sugar until a soft paste is formed, easy to spread.

Rub the margarine into the oats, flour and baking soda. Add the sugar until the mixture looks like crumbs. Press half the mix into an 8-inch-square tin. Spread with the filling, cover with the rest of the oatmeal mixture. Press down well and bake at 350°F (gas 4) for 40 minutes. Cut into fingers whilst hot.

M.H.M.

Festival gingerbread

1 lb self-raising flour
1 oz ground ginger
1 teaspoon cinnamon
8 oz butter
8 oz brown sugar
8 oz currants
8 oz sultanas
4 oz candied peel
4 oz crystallized ginger
¼ pint milk
3 eggs
8 oz black treacle
1 teaspoon bicarbonate of soda
ICING
8 oz icing sugar
¼ teaspoon cinnamon
Juice of 1 orange
Warm water
Cherries
Almonds
Angelica

Sift together the flour and spices. Rub in butter until the mixture is like fine crumbs. Stir in sugar, currants, sultanas, chopped peel and chopped ginger. Warm the milk to lukewarm and add eggs, treacle and bicarbonate of soda. Pour this mixture into the dry ingredients and mix well. Bake in a rectangular tin (8 by 12 inches) which has been greased and lined, at 350°F (gas 4) for 1½ hours. Make the icing by mixing sugar, cinnamon and strained orange juice and enough warm water to make a thin paste. Pour over the cake and decorate with cherries, angelica and almonds.   M.N.

Crunchies

6 oz porridge oats
4 oz margarine
4 oz demerara sugar

Melt the margarine and sugar in a saucepan. Add the oats and spread on to a well-greased Swiss-roll tin. Bake slowly for about 1 hour on the middle shelf at 350°F (gas 4). Cut into pieces whilst hot, leave in the tin to cool.   M.H.M.

Biscoitos de Coimbra
Coimbra biscuits

¼ pint milk
1 teaspoon baking powder
3½ oz butter
9 oz sugar
1 tablespoon cinnamon
Flour

Mix together in a bowl, the milk, baking powder, cinnamon, butter and sugar. Blend well. Add flour little by little until you get a firm dough. Shape into biscuits and cook in a moderate oven on greased baking sheets.   C.W.

Oatmeal cookies

8 oz flour
8 oz medium oatmeal
2 tablespoons margarine
4 oz brown sugar
1 teaspoon baking soda
1 teaspoon salt
¼ teaspoon cinnamon
¼ teaspoon nutmeg

Rub the margarine into the flour and oatmeal, stir in the other ingredients and mix to a stiff paste with a little water. Roll out and cut into biscuit shapes. Bake quickly at 425°F (gas 7) until brown.   M.H.M.

Jacks

3 oz unsalted butter
Grated rind of ½ lemon
4 oz caster sugar
1½ beaten eggs
4 oz flour
Pinch of salt
Generous ¾ teaspoon baking-powder
2 oz chocolate chips
1 teaspoon milk

Cream butter with lemon rind, beating until light and fluffy; beat in sugar very gradually; beat egg with fork and then beat by tablespoon into mixture. Sift flour with salt and baking powder. Sift again over creamed ingredients, add chocolate chips and milk. Fold lightly until just combined. Spoon into a buttered loaf pan, measuring 7 by 3 by 2½ inches, with a piece of buttered paper in the bottom, making a slight trough down centre of batter, and bake at 350°F (gas 4) for 45-50 minutes.
A.S. (1)

Ashbourne gingerbread

8 oz butter
5 oz caster sugar
10 oz plain flour
2 level teaspoons ground ginger
Pinch of salt
2 oz candied peel

Cream together the butter and sugar. Sift in the flour, ginger and salt, and work together until smooth. Add the finely-chopped peel. Press into a swiss roll tin and bake at 350°F (gas 4) for 25 minutes. Mark into squares and leave in the tin until cold.   M.N.

Cornish gingerbread

1½ lb plain flour
8 oz brown sugar
2 oz ground ginger
2 oz mixed candied peel
Pinch of mixed spice
8 oz butter
1 lb black treacle
1 oz bicarbonate of soda
2 tablespoons milk

Mix together flour, sugar, ginger, chopped peel and spice. Stir in butter melted with the treacle. Dissolve the soda in the milk and stir into the mixture. Work until well blended. With the hands, roll out portions of the mixture into long sausage-shapes, cut into small pieces, and roll each piece into a ball about the size of a walnut. Put on greased baking sheets, allowing room to spread, and bake at 400°F (gas 6) for 10 minutes. Cool on a wire rack and store in an airtight tin.   M.N.

PUDDINGS AND BAKING

Brownies

6 oz butter or margarine
2 level tablespoons cocoa
6 oz caster sugar
2 eggs
2 oz plain flour
2 oz chopped walnuts
A 7-inch square cake tin, greased and
*   base lined*

Melt 2 oz of the fat, stir in the cocoa and set aside. Cream remaining fat with the sugar until lighter in colour and texture. Gradually beat in the eggs. Fold in the sieved flour, walnuts and cocoa mixture. Turn into prepared tin and bake in a moderate oven 350°F (gas 4) for about 45 minutes until cooked. Leave to cool in the tin. When cold, turn out and cut into 16 squares. Sprinkle with sugar.

K.K.

Parkin

8 oz medium oatmeal
8 oz plain flour
7 oz butter
8 oz black treacle
¼ teaspoon nutmeg and mace (each)
½ teaspoon ground ginger
1 teaspoon bicarbonate of soda
1 tablespoon cream
¼ teaspoon salt

Rub the butter into the oatmeal, flour and salt. Mix in the spice and baking soda. Warm the treacle and cream and stir into the dry ingredients. Leave to stand overnight. Next morning, bake in a flat tin in a moderate oven for about an hour. When cool, wrap and store for at least one week.

M.H.M.

Oatie biscuits

Shortcrust pastry made with 6 oz flour
3 oz rolled oats
3 oz sugar
1½ oz butter

Mix the oats, sugar and butter with the pastry, kneading to a smooth paste, using a tablespoon milk to moisten. Roll out, cut into 2-inch rounds and bake in a hot oven until pale brown. Remove from tin at once. Spread with honey.

M.H.M.

Lamingtons

Slightly stale sponge or madeira cake
2 tablespoons butter
6 tablespoons water
2 tablespoons cocoa powder
12 oz icing sugar
½ lb desiccated coconut

Melt the butter, add water and dissolve cocoa powder in this. Sieve icing sugar and also mix. Keep warm.

Cut the sponge into two-inch squares, coat on all sides with the mixture, roll in coconut. Leave to dry. Extra delicious if split and filled with whipped cream.

SERVES 4.

G.C.

Oatmeal scones

7 oz flour
3½ oz fine oatmeal
3 oz sugar
3 oz butter
1 oz lard
1 teaspoon baking powder
1 egg
Salt
¼ cup cold water

Melt the butter with the lard and mix into the dry ingredients. Beat the egg in cold water, mix into the rest. Roll out the dough thinly, cut into 2-inch rounds, and bake on a well-greased sheet in a moderate oven until golden.

M.H.M.

Sablés de Caen

These little biscuits are so called because of the sand-like sprinkling of sugar on the surface.

4 oz butter
8 oz caster sugar
2 egg yolks
1 tablespoon double cream
1 tablespoon grated lemon rind
8 oz plain flour
1 teaspoon baking powder
Sugar for dredging

Beat together the butter and sugar until the mixture resembles coarse crumbs, then stir in the egg yolks, cream and lemon rind and mix well. Sieve in the flour and baking powder and work into the creamed mixture thoroughly. Knead the dough lightly with the finger tips to form a smooth, slightly tacky dough. Wrap in foil or film and chill in the refrigerator for about 1 hour until firm.

Working with only a little of the dough at a time, roll thinly on a lightly-floured board and stamp out shapes with biscuit cutters. Carefully transfer the biscuits to a greased baking sheet and sprinkle generously with sugar. Bake at 350°F (gas 4) for approximately 8 minutes until pale brown in colour. Remove from the sheet while still warm and cool flat on a wire rack. Makes 30-40 biscuits. Store in an airtight tin. Serve with coffee, or a sweet cider.

L.B. S.H.

Petits fours

Most of the *petits fours* given below may be made fairly well in advance.

CHOCOLATE CUPS: Tiny chocolate cases filled with a delicious chocolate rum cream. Very rich—and perfect with coffee.

4 oz plain chocolate
1 tablespoon double cream
1 tablespoon rum

Make about one week in advance and store in air-tight containers in the refrigerator.

Melt 2½ oz of the chocolate in a basin over hot water just to a smooth, thick consistency and texture. Spoon into *petits fours* cases, distributing evenly around sides and bottom. Leave in a cool place to set for two hours. Test by carefully peeling away one case. If the chocolate begins to crack, add an additional chocolate layer to each case.

Melt the remaining chocolate with the cream and rum and leave to cool and thicken, then whisk to a smooth light-coloured cream. Pipe small rosettes into the prepared cases.

MAKES 15 *petits fours*   L.B./H.B.

MINTS: Mix together to a smooth stiff paste 8 oz icing sugar, a squeeze of lemon juice and approximately ½ egg white. Add a few drops of peppermint essence to taste and colour as liked with red, yellow, or green colouring. Roll out to ¼ inch thick on a board dusted with icing sugar and stamp out with biscuit cutters. Carefully place the mints into a container with an air-tight cover. Do not pack more than one layer deep. Cover and store in a cool place for one to two weeks.

GLACÉ FRUITS: Strawberries, redcurrants, or cherries which are frozen in their season (on the stems) are delicious. To glaze them: dissolve 8 oz sugar in 2½ fl oz of water. Wash down the sides of the pan with a wet brush then let the mixture boil to 290°F without stirring. Remove the pan from the heat and dip each piece of fruit individually into the syrup using the stem to hold with a pair of tongs. The fruits should be left completely frozen until they are dipped.

To cool the dipped fruit, set on to greased paper on a tray. Put into *petits fours* cases, if liked, to serve.

MARZIPAN DATES: To stuff twelve dates approximately, 3 oz marzipan is necessary and when the dates are filled they can be rolled in sugar to give a professional finish. Pack the finished dates into air-tight boxes; store for up to one month in the refrigerator or freezer.

L.B./N.C.

Danish pastries

¼ pint milk, boiled then cooled to
*   lukewarm*
1 tablespoon dried yeast
2 oz sugar
12 oz strong plain flour
Large pinch of salt
9 oz butter
1 egg, beaten
Glacé icing and flaked almonds to
*   decorate*
FILLINGS TO TASTE: *almond paste, lemon*
*   curd, apricot jam, redcurrant jelly,*
*   cinnamon and sugar mixed with butter*

Add 1 teaspoon of the sugar to the cooled milk and sprinkle the yeast over the

folds to make the teeth fan out. Brush with beaten egg.

CRESCENTS: Roll the remaining piece of dough into a circle about 10 inches in diameter and cut into four equal wedges. Put a little filling at the wide edge, brush the sides of the wedge with egg then roll up from the wide edge. Shape into crescents as you place the pastries on a greased baking sheet. Brush with beaten egg.

Put the pastries on their trays into large plastic bags and leave to rise until puffy in a warm place but away from direct heat—approximately 20 minutes. Bake until golden brown, about 15 minutes at 400°F (gas 6). Cool on a wire rack, and decorate with a little glacé icing and flaked almonds, if liked.

L.B./A.C. (2)

Canadian pastry

Particularly suitable for pies with a top crust only, for double crust pies, or for tarts where the pie can be served from the baking dish or tin.

10 oz strong flour (bread flour)
4 oz butter
4 oz lard
5 tablespoons (approx) cold water

Start with cold fats and cut them in small chunks into the flour. Rub the fat coarsely into the flour with the finger tips, leaving flat flakes of fat throughout. Stir in sufficient cold water to form a dough, knead only lightly then wrap the dough in foil or film and chill until quite firm.

Before rolling the pastry, work it lightly with the hand to make a dough which has no cracks and which can be rolled without breaking apart. Roll on a lightly floured board to about the thickness of a coin.

The pastry freezes well but should be formed into blocks not more than about an inch in thickness before being wrapped for freezing. L.B.

English shortcrust pastry

8 oz plain flour
2 oz butter
2 oz lard
2-3 tablespoons cold water

Cut the fat in small pieces into the flour, then rub in with the finger tips until the mixture forms very fine crumbs. Shake the bowl to ensure there are no large balls of fat not mixed in and continue until the whole mixture is even. Stir in only enough cold water to form a smooth paste which can be rolled. Knead very lightly and roll out on a lightly floured board. L.B.

surface. Leave until the yeast has all dissolved and formed a good froth on top—10-15 minutes.

Sift together the rest of the sugar with the flour and salt. Rub 2 oz of the butter into the flour, then stir in the egg and the yeast mixture. Mix to form a smooth dough, put the bowl into a large plastic bag and leave in a warm place away from direct heat for about 1½ hours or until the dough is puffy in appearance, springy to the touch and holds the imprint of a finger.

While the dough is rising, prepare the remaining 7 oz butter: cut it into two parts and divide each part into an equal number of small pieces, keeping each group of pieces on a separate sheet of greaseproof paper. The butter should be soft enough just to flatten with a knife but not so soft as to be sticky—if necessary, keep the prepared butter in the refrigerator, but if it is too hard it will tear the dough. Flatten all the little pieces of butter with a knife.

When the dough has risen adequately, turn it out on to a table or board and lightly knead it, then roll to a regular-shaped rectangle. Dot one portion of the butter pieces over the top two-thirds of the dough, leaving a border around the edge of about 1 inch. Fold up the bottom third of pastry, fold down the top third, and seal the edges by pressing with the rolling pin. Give the dough a quarter turn and, with the fold on the left, roll out thinly. Once more fold up the bottom third and fold down the top third, then again seal the edges, but this time wrap the dough in aluminium foil and chill in the refrigerator for ½ hour.

Repeat the rolling in of the butter and the folding of the pastry to use the second portion of butter pieces. When the pastry is complete, wrap and chill for half a day or overnight before using. When shaping the pastries, it is best to work with only part of the dough at a time, leaving the remainder in the refrigerator. The recipe makes about a dozen pastries, depending on your skill in rolling and shaping.

The following are instructions for making some popular shapes.

WINDMILLS: Roll approximately one quarter of the dough to a rectangle 15 inches by 5 inches and cut into three equal squares. Make cuts from each corner of the pieces in to within 1 inch of the centres. Put a teaspoon of filling in the centres and turn alternate corners of the triangles in to the centre. Brush with beaten egg, and place on a greased baking tray.

SNAILS: With slightly less than one quarter of the dough, roll a rectangle 10 inches by 5 inches. Spread with cinnamon sugar, roll up like a swiss roll, starting from a short side. Cut into three equal slices, flatten slightly and place on the greased tray. Glaze with beaten egg.

COCKS' COMBS: With a little over one quarter of the dough, roll a rectangle 12 inches by 5 inches, then cut into three equal parts. Spread filling across the centre of the pieces, brush the edges with egg, then fold in half like a sandwich. Press gently along the outside edges and slash at ½-inch intervals along the long side to create the effect of a comb. As you transfer the pastries to the baking tray, bend them backwards along the

INDEX

CONTRIBUTORS

At the end of each recipe, the contributor's initials are given. Their names are as follows:
V.A. Valerie Akers; J.A. Jennifer Angrave; S.A. Sally Ardley; L.B. Lucille Barber; H.B. Helen Beaumont; G.B. Guy Bentinck; M.B. (1) Mary Berry; J.B. (1) Juliano Biguzzi; M.B. (2) Maggie Black; A.B. (1) Alison Bold; F.B. Fiona Booth; S.B. Sarah Bosley; M.B. (3) Mary Brand E.B. (1) Elizabeth Brocklebank; E.B. (2) Eileen Brunning; J.B. (2) Jane Bullough; J.B. (3) Judy Burn; A.B. (2) Alison Burt; J.C. (1) Julia Carpenter; N.C. Nicola Cattrall; A.C. (1) Anne Chamberlain; A.C. (2) Anne Chappell; F.C. Fletcher Christian; G.C. Glynn Christian; M.C. Maxine Chung; J.C. (2) Jayne Collings; H.C. (1) Hilary Cooper; H.C. (2) Helen Corrie; J.D. (1) Jill Davies; J.D. (2) James Denny; M.D. Marion Deschamps; V.D./ V.W. Victoria Dickie/Vanessa Wauchope; A.E. Alison Edgeler; J.E. (1) Josephine Emery; J.E. (2) Jane Evans; C.F. Christine France; T.F. Toni Fyson; G.G. Geralyn Glicker; P.G. Paula Goard; S.G. Sue Gold; J.G. (1) Jolle Gotsaed; W.G. Winifred Graham; A.G. Alison Granger; J.G. (2) Jill Green; D.G. Diane Greenberg; V.G. Vivienne Griffiths; M.H.M. Mary Hanson Moore; L.H. (1) Linda Harvey; S.H. Susan Hersfall; L.H. (2) Lee Highton; V.J. Virginia Jackson; R.J. Rosalind Jenkinson; E.J. Elizabeth Jewison; A.K. Alison Kelsall; K.K. Katherine Kleber; N.L. Nico Landenis; H.L. Hilary Lane; R.L. Roger Lasham; D.L.

(1) Dawn Leamont; C.L. Catherine Lefley; P.L. Prue Leith; D.L. (2) Deborah Lindsay; M.L. Moira Lister; K.L. Karl Löderer; G.L. Gill Longdon; M.M. Monda Massey; P.M. (1) Penelope Maxwell; D.M. Deborah McGlynn; F.M. Fiona Mellor; I.M. Inge Mitchell; P.M. (2) Penelope Mardon; J.M. James Mortimer; S.N. Sandra Nixon; M.N. Mary Norwak; M.O. Michael O'Mahony; C.P. (1) Caroline Palmer; A.P. Amanda Pearce; C.P. (2) Claire Pearce; S.P. (1) Susan Pearson; B.P. Barbara Perkins; S.P. (2) Sheila Perrins; M.P. Margaret Peters; W.L.P. Wai Lim Poon; M.O. Margaret Ouin; C.R. (1) Clare Randall; L.R. Lindsay Redman; A.R. (1) Annette Reilly; A.R. (2) Astrid Rejnholm; S.J.R. Sarah Jane Richards; C.R. (2) Catherine Robinson; M.R. Michel Roux; G.R. Gillian Rowe; A.S. (1) Alice Salmon; B.S. (1) Bridget Scatchard; W.S. Werner Seeberg; H.S. Helen Sheppard; B.S. (2) Barbara Simpson; E.S. Elizabeth Simpson; M.S. Michael Smith; J.S.C. Jesus Soane Corral; A.S. (2) Anne Stock; U.S. Una Stubbs; L.T. (1) Lynne Taylor; J.T. Julian Tennant; M.T. Mary Terrell; E.T. Enid Thomas; L.T. (2) Lynne Titchiner; S.T. Silvino Trompetto; C.T. Carol Tuck; J.V.Z. John van Zuilecom; D.V. Dione Venables; A.V. André Villon; W.V. Werner Vogeli; H.W. Hilary Walden; S.W. (1) Sarah Webb; G.W. (1) Gail Weston; J.W. Judy Whalley; S.W. (2) Suzanne Wilkinson; K.W. Kathryn Willouby; S.W. (3) Sandra Wingrove; R.W. Rachel Winnington; G.W. (2) Gillian Wootton; C.W. Carol Wright.

METRIC CONVERSION

For most recipes, there is no need to be exact in converting ounces to grammes and vice versa. 1oz is equivalent to 28·350 grammes but as a convenient rule, 1oz is *approximately* equivalent to 25g. Thus, 4oz is 100g, 6oz is 150g and so on. For liquids, 1 pint is equivalent to approximately $\frac{1}{2}$ litre or 500 millilitres.

British oz	Grammes	Pints	Milli-litres	British fl oz	Metric litres
$\frac{1}{2}$oz	5gm	$\frac{1}{4}$ pint	150ml	2oz	$\frac{1}{2}$dl
1oz	25gm	$\frac{1}{2}$ pint	300ml	5oz	$1\frac{1}{2}$dl
4oz	100gm	$\frac{3}{4}$ pint	450ml	10oz	3dl
8oz	225gm	1 pint	600ml	14oz	4dl
16oz	450gm			25oz	$\frac{3}{4}$ litre
				33oz	1 litre

OVEN TEMPERATURES

	ELECTRIC		GAS
	Fahrenheit	Centigrade	
Cool	200°F	95°C	$\frac{1}{4}$
	225°F	110°C	
Slow	250°F	130°C	$\frac{1}{2}$
	275°F	140°C	1
	300°F	150°C	2
Moderate	325°F	160°C	3
	350°F	180°F	4
Fairly Hot	375°F	190°C	5
	400°F	200°C	6
Hot	425°F	220°C	7
	450°F	230°C	8
Very Hot	475°F	240°C	9
	500°F	260°C	

PHOTOGRAPHERS

Robert Golden, Cover; James Mortimer, Halftitle; Eric Carter, Title; James Mortimer 6; John Wingrove 9; John Wingrove 10; Chris Drake 13; John Wingrove 15; John Wingrove 16; James Mortimer 18; Bob Croxford 21; James Mortimer 23; Julian Nieman 24; Eric Carter 27; Fotiades 28; Kjell Nilsson 31; James Mortimer 34; John Wingrove 38; James Mortimer 41; James Mortimer 42; Eric Carter 45; Eric Carter 49; Eric Carter 50; Andrew Whittuck 52; James Mortimer 55; James Mortimer 56; Jacques Primois 58; Eric Carter 61; James Mortimer 65; Eric Carter 66; Bent Rej 69; James Mortimer 71; Portuguese Tourist Office 72; Fotiades 74; Eric Carter 77; John Wingrove 78; Eric Carter 81; James Mortimer 82; James Mortimer 86; Bryan Douglas 91; James Mortimer 92; Eric Carter 95; Ray Williams 96; Eric Carter 99; James Mortimer 102; James Mortimer 108; John Wingrove 113; James Mortimer 116; Julian Nieman 120; Paul Kemp 122; Spike Powell 129; Eric Carter 132, 134, 139, 143, 144, 148, 149, 150; James Mortimer 153. DRAWINGS: Thelma Lambert.

PDO 80-704